Richard Channing Moore (1762-1841), first Rector of Monumental Church, Richmond, and later Bishop of Virginia. Died in Lynchburg, and is buried in Richmond. From life by William Henry Brown, lithograph by E. B. and E. C. Kellogg. Photographed from the copy of the silhouette in the Mayo Memorial House, Richmond. Courtesy of Dr. G. McLaren Brydon.

The OLD *and the* QUAINT *in* VIRGINIA

BY

GEORGIA DICKINSON WARDLAW

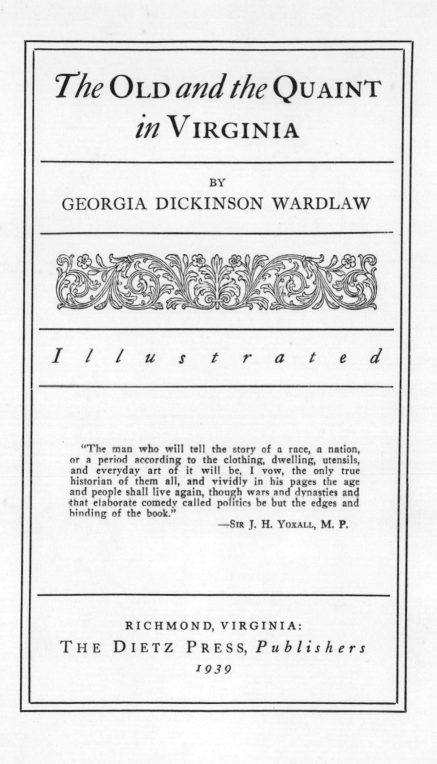

I l l u s t r a t e d

"The man who will tell the story of a race, a nation, or a period according to the clothing, dwelling, utensils, and everyday art of it will be, I vow, the only true historian of them all, and vividly in his pages the age and people shall live again, though wars and dynasties and that elaborate comedy called politics be but the edges and binding of the book."

—SIR J. H. YOXALL, M. P.

RICHMOND, VIRGINIA:

THE DIETZ PRESS, *Publishers*

1939

TO

ROBIN

WHO I HOPE MAY ONE DAY SHARE
HER MOTHER'S LOVE FOR THE
OLD AND THE QUAINT.

PREFACE

IKE Oliver Goldsmith, "I love everything that's old: old friends, old times, old manners, old books, old wine." To this pleasing list I would add those quaint and irresistible "old things" whose colorful stories have been woven into the fabric of this book.

Who can resist the appeal of an old sampler or patchwork quilt; the fascination of a bold black silhouette, or a faded and lacy old valentine; the fragile beauty of an old fan; the lovable qualities of an old clock or piece of furniture; the splendor of old silver; the charm of old china; or the age-old allure of a doll—particularly an *old* doll? Certainly not I.

Gathering material for *The Old and the Quaint in Virginia* has taken several years, during which time hundreds of sources of reference have been read and carefully examined: old letters, diaries, wills, inventories, orders, advertisements, books both old and new, magazines, and newspapers. Much time has been spent in Museums and Historical Societies studying their valuable exhibits; and countless happy and never-to-be-forgotten hours in hospitable homes throughout Virginia, seeing prized heirlooms and listening to the many tales and traditions so inseparably a part of these old relics.

The quest of the quaint is never-ending in Virginia. One may begin the happy pilgrimage in search of old

Lowestoft, only to find blue Staffordshire instead, but the trail leads far and wide, and into many unexpected and delightful by-paths. Laurence Sterne made a statement almost two hundred years ago, which is just as true today. He said:

"What a large volume of adventures may be grasped within this little span of life, by him who interests himself in everything, and who, having eyes to see what time and chance are perpetually holding out to him as he journeyeth on his way, misses nothing he can fairly lay his hands on."

I have found both truth and inspiration in his words.

GEORGIA DICKINSON WARDLAW.

Richmond, Virginia,
September 25, 1939.

ACKNOWLEDGMENTS

ERTAIN material used in several of the following chapters has been taken from articles written by the author, which first appeared in the Sunday Magazine of the Richmond *Times-Dispatch*. The use of this is gratefully acknowledged.

The author wishes to record her deep gratitude to those who aided in her research, and in various ways and capacities have lent able assistance; who generously put at her disposal family journals, histories, letters, papers, and clippings, for perusal and use; who gave unstintingly of information regarding their priceless relics, and permitted them to be photographed especially for this book.

The long list of names include:

Miss Helen G. McCormack, Director of the Valentine Museum, and Mrs. Fitzhugh Lafferty, Assistant to the Director; Mr. Robert A. Lancaster, Jr., Secretary of the Virginia Historical Society, and Mrs. J. A. Johnston, Assistant Secretary; Miss India W. Thomas, House Regent of the Confederate Museum; Miss Coralie H. Johnston, Reference Librarian, Virginia State Library, and Miss Dandridge Lambert, Assistant Reference Librarian; Miss Emerald C. Bristow, Lecturer on Decorative Arts, The Virginia Museum of Fine Arts; Miss Mary Nokely, Secretary of the Richmond Academy of Medicine; Mr. F. A. Dabney and

Mr. A. P. Ward of the Metropolitan Engraving Company; Major Francis E. Turin, Manager, Norfolk Advertising Board; Mr. Howard Corning, Secretary of the Essex Institute, Salem, Massachusetts; and Miss Anne Kinnaird, Assistant Archivist, Missouri Historical Society, St. Louis, Missouri.

Also, Miss Ellen Glasgow, Mrs. Margaret Dashiell, Mrs. Barton H. Grundy, Mrs. Bradley W. Johnson, Mrs. W. W. LaPrade, Mrs. M. R. Turnbull, Mrs. J. F. Biggs, Miss Catherine Gordon, Miss Jennie Pritchett, Mr. J. Bernard Robb, Dr. Churchill J. Gibson, Reverend G. MacLauren Brydon, Mr. August Dietz, Sr., Mr. August Dietz, Jr., Mr. J. Powell Wardlaw, Major and Mrs. Bernard H. Baylor, and Mr. and Mrs. S. Willard Ahalt, of Richmond, Virginia; Mrs. Stephen Decatur Mayo, of Gloucester County, Virginia; Mr. F. Otway Byrd and Mrs. Robert W. Daniel, of Brandon, Virginia; Mrs. Robert Voss Gordon, Miss Eliza Roy, and Miss Elsie W. Lewis, of Fredericksburg, Virginia; Miss Anne E. Gammon, of Norfolk, Virginia; Mrs. William H. Hartt and Mrs. Somerville Judick, of Portsmouth, Virginia; Miss Helen Siebold Walter, of Staunton, Virginia; Mrs. William W. Richardson of Hampton, Virginia; Mrs. Harrison Trent Nicholas, of Lynchburg, Virginia; Mrs. Arthur Peyton McCarty, of Washington, D. C.; Mr. Harold G. Brown, Winchester, Virginia; Mrs. Louis E. Fagan, of Philadelphia, Pennsylvania, and Miss DeWees Cochran and Miss Claribel A. Wheeler, of New York City.

CONTENTS

LIST OF ILLUSTRATIONS

The Sampler's Story

"When I was young and in my Prime,
You see how well I spent my Time.
And by my sampler you may see
What care my Parents took of me."

   —RHYME FOUND ON AN OLD SAMPLER.

CHAPTER I

THE SAMPLER'S STORY

HE story of the sampler, no matter how simply told, is one of patience and pathos, romance and religion, character and charm. One has only to examine any sampler of the late eighteenth or early nineteenth century, to at once realize what infinite patience went into its making. On a square of linen, measuring anywhere from six to eighteen inches in width and depth, were worked hundreds of infinitesimal stitches, done in various sizes and styles with the finest of silk thread. Often tears and heartache left their imprint on the finished sampler, as is evidenced in the one begun by little Martha Carter Fitzhugh of Virginia in 1790, and finished by unknown hands after her death in 1793.

How this quaint and appealing sampler found its way into a New England Museum, where today it is seen by thousands of visitors annually, is one of the mysteries the antiquarian must leave unsolved. He may thank his stars that, if not in its native surroundings, this old and exquisitely wrought piece of needlework, begun by the deft and nimble fingers of little Martha Carter Fitzhugh and left unfinished at her death, is at least safely preserved for posterity.

According to Mr. Howard Corning, Secretary of the Essex Institute at Salem, Massachusetts, this sampler came into the possession of the Institute before a regular system of recording articles was installed, for the date of its receipt and the source from which it came are both unknown; also it is believed to be the only sampler in their entire collection from Virginia.

The very name of Fitzhugh at once brings to mind such famous homes in Virginia as "Boscobel," "Belle Air," and "Chatham," built by members of this notable family. Of the three, "Chatham" still stands—serenely beautiful—with a sweeping view of the spires and towers of Fredericksburg from its terraced garden overlooking the Rappahannock.

The master of "Chatham" was William Fitzhugh III. He had been a classmate of William Pitt, Earl of Chatham, at Eton and Oxford, and according to tradition, the Earl commissioned Sir Christopher Wren to draw the plans for this splendid house, that he might present them to his friend. William Fitzhugh was one of the wealthiest men of his time in Virginia, and his great house was proverbial for its hospitality. A frequent and distinguished guest at "Chatham" was George Washington. Years later a celebrated Confederate General-to-be—Robert E. Lee wooed and won the fair Mary Custis here, and so tender was his regard for the scene of his courtship with her who had become his wife, that he refused to allow Confederate guns to be turned in its direction, even when "Chatham" was the headquarters of General Sumner during the Battle of Fredericksburg.

The union of William Fitzhugh and Ann Randolph of "Chatsworth" was blessed with many children, as little Martha Carter Fitzhugh's sampler records. One of the girls, Mary Lee Fitzhugh, who was five years old when her sister Martha died, married George

Sampler begun by Martha Carter Fitzhugh of "Chatham," who died
September 29, 1793, leaving it unfinished. Courtesy of The Essex Institute.

Washington Parke Custis, and it was their daughter, Mary Randolph Custis, who was courted beneath the great oak at "Chatham" by young Robert E. Lee.

Time has faded the silken stitches worked so painstakingly into little Martha Fitzhugh's sampler, but one can still clearly read the genealogical record and pathetic inscription, as begun by this little girl, sometime between the age of four and seven.

"William Fitzhugh born September 4, 1741. . Ann Randolph born May 13, 1747. . They were married April 2, 1763. . Lucy Fitzhugh born November 2, 1771, died September 29, 1777. . Betty Randolph Fitzhugh born November 20, 1773, died October 10, 1774.

> Here Innocence and Beauty lie whose Breath
> Was snatch'd by early, not untimely Death.
> Hence did they go, just as they did begin
> Sorrow to know, before they knew to Sin.
> Death that does Sin and Sorrow thus prevent,
> Is the next Blessing to a Life well spent.

Ann Randolph Fitzhugh born June 30, 1783. . Martha Carter Fitzhugh born February 28, 1786, died September 29, 1793 leaving this sampler unfinished, the word Hence, which was the last she marked being prophetic of her lamented Death. . . . .

> Her Name shall live and yield a sweet Perfume,
> And (tho in dust) her Memory shall bloom.
> Tho' I Deplore my Loss and wish it Less,
> Yet will I kiss the Rod and acquiesce.

Mary Lee Fitzhugh born April 2, 1788. . . . .
William Henry Fitzhugh born March 9, 1792. . . . ."

Research into the ancestry of the sampler reveals that its family tree has roots in many European countries. Leigh Ashton in his introduction to *Samplers* says, "The sampler is an instance of widespread domestic cult, but England is its real home." Yet in Norway, Sweden, Denmark, Spain, Italy, Greece, Holland,

Switzerland, Roumania and Mexico, the sampler has long been a much practiced feminine art.

Intensive reading brings to light fascinating bits of verse and speech referring to the sampler. John Skelton, who died in 1529, sang:

> "When that the tapettis and carpetiss were lay'd
> Whereon their ladies softly might rest,
> The sampler to sew on, the lacis to embraid."

Shakespeare, too, alludes to the sampler. In *Titus Andronicus,* Marcus says:

> "Fair Philomene, she but lost her tongue,
> And in a tedious sampler sewed her mind."

And in *A Midsummer Night's Dream,* Helene breathes to Hermia:

> "We, Hermia, like two artificial gods,
> Have with our needles created both one flower,
> Both on one sampler, sitting on one cushion."

A Royal notebook speaks of "6d for the linen of a sampler." In July, 1502, Elizabeth of York "pais eight-pence for an ell of linen cloth for samplers," while in 1546 Alyes Punchbeck is bequeathed by her aunt "my sampler with semes."

During the first stages of the sampler it was used for nothing more than a record of stitching patterns, set haphazard on a roll of linen. A mother taught her young daughter a new embroidery stitch, for, as the nursery rhyme goes—Curly Locks must "Sit on a cushion and sew a fine seam." Thus the stitch was promptly practiced and preserved for reference—via the sampler.

It is told of many a maid of the seventeen-seventies, eighteen-twenties, and gay-nineties, that those thoughts which she dared not confess to her lover's face (whether of reciprocal affection or unrequited love) she worked into her sampler! The very faith of one's fathers and color of one's surroundings somehow manifest themselves in the finished sampler. Those done by the Brontë sisters—Charlotte and Emily—and still in existence, are described as having seven-lettered quotations worked with black thread on gray canvas. Shadows, themselves, of the colorless austere life of the country rectory; of *Jane Eyre,* and the melancholy Yorkshire moors of *Wuthering Heights!*

Strange as it may seem, sampler-making seems to have been relegated to the very young. Many a little girl, in Virginia and elsewhere, learned her ABC's by the careful tedious stitches she worked into her sampler, usually embroidering two sets of alphabets—one capitalized, the other in small letters, on a square of linen.

Such a sampler, full of character and charm, was made by little Mary Ambler of Yorktown, who, early in her 'teens, became the bride of John Marshall. This sampler, which is a recent acquisition to the John Marshall House in Richmond, is preserved beneath glass and securely framed, and hangs on the walls of one of the rooms. It is unusually small in size, measuring twelve inches in length and six inches in width, and is embroidered in two sets of alphabets, capitalized and small, and signed in large letters, "Mary Ambler."

How old was Mary Ambler when she made this sampler? One can only hazard a guess, but she must have been very young for she was just sixteen when she married John Marshall.

Mary Willis Ambler (for that was her full name) was the daughter of Jaquelin Ambler of Yorktown. Her mother, the famous "Belinda" of Thomas Jefferson's early dreams, was Rebecca Burwell of "Carter's

Grove" of whom Jefferson wrote to his classmate John Page at William and Mary College, "Last night, as merry as agreeable company and dancing with Belinda in the Apollo could make me, I never could have thought the succeeding sun would have seen me so wretched as I now am." Could Rebecca Burwell have told Thomas Jefferson that night after the ball at the Raleigh Tavern in Williamsburg, that Jaquelin Ambler held the key to her heart? Anyway, she married him, and little Mary Ambler came to bless the home.

It was during the late winter of 1779-80 while visiting his father, Thomas Marshall, (commander of troops at Yorktown) that John Marshall fell in love with Mary Ambler, who was then but fourteen. They became engaged, but since Mary was considered too young to wed, John Marshall began to read law under George Wythe at Williamsburg. Absorbed in jurisprudence as he was, the sentimental scribblings on John Marshall's note-books revealed the real trend of his thoughts, for from front to back was written "Miss Maria Ambler," "Miss Mary Ambler," "Miss Polly Ambler." As for the young lady herself, I like to think that like many another maid of her time, she "sewed her thoughts into a sampler" which may yet find its way into John Marshall's home, there to rest beneath glass and hang beside her earlier sampler.

Even among Royalty, sampler-making enjoyed a wide-spread vogue. The unhappy Catherine of Aragon brought a knowledge of lace and open-work stitches to England when she came to wed Henry VIII. During the Elizabethan reign, the sampler habit became firmly established in England, Good Queen Bess herself owning a linen sampler worked with her own initials and royal insignia. Edward VI is said to have owned twelve samplers as well as a parchment of patterns, and his inventory lists a "sampler worked on Normandy canvas."

The first sampler brought to America is recorded as being one of great value, made in England by Anne Gower and brought by her when she came to this country as the first wife of Governor Endicott. Made before 1628, it is described as being embroidered on cream-colored linen with a matching thread. Still more interesting is the fact that the first all-American sampler is credited to Lorea Standish, daughter of the redoubtable Captain Miles Standish of Plymouth fame. Alice Morse Earle in her delightful book, *Home Life in Colonial Days,* states this is the oldest sampler she has ever seen. The verse embroidered on it reads:

> "Lorea Standish is My Name
> Lord guide my Heart that I may do thy Will,
> And fill my Hands with such convenient skill
> As will conduce to Virtue void of Shame,
> And I will give the Glory to thy Name."

The trend of early American samplers varied. Quite often the religious note predominated, as in the above, and in many quaint and charming old samplers which are to be seen in Virginia today. In the Valentine Museum in Richmond there is a splendid collection of old samplers belonging to the late eighteenth and early nineteenth century, quite diversified as to theme and design.

The oldest of these, and by far the *quaintest,* is the one made in 1788 by little Kitty Wood of Richmond, when she was eight years old. The material is a soft hand-woven linen, light tan in color, with the familiar sets of alphabets — capitalized and small — worked across the top. The central *motif* is a little red house, *very Georgian!* with a green tree on either side, and four small trees below. The edges are badly worn, but one can still admire the trailing rose vine which forms the border of this quaint and captivating sampler.

Wisely and well is Kitty Wood's sampler being preserved for posterity, for it lies beneath glass, safe from the touch of eager hands. Beside it is the quaintest letter imaginable (there is no other word to describe it!) the author of which is little Kitty Wood herself, written from Richmond in 1789 to her "Honored Mama, at the command of her dear Pappa."

It is a difficult task selecting the most interesting samplers in the Valentine Museum collection, for they are many and varied. The sampler worked by Mildred Malone of Richmond, and dated September 8, 1812, is an outstanding example of the religious sampler. In the center is a design both painted and embroidered, depicting "Christ and the Woman of Samaria." Here we have the familiar scene of the woman drawing water from the well, while at the top of the sampler, in delicately wrought letters, are the two verses from the IV Chapter of John which so graphically tell the story of Christ's meeting with this woman.

Still another sampler of a similar trend is the one made by Ann J. Hammond. This sampler is more than a hundred years old and is in an excellent state of preservation. The material is a brown hand-woven linen, and measures eighteen inches in width and depth. The delicate stitches are worked with meticulous care, in a variety of colored threads. Rose, green, blue and yellow predominate, and are lavishly used in the alphabet, flowers, and bow-knots which offset the principal inscription. This reads:

"Jesus permit thy gracious Name to stand,
As the first effort of an infant hand.
And while her tender fingers o'er this canvas move,
Engage her tender heart to seek thy love.
With Thy dear children let her share a part,
And write Thy Name upon her heart."

An almost identical sampler, as to material and design, is the one worked by Ann Hammond's mother in the year 1801, at the age of fifteen. She was Ann Newton Collins (recorded in the family Bible as "Nancy") and was the daughter of Christopher Collins and Ann Jordan. She became the third wife of Captain Thomas Hammond of Charles Town, Jefferson County, Virginia (now West Virginia). Captain Hammond's second wife, by whom he had no children, was Mildred Washington, daughter of Charles Washington.

Another sampler whose design and verse reflect a happier and lighter vein than most of its theological and genealogical companions, is one captioned "The Cottage Girl." It is worked on a loosely woven background in red and brownish-green threads. The central design shows a young girl standing beneath a tree, looking toward a winding walk which leads to a small cottage. Beneath the scene is the verse:

"O who will buy my roses,
They are fading like my youth.
But never like these posies
Shall wither Flora's truth."

Instinctively, my gaze rested on this unusual bit of verse. There was no doubt in my mind that the author of this quaint piece of needlework was named Flora, but, I pondered, was she a spinster of sixty, or a lass of sixteen? At the bottom of the sampler was my answer. The author was Flora Virginia Holmes, and she was all of *ten years old,* when she finished her sampler on which she had so charmingly described her "fading youth."

A genealogical sampler, also in the Valentine Museum, is one worked on a square of linen measuring sixteen and one half inches in width and depth. In addition to two sets of alphabets and numerals from one to thirteen, there are recorded the names of seven members of the "Brown Family," including the quaint "Angelina" and "Lucinda" of our great-grandmothers' day. A verse follows, and then the signature of Emma Brown who "finished this sampler 28th of October, 1825, Richmond, Virginia. *North America."*

One of the oldest samplers in Virginia today is an unpretentious little square of linen, worked entirely with letters of the alphabet. It forms a part of the small but interesting collection in the Virginia Historical Society, and antedates the Revolutionary War. This quaint old sampler was made by Barbara Fox of King William County, Virginia. She was a granddaughter of Thomas Fox and Mary Tunstall, who were married in 1707. At the close of the American Revolution, Barbara Fox married Captain Drury Ragsdale, who was a charter member of the Society of the Cincinnati and held many positions of trust. Barbara Fox Ragsdale was the great-great-grandmother of Doctor De La Warr Benjamin Easter, of Washington and Lee University, and the sampler was bequeathed by him to the Virginia Historical Society.

Barbara Fox Ragsdale must have transmitted her talent for needlework to her own little daughter, Frances Ragsdale, for this young lady's quaint alphabetical and numerical sampler—made in 1797 when she was twelve years old, is among the oldest of the samplers in the Valentine Museum. In this particular instance it is interesting to compare the ideas and workmanship of mother and daughter, for strangely enough, these two are not dissimilar.

In her delightful book, *Homespun Handicrafts,* Ella Shannon Bowles reminds us that "Public buildings, meeting-houses, brick houses of the early nineteenth century, figures of children, pots of gay flowers, trees, fruits, and baskets grew as if by magic in canvas stitches." The ship followed in the eighteenth century. In the colonies the genealogical sampler appeared prior to the Revolution, and remained a popular theme for many years thereafter, while the sorrow and horror of war brought into the realm of needlework many tributes to the dead.

As for materials used to make samplers Mrs. Bowles lists "seventeenth century linens which were supplemented by wider linens, woolen tammy-cloth, tiffany, bolting-cloth and homespun linens." Tammy-cloth, she reminds her readers, is mentioned in *The Vicar of Wakefield,* and was highly glazed; tiffany was a type of gauze or very thin silk; bolting cloth was primarily a sieve-cloth, used by millers for sifting flour. "It was made" writes Mrs. Bowles in her splendid chapter on samplers, "in different degrees of fineness, and since the threads could be easily counted, was well liked for sampler embroidery."

Silk threads were used early in sampler making, as well as lamb's wool and worsteds. Toward the end of the eighteenth century, crewels, fine worsteds tightly twisted with silks, also found a place in embroidery.

Mary Washington is said to have delighted in sampler-making and needlework in general, and when she was sixty-nine years old, embroidered twelve chair cushions, four each, for three of her grandchildren. "Miss Lewis" (one of the daughters of Colonel Fielding Lewis and Betty Washington) presented hers to the Marquis de LaFayette as a memento of her illustrious grandmother. "The cushions were executed upon coarse canvas in a design of shells, worked in brown and yellow wools with the high-lights flecked with gold colored silks," states my authority.

Who finished little Martha Carter Fitzhugh's sampler, and how did it find its way to Massachusetts from down in Virginia? Who kept little Mary Ambler's childish sampler these one hundred and fifty years? Where was little Kitty Wood when she made her quaint sampler—at home or in some select school for *very young ladies?* And where, today, are the remaining eight chair cushions embroidered by the Spartan Mother of Washington? It would be interesting if we but knew!

Silhouettes: A Study in Shadows

"*If you will observe, it doesn't take
A man of giant mould to make
A giant shadow on the wall;
And he who in our daily sight
Seems but a figure mean and small,
Outlined in Fame's illusive light,
May stalk, a silhouette sublime,
Across the canvas of his time.*"
—JOHN TOWNSEND TROWBRIDGE.

CHAPTER II

SILHOUETTES: A STUDY IN SHADOWS

WAS the silhouette popular in Virginia? Did it enjoy the same vogue in the Old Dominion that it did in other sections of the country, and abroad? Judging from the imposing list of Virginians whose "shadows-in-black" were cut by the celebrated scissors-and-shadows artists of by-gone days, the answer is decidedly "Yes."

Whether it was vanity, or simply a case of satisfying a caprice, that prompted so many illustrious sons and daughters of Virginia to be silhouetted we shall never know, but we do know that the most renowned masters of that quaint art—the silhouette—had as their subjects the great and the near-great of the Old Dominion.

William Bache cut General George Washington, Martha Washington, Mrs. Bushrod Washington, Nellie Custis and George Wythe. William Henry Brown did John Marshall, Henry Clay, John Randolph of "Roanoke" and Bishop Richard Channing Moore. Edouart cut Bailey Washington and Winfield Scott; Peale did busts of Dr. James Craik, Washington's personal physician, and also Dr. Walter Jones; and Todd of Baltimore, in his priceless album of more than two thousand profiles, entered the name of "Spottswood of Virginia." And there were others, many others, less well known perhaps, but equally as interesting.

Old lap-desks and horse-hair trunks have a way of bringing to light the most unexpected things—treasures of other days—forgotten or mislaid, or, what is still more exciting, whose very existence was unknown until the happy discovery was made by the fortunate possessor of these repositories of *ante bellum* days.

Not least among these rare finds have been countless silhouettes, tucked away between yellowed pages of old Bibles and letters, while an old diary carries these lines: "Sat for my silhouette by candlelight. *My shadow startled me!*"

To a generation unfamiliar with the flashlight or snapshot method of picture-taking, the silhouette must indeed have seemed painfully realistic, and at times, dreadfully direct and far from flattering. Yet the fad flourished, and "shadowgraphs" as they were sometimes called, enjoyed widespread popularity and a decided vogue, so much so that the *élite* of two continents were silhouetted in profile and full length.

Today, anyone possessing one or more of these originals may consider himself rich in his possession, not only because the silhouette may happen to be of some distinguished person, but because silhouettes by such masters-of-the-art as Brown, Bache, Peale, Edouart, or Hubard, are becoming increasingly rare, and therefore bait for collectors.

When these artists of the scissors-and-shadows era began their American tours, the South proved to be a happy hunting ground. Throughout Maryland, Virginia, Georgia, and South Carolina, the most illustrious of statesmen and *crème de la crème* of society, sat for their silhouettes in profile, or stood for a full length shadow.

In the century-old scrapbook of William Bache

Doctor Craik & Doctor Dick

Above: George Washington, by a French officer, Poitiaux. Below: Dr. James Craik of Alexandria, and Dr. Elisha Dick, Washington's physicians, silhouetted by an unknown artist. From the collection of medical silhouettes in the Richmond Academy of Medicine.

(which is said to have been in the possession of a great-niece living in Elmira, New York, some years ago) there are over two thousand portraits, including the duplicates of those he made of Chancellor Wythe's bust as well as the full length silhouettes of George and Martha Washington, Nellie Custis (Mrs. Lawrence Lewis), Thomas Jefferson, Edmund Randolph, and other distinguished Southerners.

William Bache was an Englishman by birth, but an American by association. He was born December 22, 1771, in Worcestershire, England, but at the age of twenty-two arrived in Philadelphia where an elder kinsman, Richard Bache, who had married Sally Franklin, had already settled. Bache at once established himself in Philadelphia as a cutter of profiles, and after much success, began his tour of the South.

There is an interesting story connected with a profile of Washington, cut by machine at Alexandria in 1798, and attributed to Bache. It was presented to William Henry Brown (another famed silhouettist) who used it as the frontispiece in his *Portrait Gallery of Distinguished American Citizens,* a copy of which is in the Library of Congress in Washington. To quote Brown:

"I received it from an old lady whose son had been drowned, and of whom I took a likeness after that body was found, which was so striking that it gave great satisfaction to the mother, who, in return, presented me with the profile of Washington. It was taken by machine at Alexandria, on the General's visit to that city to deposit his vote at an election, and was given to her, then a girl, by the General's own hand, and has been highly prized by her, and never would be parted with, but in return for the great favor I had done her in bringing to mind the image of her dead son."

Alice Van Leer Carrick in her superb book on silhouettes so quaintly captioned, *Shades of Our Ances-*

tors, expresses the doubt that even George III ever posed for his profile more frequently than Washington, and William S. Baker, one of the greatest of all authorities on Washington portraits, wrote, "I doubt if any man were ever painted, engraved, or lithographed so often as our Washington."

"First in war, first in peace—and the most silhouetted of our countrymen," Alice Van Leer Carrick writes of Virginia's immortal son. "Folwell, Bache, Peale and Joseph Wright—all professionals—made shadows of him," she reminds her readers, and adds, "Doolittle engraved his profile portrait; St. Mémin etched two tiny heads for signet rings; Vallée, the unsuccessful cotton manufacturer, painted one in India ink." Samuel Powell, Washington's personal friend and Mayor of Philadelphia, also cut his likeness by lamplight, and even Nellie Custis cut his profile from a shadow thrown on a wall at Mount Vernon. Surely everyone was eager to copy the august features of this great man.

I have read that the profiles cut by Nellie Custis at Mount Vernon so long ago, of the General and his Lady, are no longer in existence. Formerly in the possession of the Everett School in Boston, they were lost when the school house was destroyed by fire some years ago. Under each head, in flowing feminine script there was written, "The within are profiles of General and Mrs. Washington, taken from their shadows on a wall."

A Southern silhouettist of considerable fame was Charles Wilson Peale. He was born in Chestertown, on the Eastern Shore of Maryland, April 16, 1741, and died in Philadelphia—the scene of his greatest and most varied activities—in 1826. It was here that Washington was profiled by Peale's silhouette machine in

1794, the silhouette department being located in the North Gallery, an attractive adjunct of Peale's Museum in Philadelphia. A witness to the cutting of this silhouette was Alice Poultney Todd, wife of James Todd, whose brother was the first husband of Dolly Madison.

Peale was what might be called a "hollow-cutter"; that is, his silhouettes were first profiled by machine, the outline then cut from white paper, leaving a hollow-cut which was promptly placed over black—usually black silk. In *Shades of Our Ancestors,* Alice Van Leer Carrick states that all of the Peale silhouettes she has ever seen—"a great many by the way, for his is not a rare name"—have been hollow-cuts. Considering that Peale did not cut his silhouettes by hand, one is very disposed to share her opinion that a decidedly unstereotyped effect enters into his finished silhouette.

Almost invariably Peale stamped his work. In all, he used three different marks: "Museum" which is the most frequently found; "Peale's Museum"—the words in smaller type and with the impress of a spread eagle above, and the name "Peale" which is the most uncommon of all.

In the Library of the Richmond Academy of Medicine, one may see what is believed to be the only collection of medical silhouettes in the world. This remarkable collection, which was given to the Academy by Dr. Joseph Miller of West Virginia, who is said to have spent years in assembling it, numbers in all sixty-six silhouettes—as varied and charming a group of profiles and full-lengths as any devotee of this quaint art could dream of seeing beneath one roof.

Here one may see the "shadows" of some of this country's most famous men of medicine a century and

more ago: a bust of Dr. James Craik, Washington's
personal physician, wearing what looks to be a
"Hessian" hat; also a bust of Dr. Walter Jones of
Lancaster County, Virginia, Physician-General in the
Revolution—both of which are by Peale; a distinguish-
ed trilogy of bust profiles of Dr. Benjamin Franklin,
Dr. Benjamin Rush, and Dr. John Redman, with a
large golden eagle above, which is attributed also to
Peale, and many other notables.

Of the sixty-six silhouettes in the Richmond Academy of Medicine collection, seven are definitely Peale's,
fifteen Edouart's, two Browne's, and one Hubard's, the
remaining twenty-five being unidentified. Peale's bust
of Dr. James Craik of Alexandria, who attended
George Washington in his last illness, is cut from white
paper and pasted over black silk, with "Peale's Museum" stamp clearly marked on the front, showing the
spread eagle.

What of Edouart? He was not of our Southland—
not even of America, but to some silhouette enthusiasts
he will always be the most ingenious silhouettist of all
time. I confess to having fallen under the spell of
anything *Edouartian;* the little man simply intrigues
me with his flair for backgrounds, and the exquisite
touch he gave to everything and everyone he cut. His
utterly charming and exquisitely done full-length silhouettes of American notables, done singly and in
groups, have made his name familiar to every lover and
collector of silhouettes, and therefore his history is
interesting.

Born in Dunkirk in 1788, Edouart settled in England
in 1815, and during the fourteen years he worked in
Great Britain prior to his famous and successful American tour (1839-49), he had travelled the length and

breadth of the British Isles—London, Oxford, Cambridge, Bath, Edinburgh, Glasgow, Dublin, Cork—where his skill had won him wide acclaim.

When one considers the cost of old miniatures on ivory, and portraits in oil, one sighs with regret and bemoans his fate that this ingenious Frenchman—Augustin Amant Constance Fidèle Edouart belonged to another age, for an English label gives his price as five shillings for a full length figure, while a profile bust cost but one shilling. This was in Bath; later, the fastidious little Frenchman raised his prices, scorning what he termed "a shilling business," and though his prices mounted his business continued to flourish like the green bay tree. Edouart knew his public, especially his *élite* public, so he must have reasoned that if his efforts were to be crowned with success and his name attain enduring fame, his silhouettes must be *recherché*. And so they were—and are!

At Abbotsford he profiled Sir Walter Scott; at Cambridge Henry Wadsworth Longfellow. He cut the paper portrait of Charles X at Holyrood, and Martin Van Buren at Washington, while an authority states "his lovely ladies at Saratoga are quite as charming as the belles at Bath." Surely no artist or photographer of today is half so popular with his public, as was Edouart. A list of his patrons would be a *Who's Who* of the forties—a *Social Register* of fame and fashion, wit and beauty.

By far the quaintest silhouette of Edouart's I have ever seen, is one in the Valentine Museum in Richmond, of Auried Stephen Thomas Clissold, age one-and-a-half years. This silhouette was given to the museum by an English collector, and differs from most other Edouarts, in that it has no pictorial background.

Master Clissold is wearing what looks to be feminine attire: a long dress which gives the impression of concealing numerous starched petticoats, with a sash that ties in a large bow in the back. He wears ankle-boots which doubtless were of Turkey leather in a brilliant shade of red, for Edouart has taken great pains to show them off to advantage.

This astonishing infant (one suspects that Edouart called him the *enfant terrible*) is shown wielding a whip with astonishing vigor, as if to say, "I shall thrash you, Monsieur, if you dare to come near me." But perhaps I am wrong. The pose may be deceiving, and Clissold may not have been a belligerent babe after all. Does not a modern photographer place in the hands of his juvenile subjects the most vicious looking plush monkeys with glass eyes, in order to pacify and amuse and quiet, that a pose may be successful?

Edouart is said to have kept a stock of "papers, letters, and sheet music, ready to be placed in his sitter's hands." It is therefore quite possible that he was also well supplied with trinkets and toys such as balls, hoops, and whips, on those occasions when he was called upon to make silhouettes of the very young. So the menacing looking whip may have been placed in the little fellow's hands by none other than Edouart himself.

Master Clissold is, of course, English, and the silhouette belongs to the period of Edouart's successful career in the British Isles. It is severely plain: a good size full-length black shadow pasted on white. Below is Edouart's small and distinct signature, written in ink—"Aug. Edouart, fecit, 1827." The *fecit* is characteristic of Edouart, signifying, of course, that Edouart made it.

Bailey Washington, son of Lawrence
Washington, half-brother of George
Washington. By Edouart. From the col-
lection of medical silhouettes in the
Richmond Academy of Medicine.

"Master Clissold" by Edouart, 1827.
From the Valentine Museum Collection.

On the back of the silhouette is a printed label which Edouart used during his English tour. It reads:

"Likeness in Profile Executed by Mons. Edouart, Who begs to observe that his Likenesses are produced by the scissors alone, and are preferable to any taken by machines, inasmuch as by the above method, the expressions of the passions, and peculiarities of character, are not brought into action, in a style which has not hitherto been attempted by any other artist. Numerous Proof Specimens may be seen at No. 3 Colonade, Cheltenham.
Full Length   5 shillings.
Ditto Children under 8 years of age, 3 shillings, 6d.
Profile Bust   1 shilling.
Duplicate of the cuttings to any quantity, are for each Full Length, 3 shillings.
Ditto, children   2 shillings, 6d.
Attendance abroad, Double, if not more than two Full Length Likenesses are taken.
Any additional Cuttings, as Instrument, Table, etc. etc. to be paid accordingly."

Of the fifteen silhouettes by Edouart in the Library of the Richmond Academy of Medicine, only one is Virginian, but the name is Washington, and the full length figure in black stands against a beautiful terraced background. Here is a typical Edouart. Bailey Washington, (for that was the distinguished gentleman's name) carries a cane, and is shown holding his high hat in his hand. The cut of his clothes show him to be a very splendid gentleman indeed, surveying what looks to be a landscaped garden from high terraced steps. The silhouette is signed by Edouart, and is dated 1841.

After a highly successful ten years in America, Edouart returned to London on board the ship *Oneida,* a small Southern vessel loaded with cotton. In a furious gale off the coast of Guernsey the boat foundered, and the twenty-six passengers narrowly escaped death. The three thousand six hundred duplicates of silhouettes, cut by Edouart on his American tour, were somehow salvaged from the sinking vessel and carried ashore by the little Frenchman himself.

Edouart, so the story goes, was taken to the house of a man named Lukis, where he recuperated from the shock and exposure of shipwreck. When able to continue his journey, in gratitude for the kind treatment he had received at the hands of his stranger host, Edouart presented the duplicates of his entire American series to Fredericka Lukis, daughter of his benefactor. From her the collection passed through several hands, finally coming into the ownership of Mr. Arthur S. Vernay of New York, who made all devotees of silhouettes his debtor, by placing the entire collection—perfectly preserved and intact—on exhibition, thus enabling hundreds of persons to see—and buy—these highly prized shades of their ancestors. Among them was found the duplicate of Edouart's silhouette of Winfield Scott.

William Henry Brown, considered by many to be the most famous of all American silhouettists, began cutting silhouettes fifteen years before Edouart reached America, for in September, 1824, he had silhouetted LaFayette at Philadelphia.

Brown was a Charlestonian by birth, the son of Quaker parents from Abbeville, South Carolina. Born May 22, 1808, he lived to enjoy a life of brilliant contacts and great distinction, and lies buried in the Circular Churchyard in Charleston.

His monumental work, *Portrait Gallery of Distin-*

guished American Citizens contains profiles and full-lengths of some of Virginia's most illustrious sons—John Randolph of "Roanoke" admiring his blooded horses; Henry Clay, John Marshall, Bishop Richard Channing Moore, and others of equal note. Brown's silhouette of the venerable Bishop is charming. He is shown standing beneath an ancient oak, surveying what well might be one of Richmond's "seven hills." Here we have one of the most delightful examples of the lithographed backgrounds Brown used for his *Portrait Gallery*. These were done by E. B. and E. C. Kellogg, and while Brown may not have designed them himself, he must have given the Kelloggs very careful instructions.

The Bishop's silhouette is the utter perfection of Brown's art. The old gentleman stands, cane in hand, wearing with great dignity a high silk hat. His silvern hair shows white against the black figure, and hangs to his shoulder. What sturdy legs the reverend Bishop had, and what a rotund figure! Brown shows him to be the picture of sartorial perfection, attired in a frock tail coat, knee breeches, and such quaint slippers! Yet one instinctively feels that the Bishop's thoughts were not upon the things of this world, when he stood for his silhouette. The finished picture gives one the impression that Brown had come upon the old gentleman quite unexpectedly—in a moment of silent reverie—surveying a verdant landscape, while the words of the psalmist might well have been upon his lips.

See for yourself. A copy of the original hangs framed on the walls of the Mayo Memorial Church House in Richmond. In the left hand corner is printed in small letters, "From life, by Wm. H. Brown" and directly opposite, "Lith. of E. B. and E. C. Kellogg."

Where and with whom does one end in the study and search for silhouettes, and the names of those who made them? No more fitting finale to the subject could be chosen than the name of Hubard—Master James Hubard, the boy prodigy who began cutting silhouettes at the age of twelve; gained international fame by the swiftness and skill of his scissors, (he is reputed to have cut silhouettes by hand in the astonishing time of twenty seconds, as against the one minute required by Brown!) and met his death—strange as it may seem—in Richmond, Virginia.

When James Hubard arrived in New York in 1824, he was already a British celebrity. He had made his *début* at Ramsgate in September, 1822, (authorities believe his age then was fifteen) where his talent had so impressed the Duchess of Kent, who was then at Townley House, that he made portraits of her entire suite. He profiled Queen Victoria "when she was a slender little princess," and was presented with a silver palette by the Glasgow Philosophical Society, in recognition of his genius. This piece of silver, measuring four by six inches, and inscribed with the words, "Presented to Master James Hubard by the admirers of his genius in the City of Glasgow, February 14th, 1824" was, for many years in the possession of Hubard's daughter in Lynchburg, Virginia. Today, its safe-keeping has been intrusted to the Valentine Museum in Richmond.

Hubard was widely advertised after arriving in America. In Boston, a notice appeared December 24, 1824, which read: "The Hubard Gallery of Cuttings, Julian Hall, Milk Street, is now handsomely decorated with evergreens. A fine large equestrian statue of Washington, cut by Master Hubard, occupies the center of the decorations, while a whole length figure of

LaFayette and DeWitt Clinton, both taken from life by Master Hubard, are allowed striking likenesses."

Later in Philadelphia, he was a pupil of Sulley's and his first painting was exhibited at the Academy of National Design in 1829. In Baltimore, where he went after leaving Philadelphia, he left two handsome bronzed whole lengths, for he had continued with his profiles as well as his paintings. Later he came to Virginia.

"Here romance, which should have been dogging the heels of so adventurous a person as Hubard, overtook him in Gloucester, where he met and married Miss Maria Mason Tabb," writes Miss Helen G. McCormack, Director of the Valentine Museum, who probably knows more about Hubard's life than any other person in Virginia, outside of his family. "Miss Tabb is shown in a miniature by her husband to be a clear-eyed, steadfast young lady, capable of recognizing in an itinerant painter a person of unusual character" she continues.

After their marriage the Hubards went to Italy where they knew Horiation Greenough and Hiram Powers, both of whom were celebrated American sculptors. In 1850 the Hubards returned to Virginia. With the outbreak of hostilities between the North and the South, and the Confederacy's clarion call to arms, Hubard showed himself a true patriot, converting his foundry which had been erected for the casting of the Houdon replica, into a foundry for cannon and shells. In February 1862 while experimenting with a ball for the Brook gun, he was killed, having literally given his life for the cause of the Confederacy.

Hubard's obituary in the *Richmond Dispatch* refers to him as "a good citizen, and a gentleman of varied accomplishments," and further adds that he was regarded as one of the most gifted artists who had lived in the South for many years.

"That Hubard was a person of unusual fascination as well as of varied accomplishments is shown by the estimates of him written by those who knew him," says Miss McCormack. "Mann S. Valentine described him as a person of bold thought, vivid imagination, and strong will. The late Edward G. Valentine, a pupil of Hubard's, remembered him as a person of great charm. But none of these knew him as a silhouettist."

How many of Hubard's silhouettes there are in Virginia today, it would indeed be interesting to know. I have seen only three; two of which are in the Valentine Museum, the other in the collection of the Richmond Academy of Medicine.

Identification of original Hubards is not difficult, for if in the lower left-hand corner of the silhouette is stamped the legend "Taken at the Hubard Gallery" one may be certain that the silhouette was made in England. If there is stencilled in ink the words "Cut with scissors by Master Hubard, without drawing or machine, at the Gallery of Cuttings and Panharmonicon Concert Room," then the silhouette can be definitely identified as having been made during Hubard's American tour.

What of the unsigned silhouette? Here is a fascinating field for study and speculation. In the notable collection of medical silhouettes in the Library of the Richmond Academy of Medicine, the "unidentified group" is perhaps the most interesting of all. There is a captivating full-length silhouette of Dr. James Craik and Dr. Elisha Dick, who attended the master of Mount Vernon during his fateful illness. Dr. Dick is

Dr. John Peter Mettauer, celebrated Virginia physician, born in Prince Edward County, Virginia, in 1787. Dr. Mettauer is shown wearing his "famous stove-pipe hat" in which he was buried. By an unknown artist. From the collection of medical silhouettes in the Richmond Academy of Medicine.

shown extending his hand in greeting to his colleague. Quaint is the word for this old silhouette, but when, where, and by whom it was made remains a mystery.

Again, there is the beautifully executed bust of Georgia's illustrious son, Crawford Williamson Long, whose use of ether as an anæsthetic in 1842, was the first recorded instance of the use of an anæsthesia in surgical history. Well may Virginians share Georgia's pride in Dr. Long's great experiment, for his mother was Elizabeth Ware, a daughter of the Old Dominion.

Nor must I fail to mention the largest, and to me, most fascinating of all the silhouettes in this unidentified group: the bold, full-length shadow of that distinguished Virginian and Doctor of Medicine—John Peter Mettauer, whose accomplishments in his chosen field, to say nothing of his idiosyncracies, but serve to enhance the charm and interest already attached to his impressive shadow-in-black. Fortunately, for those interested in his history, there is pasted on the back of his silhouette a detailed account of his life, which gives intimate glimpses into the professional, as well as the personal side of his character.

John Peter Mettauer was a native of Prince Edward County, Virginia, and was born in the year 1787, the son of Dr. Francois Joseph Mettauer, one of two brothers who came to Virginia as regimental surgeons with General LaFayette. After the battle of Yorktown Dr. Francois Mettauer's regiment was stationed in Prince Edward County, where he settled after the war and married Elizabeth Gaulding.

Here their son John Peter Mettauer was born and raised, graduating with an A. B. from Hampden-Sydney College in 1806, at the age of nineteen. Three years later he received his degree of M. D. from the

University of Pennsylvania, and later in life also received degrees of A. M. and LL. D. Of his achievements we read:

"Of the many able men the Old Dominion has given to the medical
profession, Dr. Mettauer was, unquestionably, the most remarkable.
By nature a great surgeon, he was also an able physician, and a
voluminous contributor to medical literature. His marvelous surgical
skill and ingenuity soon obtained for him such a reputation, that,
despite the fact of his work lying in an obscure country village, and
before the days of numerous railroads, patients flocked to him from
all around, some even from abroad.

"He performed almost every operation known in his day, and it is
certain that he did more than eight hundred operations for cataract.
In operations for vesical calculus, his operations exceeded by one
hundred and seventy five, Dudley's two hundred and twenty-five.

"He was the first surgeon in Virginia, and one of the first in the
United States to operate successfully for cleft palate, his first operation having been performed in 1827."

Dr. Mettauer's full-length shadow shows him dressed
in what was undoubtedly the height of fashion in his
day. The lines of his frock-tail coat are carefully cut;
his trousers are close-fitting; his shoes small and dandi-
fied. A large wing-collar is seen protruding from
under his chin, while the most conspicuous feature of
the entire silhouette is the Doctor's "stove-pipe" hat.
Trust the French to be fastidious in matters of dress!
One may safely predict that when John Peter Mettauer
entered a room, he was at once the cynosure of all eyes;
not because of his fame as a surgeon and physician, but
because of his hat! With the Doctor it was *de rigueur!*
And herein lies a tale.

Dr. Mettauer's attachment for this especial hat is a
part of the story of the man himself. He invariably
wore it (the same one that is shown in the silhouette)
and nothing under high heaven could induce him to

remove it. He is said to have worn it everywhere—
and on all occasions—even at meals, and, of all places,
in bed! Nor would he attend service in any church, a
fact attributed to his unwillingness to remove his hat.
When called upon to testify in court, he declined to
remove it, and one naturally assumes that what was
true of his conduct in the court-room was also true in
the operating-room. When Dr. Mettauer's end was
near, he left instructions that he be buried in his hat,
and his instructions are said to have been faithfully
carried out, it being necessary to have a coffin made
eight feet long, to accommodate both the deceased and
his indispensable headgear.

Some day, in the none too distant future, I hope to
see all old silhouettes in Virginia exhibited *en bloc,* in
order that those who are the proud possessors of these
quaint shades of our ancestors, may share them with
others.

The Vogue of the Valentine

"Where can the postman be, I say?
He ought to fly on such a day.
Of all days in the year, you know,
It's monstrous rude to be so slow.
The fellow's so exceeding stupid—
Hark, there he is—oh! the dear Cupid!
Hark, there he is—oh! the dear Cupid."
—LINES ON ST. VALENTINE'S DAY FROM HONE'S
Every Day Book, published in London in 1826.

CHAPTER III

THE VOGUE OF THE VALENTINE

THE quest of the quaint inevitably leads to old valentines. Rarer than samplers and silhouettes, these sentimental missives of our ancestors are more than mere flimsy trifles—they are transcripts of history. Not only do they record the tender emotions (so quaintly and gracefully expressed) of the gallants of a century ago, but reveal as well, the manners, customs, and fashions, of a day and generation that has gone forever. Even the so-called "comics," which one writer very justly describes as "not valentines at all, but vulgar vehicles of insult"—illuminate their times.

The index to many a man's character may be found in the valentine he sent to his lady love seventy-five or a hundred years ago. Was he ardent, persistent, bold— given to flattery—or was he a timid soul? Was he a man of discriminating taste, and a lavish spender? The answer lies in his valentine.

If an old valentine is of satin, gauze, and lace-paper —elaborately embossed (and possibly perfumed!) one may be reasonably certain that the sender was a gentleman of means, and one who did business with London and Edinburgh firms. And if, in addition to the amorous verses printed on the valentine, he chose to inscribe with his own hand, expressions of high esteem and undying devotion, then, manifestly, he was the perfect lover.

Such a gentleman, I am sure, was James David Gammon, of Princess Anne County, Virginia, whose valentine to Margaret Ann Murray, also of Princess Anne, is the most exquisite and elaborate bit of "love-and-lacework" I have ever seen. They were married in the year 1856, and since the valentine was sent several years previous to their nuptials, it can definitely be classed as "old." It is the treasured possession of their daughter, Miss Anne Eliza Gammon of Norfolk, who keeps it between the folds of tissue, carefully boxed, as though it was really a bit of lavender and old lace.

Then there is the faded and tear-stained old valentine which a Richmond youth sent to his sweetheart in Montgomery County, Maryland, just before the outbreak of the War Between the States. When the call to arms was sounded, the young lover joined the Confederate Army, and like many of his contemporaries, never returned. Crushed by her loss, and faithful to his memory, the girl never married. Her soldier's last token of love remained her dearest treasure, and on her death-bed she gave it to a faithful slave, who had comforted her during the years of her sorrow.

Many years thereafter, the valentine fell into the hands of an antique dealer, who sent it as a token of high regard to Virginia's distinguished authoress, Miss Ellen Glasgow. In his letter to Miss Glasgow, giving the valentine's history, the Maryland dealer wrote: "If you conclude to keep the valentine, it will at least be near the home it started from." Miss Glasgow presented it to Mrs. Margaret Dashiell of Richmond, whose dominant interest is old prints, but who became

Valentine sent by a Confederate soldier from Virginia, to his sweetheart in Frederick County, Maryland. Acquired several years ago by a Maryland antique dealer, who sent it to Miss Ellen Glasgow, of Richmond, as a token of esteem. Given by Miss Glasgow to Mrs. Margaret Dashiell of Richmond.

interested in old valentines many years ago while collecting prints. Mrs. Dashiell has sold or given away most of her valentines, but this faded and worn one, around which the aura of romance and tragedy still clings, remains one of her most prized possessions.

"Romance is always young," writes the poet Whittier, and well do we know that the whole world loves a lover. How else explain the vogue of the valentine, which has increased rather than diminished with passing years, until today, more valentines are sold than any other type of greeting, except Christmas cards?

Few people realize that when they celebrate St. Valentine's Day, they are really celebrating a feast that dates back to ancient Rome, when Lupercalia, the Feast of Mating Birds, was celebrated by the young men and maids of that time. This signified the advent of spring, when every man had the right to express his affection, and every maid as well. The procedure was for each to draw the name of his or her valentine from an urn.

Another explanation of the origin of Valentine's Day is that among the ancient Romans, it was the custom to draw the names of girls in honor of their goddess, Februata-Juno, on the fifteenth of February, in exchange for which certain Catholic priests substituted the names of saints, in billets given the day before—February fourteenth. Thus it may have been that Saint Valentine's name was drawn first, and its poetic beauty so lingered in the minds of the young folk, that eventually the day became Saint Valentine's Day.

Most authorities agree on one point—that only by accident has Valentine's Day always been associated with the benevolent Bishop Valentine, who was martyred in 306 A. D. The Christian Church, forced to recognize the day, dedicated it to the martyred saint, but even this failed to give it a religious significance. Eventually, the celebration died out on the Continent, but in England it became a popular festival, with poems and gifts the order of the day.

Charles, Duke of Orleans, who had been captured at Agincourt and taken to England (where, clearly, he made himself at home), penned ardent valentines to his lady love while confined in the Tower of London. Another famous Royal Valentine is the one John Lydgate wrote to Catherine, wife of Henry V.

Chaucer, Spenser, Michael Drayton, and John Donne all wrote valentines, and the Cavaliers and Victorians who followed them continued the practice. Was it not Edmund Spenser who gave to the world— over three hundred years ago—the now-famous line, "Roses red and violets blew,"—amaranthine flowers to the valentine?

Even in Shakespeare's day the custom of challenging one's valentine had already commenced, for in *Hamlet,* Ophelia says:

> "Good Morrow! 'tis St. Valentine's Day,
>   All in the morn betime,
>   And I a maid at your window
>   To be your valentine."

As a rule, the custom simply demanded saying the words, "Good Morrow! 'tis St. Valentine's Day," and he or she who said it first on meeting a person of the opposite sex, received a present. There were, to be sure, ways of preventing mishap. Mrs. Pepys for instance, "set her mind" on having Will Bowyer for her valentine, (this was evidently before her marriage to the famous diarist), and so afraid was she that her eyes might fall on one of the painters working in the house, that she covered them with her hands, until Will appeared on the scene to claim her.

In an old issue of *Poor Robin's Almanac,* under the caption of St. Valentine's Day, reference is made to the custom of drawing valentines:

"Now Andrew, Anthony, and William,
    For Valentines draw Prue, Kate, and Jilian."

Early custom demanded that presents should be exchanged, but later, a gallant ruling was enacted, whereby the gentleman alone was required to present the gift. In his famous diary, the gossipy Pepys makes annual reference to the custom of drawing one's valentine, rejoicing on one occasion that he had drawn his wife, since by having her "it would be cheaper."

In 1664, Mrs. Martha Batten was Pepys' valentine, and his present to her—a pair of gloves—cost him the painful sum of forty shillings, but as Mrs. Pepys was Sir William Batten's valentine, and received from him not only gloves, but silk stockings and garters as well, the thrifty Pepys emerged from this pleasant little sport far from being the loser.

He records another instance when an English belle got from the Duke of York a jewel valued at three thousand three hundred dollars, His Royal Highness being "once her valentine." This same lucky lady had as her next year's valentine a gentleman by the same romantic name—none other than Lord Valentine himself, who, having drawn her name, presented her with a ring costing the tidy sum of one thousand three hundred and fifty-five dollars.

Mission, a learned traveller, who died in England in 1721, describes the amusing practices of his times, and of Valentine's Day writes:

"On the eve of the fourteenth of February—St. Valentine's Day, the young folks in England and Scotland, by a very ancient custom, celebrate a little festival. An equal number of maids and bachelors get together, each writing their true or some feigned name upon separate billets, which they roll up and draw by way of lots—the maids taking the mens billets, and the men the maids, so that each of the young men lights upon a girl that he calls his valentine, and each of the girls upon a young man she calls hers.

By this means each has two valentines. Fortune having thus divided the company into so many couples, the valentines give balls and treats to their mistresses, who wear their billets several days upon their bosoms or sleeves, and this little sport often ends in love."

Walsh, in his splendid reference work, *Curiosities of Popular Customs,* gives the following quaint pen-picture of valentine-making and sending in the days when the *élite* carried their snuff-boxes, dined and danced by candle-light, travelled by coach-and-six, and wrote their *billets-doux* with a graceful quill pen.

"In the days of quill pens and dear postage, the transmission of valentines through the post was an expensive luxury. The amorous swains of that period had to content themselves and their idolized fair ones with thick sheets of gilt-edged paper—(envelopes had not then come into use, and book postage was still unknown) the first of each sheet being adorned with a gilt cupid carefully gummed on, surmounting a few lines, the favorite formula announcing in terms held sacred to St. Valentine's that because 'the rose is red and the violet blue' therefore the recipient is as sweet as sugar."

The amusing account continues:

"With the reduction of the heavy postal charges, printed valentines gradually came into use. They generally consisted of a gaudily colored picture, representing a loving couple seated in a bower, with a church in the distance, and a few lines descriptive of the sentiments of the person forwarding the same.

The designers of these amatory billets seemed to have entertained rather singular notions respecting the proper attire of the ladies and gentlemen of whose feelings they sought to become the interpreters. The lady was invariably dressed in a scarlet gown with a blue or

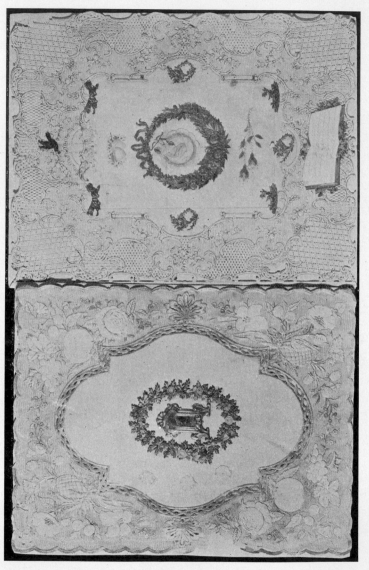

Front and back of imported valentine, made of embossed lace paper, satin, and gauze. This exquisite sentimental missive was sent by James David Gammon of Princess Anne County, Virginia, to Margaret Anne Murray, also of Princess Anne, prior to 1856, the year in which they were married. Owned by their daughter, Miss Anne E. Gammon, of Norfolk.

green shawl; the gentleman was attired in lavender trousers, yellow waistcoat, blue surtout, and green or crimson cravat. The effect thus obtained was, as might be imagined, somewhat striking. . ."

Whether these "fashion-plate" valentines were of English or American make I do not know, but the costlier creations were frequently embossed with the names of their manufacturers. Signatures of Kershaw of London, or Lloyd of Edinburgh, had the same meaning as the hallmark of famous silversmiths, and today, in the eyes of collectors, the *cachet* of these two manufacturers is the most coveted mark a valentine can carry.

Reference has been made to the "dear postage" involved in the transmission of valentines through the post, long long ago. These of course were the days before postage stamps, and the postal tariff—regulated on the basis of distance—was altogether exhorbitant, when viewed in the light of present-day postal rates. The cost of sending one sheet of paper not exceeding thirty miles, was six cents; more than thirty miles and not exceeding eighty, ten cents; more than eighty miles and not exceeding one hundred and fifty miles, twelve and a half cents; more than one hundred and fifty and not exceeding four hundred miles, eighteen and three-fourths cents; over four hundred miles, twenty-five cents. Two sheets cost twice as much, three sheets three times as much, and so on.

In spite of the "dear postage" of those days, the vogue of the valentine continued, the proof of which may be seen today in many privately owned collections, and those in Museums.

In the novels of Sir Walter Scott and Charles Dickens the status of the valentine is clearly shown. What lass was ever known to make more satisfactory use of the valentine than Catherine, Scott's *Fair Maid of Perth,* in her dealings with Hal of the Wynd? He had done her chivalrous service, so after due deliberation, she concluded with sound Scotch logic:

"I will not wait till my father compels me to receive him as my valentine for the year; I will seek him out and choose him myself. I shall thus best please my father, and but discharge the rites due to the good St. Valentine by showing my gratitude to this brave man."

Then there is the episode in *Pickwick Papers* that describes Sam Weller's sending a valentine to Mary, the winsome Ipswich housemaid. You recall that it was a shop window which first suggested the amatory approach to Sam, for therein he saw, "a highly colored representation of a couple of human hearts, skewered together with an arrow, cooking before a cheerful fire, while a male and female cannibal in modern attire were approaching the meal with hungry eyes. A decidedly indelicate young gentleman in a pair of wings and nothing else, was depicted as superintending the cooking."

Poor Sam, thus incited, straightway proceeded to purchase a sheet of gilt-edged writing paper and a hard-nibbed pen, and equipped to declare himself, did set down his sentiments and emotions toward the fair Mary, who ultimately became Mrs. Samuel Weller.

Alas, the valentine did not retain its individuality for long. In 1760, young men and maids in love were making their own valentines, but by 1783 tradesmen had taken over the idea, and what had heretofore been personal and individualistic, became as common-place as a present-day telegraphic sample greeting.

These Tradesmen's Valentine Booklets were issued annually, much after the fashion of almanacs, and ante-dated all forms of manufactured valentines. The publishers invariably stressed the fact that the poems used in each booklet were new and original, and every known trade under the sun was represented in this singular series. For the small sum of sixpence, the butcher, the baker, and the candlestick-maker could advertise their wares in the most subtle ways, and in one of these old booklets, called *The New Tradesmen's Valentine Writer,* various and sundry verses are furnished for such people as dancing masters, army officers, coach-makers, saddlers, weavers, stay-makers, brewers, et cetera.

The weaver's valentine began:

"Oh, love so *warps* my heart. . ."

while the stay-maker's verse ran something like this:

"To *shape* the temper is to. . ."

The entire verse recommended for the sentimental brewer of that day ran thus:

"As *malt* in water yields good *beer,*
When *brewed* with care and skill,
Just so your charms within my heart,
Love's sweetest pangs instil;
As *hops* infused, preserve the *beer,*
And keep it good for years,
So may your kindness foster love,
Your smiles dispel my fears."

What of the first American-made valentines, and the origin of the valentine industry in this country? The credit goes to New England, and a daughter of Massachusetts, Miss Esther A. Howland. In England, in 1825, lace and embossed paper was first manufactured. The first valentine made of this material to appear in America, was sent to Miss Howland who lived in

Worcester, Massachusetts, the present home of the world's largest manufacturers of valentines.

In this old New England town, Miss Howland's father and brothers were in the stationery business. Pondering over the practicability of the valentine as a business venture, (and ingenious to a marked degree) Miss Howland decided to try her hand at this quaint art, and to improve on the valentine imported by her father which had been sent her as a souvenir.

When one of Miss Howland's brothers who travelled for the firm left on a business trip, he took with him samples of the valentines his sister had made. On his return home, he brought with him orders totaling five thousand dollars, and thus dawned the beginning of the valentine industry in this country.

There is a romantic story concerning John Page of "Rosewell" (who was later Governor) and his courtship with Margaret Lowther of New York, which has as its setting a Valentine Ball. As a young man—just turned twenty-one—John Page had married Frances Burwell, daughter of Colonel Robin Burwell and Sallie Nelson of Yorktown. She became the mother of twelve children (three of whom died in infancy), and passed on to her reward nineteen years after her marriage to the master of "Rosewell."

At forty, John Page found himself a lonely widower, with nine young children on his hands. How sad and empty life had suddenly become. Then, a few years later, a note of spring sounded in the old man's heart (for so a man was considered in Virginia in those days, with forty summers behind him!). John Page met the fair daughter of William Lowther of Scotland, and suddenly life held a new meaning for him. Margaret Lowther is said to have been "young and sprightly, with a pretty wit and a knack for writing verses which delighted her elder beau," and, continues the old chronicle, "there were many encounters between them in which the lady had the last and smartest word."

Then came the Valentine Ball (could it have been in Williamsburg?) when Margaret dropped her glove, which her admirer returned to her in the most cavalier fashion, with the following couplet concealed inside:

> "Take G from Glove, and that leaves Love,
> 'Tis that I offer thee."

Quickly adding two more lines, the clever and captivating Miss Lowther returned the note, and John Page read:

> "Take P from Page, and that leaves Age,
> Too old thou art for me!"

But the aged Mr. Page had the last word, and in 1789, in New York City, Margaret Lowther became his wife. She did almost as nobly by her husband as did Frances Burwell, for eight children blessed their union. Long years after John Page had died, his widow was visited by Lafayette at Williamsburg, on October 20, 1824, when he was *en route* to Richmond from Yorktown, during his last visit to America.

The oldest known valentine in an American collection is the one which a certain Edward Sangor, of Tower Hill, London, sent to the lady of his dreams in 1684. It is included in the celebrated collection of Mrs. L. N. Stone of New Jersey.

Another old and quaint valentine which carries the date 1753, and is redolent of Colonial Virginia, is today in the famous collection of Mr. Frank H. Baer of Cape May, New Jersey, formerly of Cleveland, Ohio. This old valentine is of the most delicate and intricate cutwork, so fashionable during the Georgian era, and depicts three hearts, pierced with arrows. It is cut from white paper, and shown against a black background in the illustration which R. A. Brock used in *Virginia and Virginians.* For many years this old valentine was owned by Dr. Brock's sister, but later was acquired by Mr. Baer from a Richmond collector.

The oldest valentine I have found in Virginia belongs to Mrs. Bradley S. Johnson of Richmond, *née* Anne Seddon Rutherfoord. It is in the shape of a large heart, and is cut entirely by hand from white paper which is almost as thin as tissue. At first glance, one might easily mistake it for a *motif* in point-lace or ivory filigree, so intricate is the cut-work and so exquisitely executed is the entire design.

This lovely old love-token was made sometime before 1817, by Mrs. Johnson's grandmother, Anne Seddon of Fredericksburg, who married William H. Roy of "Green Plains," Matthews County, Virginia, in that year. "She was a very unusual character," Mrs. Johnson remarked to me. "She wrote for the newspapers." I smiled, and told her that I too, had written for newspapers. "But in those days, such a thing was almost unheard of," she added. "Here is the name of one of the papers she wrote for—*The Political Arena,* (an old Fredericksburg paper I believe) and yonder is her portrait."

In the *Richmond News Leader Bicentennial Supplement* — 1737-1937 — there appeared a picture of Anne Seddon Roy, who later became Mrs. John Coles Rutherfoord. It is captioned "The Flower of Virginia," and justly so, for the copy of the Hubard portrait shows her to to be a most beautiful woman. She was the daughter of the above Anne Seddon of Fred-

Hand-cut Valentine made before 1817 by Anne Seddon of Fredericksburg, who married William H. Roy of Matthews County, Virginia. Owned by their granddaughter, Mrs. Bradley S. Johnson of Richmond.

cricksburg, and the mother of Mrs. Johnson. She
was a reigning belle and beauty in Virginia at the
time of her marriage to John Coles Rutherfoord of
Richmond, and "Rock Castle" on-the-James, and in
later life penned some delightful recollections of
canal-boat days on the James and Kanawha, which have
since been published.

The old valentine, which has been treasured and kept
for three successive generations by this distinguished
family, lies today between the hallowed pages of the
old Seddon-Roy family Bible, and is in a remarkable
state of preservation. It is a work of art as well as
a symbol of devotion, and to me will always be an
original piece of "Queen Anne's Lace."

Another old and interesting valentine in Virginia is
the one which William Henry Harrison of "Bicars"
and "Racefield" in Prince George County, sent to his
lady love, Agnes Peeples Heath, also of Prince George,
prior to their marriage in 1826.

This is another quaint example of the hand-cut
valentine, and was made by William Henry Harrison's grandmother, Henrietta Maria Hardyman who
married Robert Harrison in 1779. What nimble
fingers and keen eyesight this dear old lady must have
had, when she made this elaborate valentine for her
young and romantic grandson! One suspects he must
have been her favorite, for endless hours of labor undoubtedly went into the cutting of this fanciful love-
token.

The valentine is cut in the shape of a large oval,
with eight scolloped edges, and an open center. In
each scollop two tiny hearts have been cut with fluted
edges, and below each heart, the initial "H" is simi-
larly cut. The material is a lightweight cream paper,

and the design as a whole resembles an elaborate cut-work doily.

In each of the eight scollops young Harrison inscribed, in his own hand, tender lines of poetry to the fair Agnes, the sixth verse pleading his cause in this wise:

> "Oh! if I were rich as Crœsus of old,
> And had all the silver and the gold,
> They would not any true comfort give,
> Were I destined this weary life to live
> Denied of kind nature's choicest treasure
> And her who would fill the heart with pleasure."

And he climaxes the whole with this:

> "If this you think to you comes from a friend,
> A present from your hands you may him send,
> But if the writer of this you disdain,
> Pray quickly send this back to him again."

That Agnes Heath did not "quickly send this back to him again" we know, for today it is an enduring valentine, treasured by Mrs. William W. Richardson of "Little Berkeley," Hampton, Virginia, and her sister Miss Jennie Pritchett of Richmond, granddaughters of William Henry Harrison and Agnes Peeples Heath.

In the Valentine Museum in Richmond, there is a small but interesting collection of valentines dating from 1830 through 1850. Perhaps the most unusual as well as amusing of these sentimental missives is one captioned "A Trifle Towards Housekeeping." It is rather large, and of the conventional type manufactured a hundred years ago—lace paper border, with sprays of appliquéd and painted flowers. At the top there is a small envelope containing two knives, forks, spoons, and plates. This was sent to a Miss Margaret Robinson in 1830.

Another, inscribed in a decidedly facetious vein, is a hand-colored lithographed valentine, made in England in 1850. Here a sailor and his lass are shown standing arm in arm, with his ship anchored in harbor. At the bottom of the valentine is the following bit of nautical verse:

> "Come haul me an answer, my Fair,
>   Be calm, let us have no foul weather—
> I'll take you in tow if you dare,
>   For Hymen's we'll both sail together."

When one reflects that the vogue of the valentine has survived these many years, in spite of wars and depressions, changing fashions and human caprices, one agrees with Mrs. L. N. Stone, whose monograph on the valentine carries these lines: "Good old Bishop Valentine, who long ago passed to his reward and later to sainthood, will, on judgment day, have much explaining to do."

Patchwork: A Pageant of Years

"She wrought so well in needle-worke, that shee,
Nor yet her workes shall e'er forgotten be."
—JOHN TAYLOR.

CHAPTER IV

PATCHWORK: A PAGEANT OF YEARS

I LOVE to contemplate an old and faded patchwork quilt; to try and visualize the woman who made it, the place and period in which it was made, and the conditions under which it was made. What an index to a woman's character are these treasured relics of a past industry, and how eloquently do they speak of her various traits. The thousands of small stitches tell the story of her infinite patience; the careful fitting—neat piecing— and artistic patchwork—of her pride in her work; and the once bright combinations of reds and greens, blues and yellows, lavenders and pinks—of her feminine love of color, and longing for ornamentation in her home.

Nor is this all of their story. An old quilt has much to tell of the religion and patriotism of its maker; of the history that was in the making when an unhurried woman recorded it—not in a book or diary, but in her *needlework*; of the romance and tragedy that touched her life; of the home and loved ones she left behind when she braved unknown dangers and "went West" as a bride; of the trails that were blazed and territories formed; of the home that was established and the friendships made; of the harvest and year-round bounty of the good earth. In an old patchwork quilt, we can, if we will, behold *a pageant of years*.

Marie D. Webster, in her introduction to *Quilts,
Their Story and how to make them,* says:

"The quilt has a tradition of long centuries of slow but certain
progress. Its story is replete with incidents of love and daring, of
sordid pilferings and generous sacrifices. It has figured in many a
thrilling episode. The same type of handiwork that has sheltered the
simple peasant from wintry blasts has adorned the great halls of
doughty warriors and noble kings. Humble maids, austere nuns,
grand dames, and stately queens; all have shared in the fascination of
the quilter's art and have contributed to its advancement. Cottage,
convent, and castle; all have been enriched, at one time or another,
by the splendors of patchwork and the pleasures of its making."

Since time immemorial women have worked on
quilts. In the common life of the tribe quilts were a
necessity, especially for those tribes living in cold regions. Gradually the desire for design entered into
the art of quilting. This was particularly true in some
parts of Eastern countries where tapestry and rug making had developed to a high degree.

The most ancient example of patchwork known to
man is a colored gazelle hide, which is preserved in
the Museum of Cairo. The colors of the different
pieces of skin reflect the marvels of Egyptian dyes—
deep golden yellow, pale blue, bright pink, bluish
green, and pale primrose. This piece of patchwork
dates from 960 B. C. and was used as the canopy or
pall of an Egyptian queen.

Today, Egyptians make patchwork that is inspired
by the very same art practiced in the days of Rameses
and Cleopatra. These designs are typically Egyptian,
many pieces being adorned with hieroglyphics and
replicas of paintings found on tombs and temples. The
natives of the warm Nile valley do not convert their
patchwork into bed coverings, but instead, display their

vivid patterns in wall hangings, covers for cushions, and panels for screens.

Long before the Renaissance, the use of patchwork was known in different parts of Europe, but its introduction into Italy is credited to Botticelli (1446-1510). The *applied* work of the Armenians is said to have so appealed to the great Florentine painter, that he used it on hangings for Church decoration.

Among the magnificent furnishings belonging to the Tudor period were great hangings of applied work, which enclosed beds, screened archways, and covered vast spaces of cold palace walls. This was before the introduction of the huge and beautiful French tapestries, which later took the place of the English *appliqué* wall hangings and bed draperies.

During the reign of Henry VIII, exquisite specimens of embroidery and patchwork were made, many of which today are preserved in various museums. "It was really patch upon patch," says Marie D. Webster, "for before the motives were applied to the foundation they were elaborately embroidered in intricate designs; and after being applied, they had their edges couched with gold and silver cord and ornate embroidery stitches."

In 1540, Katheryn Howard, one of the many wives of Henry VIII, was presented with "twenty-three quilts of Sarsenet, closely quilted, from the Royal Wardrobe." Poor woman! How many gruesome nights she must have lain in her castle bed, shivering beneath some of these very quilts, as she awaited her inevitable doom.

The ill-fated Mary Queen of Scots is said to have been devoted to the needle and expert in its use. During her long days of imprisonment she found solace and consolation in her needle—to what extent we may judge from the following comment of one of her attendants, who is quoted as saying "that all day long she wrought with her nydil and that the diversity of the colours made the work seem less tedious and that she contynued so long at it that veray payn made her to give over." Hardwick Hall, so intimately associated with the young queen's life, is described as "rich in relics of her industry," and in one of the rooms named for her are bed curtains and a *quilt* made by her own deft and nimble fingers.

In 1631, Charles I permitted many Eastern products to be brought into England, among the articles listed being "Quilts of china embroidered in Gold." In his delicious and inimitable diary, the gossipy Pepys often penned his now-famous words, "and so to bed," which are better appreciated after reading the following lines from his sprightly journal: "Home to my poor wife, who works all day like a horse, at the making of her hangings for our chamber and bed." Which leads one to assume that Mrs. Pepys saw to it that her good husband's place of sleep, was one of rest and comfort as well.

Just when the quilt made its appearance in America is unknown, but the introduction of the arts of patchwork and quilting in this country are credited to the English and Dutch. Old wills and inventories both in New England and the South, attest to the existence of quilts in the colonies long before the Revolution. In Mary Washington's quaint and interesting will, dated May 20, 1778, she bequeathes to her son, General George Washington, "my quilted blue-and-white quilt," which is proof of the esteem in which these beautifully executed coverlets were held by our ancestors.

The definition of quilt and the origin of the word are interesting. Webster defines a quilt as "A cover or coverlet made by stitching one cloth over another with some soft substance between them; to sew in the manner of a quilt; to stitch through and through." The word is derived from old French *cuilte, coutre, coultre,* which is derived from the Latin *culcitra, culcita*—a bed, a mattress, a pillow. Thus, broadly speaking, any article made up with an interlining may be called a quilt, though in the United States the word is generally accepted as being a light weight, closely stitched bedcover.

How did our grandmothers and great-grandmothers go about their quilt making? Alice Morse Earle in one of her delightful and informative books, *Home Life in Colonial Days,* gives us an interesting pen-picture of the usual procedure. The first step was of course to decide upon the pattern and the material. After this momentous decision was reached, the problem of cutting came next. Strange as it may seem, this phase of quilt-making is said to be the least interesting and most tedious. Old-time quilting patterns were few compared to the great number of designs for patchwork. There were approximately a dozen standard patterns: diamonds, crescents, shells or scallops, stars, hearts, circles, ovals, cables; tulips, roses, buds, leaves, running vines; birds, baskets, pineapples, harps and feathers. Of course squares, rectangles, triangles, hexagonal blocks, circles, and bands for borders were ever-present in the vast array of "pieces," which, by the hundreds, went into the finished quilt.

"To set a 'Job's Trouble'" writes Mrs. Earle "was to cut out an exact hexagon for a pattern (preferably from tin, otherwise from firm cardboard); to cut out from this many hexagons in stiff brown paper or letter paper. These were covered with bits of calico with the edges turned under; the sides were sewed carefully together over and over, till a firm expanse permitted the removal of the papers."

The three essential parts of a quilt are the top, the lining or back, and the interlining. The top is the most important feature of every quilt, and may be entirely of a plain piece of cloth; or it may be pieced together from many small pieces, varying in size, color, and shape; or adorned with fanciful designs cut from fabrics of various colors and appliquéd to the foundation. There is a fine line of distinction to be drawn between the verbs "to piece" and "to patch," when used in connection with quilting. Ruby Short McKim reminds us, in her valuable work on quilting entitled *One Hundred and One Patchwork Patterns,* that contrary to the general belief, the *patched* quilts are the aristocrats of the quilt family, while the *pieced* quilts are the poor relations.

Not only is there a fascination about the names of old quilts, but there is a fascination about their materials as well. Many of the bright blocks and hexagonals that smile at us today from their varied and charming patterns, were cut from pieces of "India Chince" brought to this country in ships belonging to the East India Trading Company. And from "far Cathay" came the glazed and unglazed materials in their dazzling and brilliant colors and *motifs,* some reflecting the Persian influence, particularly the "Persian Pear" which women called the "pickle pattern" or "gourds;" others with full-sized peacocks, exotic flowers, pineapples and pomegranates—the exquisitely unreal splendors of the Orient.

There were "sprigged and flowered callicoes" from England, and woven cloths advertised from 1715 on, such as pealong, fustian, demity, musling, cambric; various grades of duck, lawn, and searsucker, and nankeen the ancestor of "blue denim." Ruby Short McKim, widely known contemporary authority on old quilts and quilting says that of the many materials that found their way into patchwork, "the dearest and most suitable of all was calico." One authority who treats this history in full, writes that "the mainstay of the patchworker was from 1700 to 1775 callicoe, from 1775 to 1825 calico, and from 1825 to 1875 calico!"

Alice Morse Earle adds her valued opinion in these words:

"There was the one satisfactory condition in the work, and that was the quality of the cottons and linens of which the patchwork was made. They were none of the slimsy, composition-filled, aniline-dyed calicoes of today, (1892). A piece of 'chaney,' 'patch,' or 'copperplate' a hundred years old will be as fresh today as when woven. Real India chintzes and palampours are found in these quilts, beautiful and artistic stuffs, and the firm, unyielding, high-priced 'real' French calicoes."

Here were materials to "dream over;" colors to elicit endless expressions of admiration; patterns to dazzle the most staid and sensible woman. Thus, with a spirit of pride, patience, and keen delight, did our grandmothers and great-grandmothers start and finish their patchwork quilts. When the patchwork was at last completed, it was laid flatly on the lining, with layers of wool or cotton wadding between, and basted around the edges. The tense moment had now arrived, for in old-fashioned parlance, the quilt was "ready for the frames."

In colonial and pioneer days, one or more quilting frames were the common equipment of every home.

These were seldom more than four bars of wood, about ten feet long, made into an oblong frame by fastenings of bolts or pegs. Sometimes two of the bars were longer than the quilt, and two shorter. Each side of the quilting frame was tightly wound with cotton strips, and to the completed frame was stretched the quilt, which was sewed to it with stout thread, and the whole raised on chairs to a convenient height.

Thus a dozen quilters could gather around the outstretched quilt, "running the whole together with fanciful set designs of stitching," or one woman, in her "spare time" ply her needle, in rythmic fashion forward and backward and across the whole, silently meditating upon the pleasures and problems of life, and perhaps saying aloud the lines of James Maxwell, the weaver-poet,

> "With cheerful heart I work and sing
> And envy none beneath the skies."

When many of the old quilts we prize today were made by our diligent and beauty-loving ancestors, "one dollar per spool" was the usual price paid for quilting, when "hired help" was required. Two hundred yards to the spool is the customary measure today; what it was a hundred or more years ago would be interesting to know.

Just as quilting had its price-rules and regulations, so it had its superstitions. One of these was that a bride-to-be could "snap" her "Bride's Quilt" but that was all; *she was not allowed to quilt it!* Among the loveliest of all old patchwork quilts are the various patterns conceived especially for brides. One of these, frequently called "The Album" quilt, was made when a group of friends met, and each pieced a gay-colored block and embroidered her name upon it. Another favorite, even more elaborate and beautiful, was made of several dozen appliquéd designs, each different, yet with balance maintained, in a variety of exquisite materials and colors worked on a solid foundation, usually of white.

One of the most beautiful and notable American quilts of this kind is the "Baltimore Bride's Quilt," made in Baltimore, Maryland, in 1851. This elaborate and exquisite piece of needlework has twenty-five appliquéd designs, each one made by a friend of the bride-elect. In its entirety it is a kaleidoscopic picture of flower-laden baskets, and horns-of-plenty pouring forth fruits in luxurious profusion; exotic birds and cooing doves, nosegays and wreaths and flowering trees; harps and anchors encircled with greenery; a little red house; a ship sailing toward the port of bliss; an old apple tree with a playful brown dog standing in its cooling shade—in fact everything fanciful and colorful that the mind of a romantic maid of that day could conceive as fitting to adorn her best friend's bridal quilt. The central *motif*—bespeaking considerable patriotic fervor—is a spirited American eagle, the American flag and shield, beneath which on a narrow scroll is inscribed *E Pluribus Unum.* Here symmetry, beauty, and artistry are combined to an almost unbelievable degree, and the finished quilt a work of exquisite perfection.

Someone has said that the names of old quilts are more comforting, if not more enduring, than words graven in stone. To read the long list is to agree, with one's eyes lingering on such names as "World Without End," "Delectable Mountains," "Star of Bethlehem," "Alpine Rose," "Cross and Crown," "Job's Tears," "Mother's Fancy," "Folded Love Letter,"

"Pine Tree," "Chimney Swallows," "Christmas Tree," "Evening Star," "Little Beech Tree," "The Little Red House," "Morning Star," "Rainbow," "Snowflake," "The Two Doves," and "Wedding Knot".

Not least among the fascinating features of quilt lore are the number and variety of names given to the various fanciful designs. Marie D. Webster in her superb book on quilts, reminds her readers that history, politics, religion, nature, poetry, and romance, have all exerted their influence on quilt appellations, and adds, "Careful consideration of a large number of quilts reveals but few that have been named in a haphazard way; in nearly every instance there was a reason or at least a suggestion for the name."

There is an historical hint to such names as "Confederate Rose," "Union," and "Star Spangled Banner." Politics speaks boldly in such old quilt names as "Democrat Rose," "Whig Rose," "Clay's Choice," "Lincoln's Platform," "Tippecanoe and Tyler Too." Pioneering days come vividly to the fore in such names as "Wagon Tracks," "Road to California," "Log Cabin," "Arkansas Traveler," "Oklahoma Boomer," "Kansas Troubles," "Cactus Basket," "Prairie Queen," "Indian Hatchet" and "Texas Star." Insect and bird reminders are found in old quilts with quaint names such as "Spider Web," "Shoo Fly," "Swarm of Bees," "Crow's Foot," "Dove in the Window" and "Bluebird," while the barnyard inspired such amusing names as "Goose Tracks," "Duck and Ducklings," "Hen and Chickens," and "Turkey Tracks."

Commonplace things of farm and home gave rise to such humble names as "The Pickle Dish," "Cake Stand," "Churn Dash," "Flower Pot," "Hour Glass," "Needle Book," and "Album." Quilts that originated in sea coast settlements abound in nautical names like "Ocean Wave," "Lost Ship," "Star and Compass" and "Storm at Sea." Seemingly every flower under the sun gave its name to some lovely old quilt: "Morning Glory," "Sunflowers," "Poppy," and roses on end— "Rose of Sharon," "Rose of Dixie," "Rose of the Carolinas," "Wild Rose," "Mexican Rose," only to mention a few.

Names that seem grotesque, yet invariably provoke smiles or a hearty laugh are "Hairpin Catcher," "Tangled Garters," "Hearts and Gizzards," "Swing-in-the-Center," "Eight Hands 'Round." There was a strain of dry humor in many a quilt-maker of long ago, for when names gave out and a new quilt was about to be born, even the wag of the family suggested such names as "Drunkard's Path," "Old Maid's Puzzle," "Blind Man's Fancy."

Geometric patterns inspired "Beggar's Blocks," "Pin Wheels," "Roman Cross," "Memory Circle" and "Diamond Cubes." Stars lead all other names of quilts, there being more than fifty known quilts bearing a star name. The woman who read her Bible never ran short of names for her quilts. Among the old favorites closely associated with religious stories and teachings are the "Garden of Eden," "Solomon's Temple," "Jacob's Ladder," "Joseph's Coat," and "Hosannah."

Places, persons, and events of historical interest often inspired especially designed quilts. One of the most beautiful of early American patchwork quilts is "The Charter Oak," named for the famous Connecticut oak that played such an important rôle in colonial history. The central *motif* suggests the famous oak, while its patriotic association is exemplified in the American eagle with outspread wings, which adorns the quilt's border.

As might be expected, that magnetic and beloved Frenchman, the Marquis de LaFayette, not only gave his name to a famous American patchwork quilt, but really inspired it: the quilt known as the "LaFayette Orange Peel." The story goes that when LaFayette was fêted in Philadelphia during his American tour in 1824, a fair young guest at the banquet which had been given in his honor, took home as a souvenir a most beautiful fruit—an orange imported from Barcelona. To preserve her treasure and the memory of her gala evening, a pattern was carefully cut from the pared rind of the golden fruit, and a vivid and colorful design for a quilt evolved from the quartered skin.

That dear old lady who, through succeeding generations has answered to the call of 'Grandma"—"Grandmere"—and "Grandmother"—had many a quaint and charming quilt named in her honor. There was "Grandmother's Cross," "Grandmother's Fan," "Grandmother's Choice," "Grandmother's Dream," "Grandmother's Own," and last, but by no means least, "Grandmother's Flower Garden." Without even seeing it, one is certain that this last named quilt would be his or her favorite, for it instantly conjures up visions of all of the bright and fragrant flowers that flourished in old-fashioned gardens: lilacs, larkspur, iris, poppies, peonies, roses, tulips, lilies, morning glories and four o'clocks.

Among several beautiful and treasured old patchwork quilts belonging to Mr. and Mrs. S. Willard Ahalt, of Richmond, is one of the pattern known as "Grandmother's Flower Garden." This lovely old quilt was made in Frederick County, Maryland, one

Patchwork Quilt of intricate hexagon design known as "Grandmother's Flower Garden." Made in Frederick County, Maryland, in 1799, by Annetta Ahalt, and owned by her great-grandson, Mr. S. Willard Ahalt of Richmond.

hundred and forty years ago by Mr. Ahalt's great-grandmother, Annetta Schloesser Ahalt, wife of Samuel Ahalt, and is today in a remarkable state of preservation.

This old pattern, sometimes called the "French Bouquet," is one of the most beautiful of all hexagon block quilts. On a foundation of all-white, there are appliquéd forty-two hexagonal designs, each design composed of nineteen different colored hexagon blocks.

The materials used in the seven hundred and ninety-eight hexagon blocks that form the fanciful "flower garden" on Mr. Ahalt's old quilt, are as varied as are the exquisite colors themselves, which run the gamut of the rainbow. Here one feels and sees all of the firm, unyielding, high-priced materials Mrs. Earle mentioned as being one of the joys and satisfactions of quilt making a hundred or so years ago—the real French calicoes, India chintzes, and palampours. Around the entire quilt there is a seven-inch border of flowered chintz with a tan background. Here, exotic birds and flowers are seen in riotous colors. All of the various old materials in this beautiful quilt seem to possess "life everlasting" and colors amaranthine.

If you are young, and fortunate, and eager to learn from the past, the owners of priceless relics of other days more often than not will tell you the story of their prized possessions. So it was that Mr. Ahalt told me how he came to have the old quilt made by his great-grandmother almost a century and a half ago, and five others as well. Around twenty years ago, at a family reunion held at the Ahalt home in Frederick County, Maryland, (the same in which Annetta Schloesser Ahalt made all of her forty-odd quilts) a division of the old family quilts was decided upon. Three large quilt chests were removed from the attic where they had stood for several years packed full of these colorful coverlets, and the quilts removed and spread out in a row. In order that no partiality be shown any of the seven great-grandchildren of Annetta Ahalt, each drew lots for first choice, and on down the line until the last quilt was in the hands of its new owner. Mr. Ahalt feels that in "Grandmother's Flower Garden" he got the pick of the lot, and after looking at the beautiful workmanship and colorful materials that went into this lovely old quilt, one feels certain (without seeing any of the others) that he did.

Virginia gave her proud name to many a famous quilt, among them the "Virginia Gentleman," "Virginia Star" and "Virginia Rose." Perhaps one day my quest of the quaint will lead me to an old Virginia homestead that boasts *at least* one of these famous quilts. It will matter very little if the colors are faded and the edges frayed. So long as the old quilt goes by the proud name of the "Virginia Gentleman" or "Virginia Rose," I shall see in it only a reminder of the patient and beauty-loving woman who made it; the old Virginia gentleman whose house was proverbial for its hospitality, and whose great high beds were never empty of guests; and a peaceful and beautiful Virginia countryside whose story has been told a thousand times.

My Lady's Fan

"In olden time, as in our present day
The sceptre in Kings' hands o'er men held sway—
Mightier the fan, which even Kings obey!"
                                        —MERARD SAINT-JUSTE.

"A thousand times in her faire hand it lay,
A thousand times its jewel'd face she scann'd."

CHAPTER V

MY LADY'S FAN

AN old fan is an irresistible object. In the hands of a clever and beautiful woman it was more than a costly and beautiful trinket; it was a powerful weapon, used to bewitch and charm; to sway the hearts of men and the destinies of nations. Even today, imprisoned beneath glass as most museum specimens are, these exquisite feminine "trifles" still have power to charm and delight.

To behold an old fan in all of its splendor and fragile beauty, is to be transported, as if by magic, to the grandeur of palaces and kings, balls and fêtes, queens and their ladies-in-waiting. It is to meet famous women of history, in whose jeweled hands the fan was displayed in all of its costly and dazzling finery. From the storied mists of the past their harmless phantoms stand before us, clothed in regal raiment. Whom do we see?

Mary Queen of Scots, the Stuart beauty, whose fans were ornate and costly creations. Elizabeth of England—vain, selfish, cruel, for whom ships plied home with jewels to satisfy her "inordinate passion" for them. Every picture of the Virgin Queen shows her ablaze with jewels, and in many she carries a royal fan, resplendant with exotic feathers caught in a jeweled clasp.

Catherine of Russia, the poor princess who made up for her scanty trousseau with a fabulous wardrobe when Empress. One gasps in admiration at the mere description of her magnificent fans culled from the great art centers of Europe. Madame du Barry, the beautiful little milliner whose red-gold beauty enraptured a king. Like her exquisite miniatures, her fans were the creations of famous artists. Far more powerful than the sceptre of Louis XV, was the fan of a Pompadour or Du Barry!

Marie Antoinette, enchanting and extravagent young Queen of France, who matched her jewels to the blue of her eyes. Visualize if you can, the exquisite creations designed especially for this fascinating and ill-fated young Austrian—fans of gauze and mother-of-pearl, of lace and ivory, of parchment and filigree; satin fans painted in lovely pastorals, ivory ones in miniatures; fans embroidered in exotic flowers, humming birds, and butterflies; fans of ostrich, of sandal-wood; fans that shimmered with gold and silver spangles. These were the fans of the once care-free and light-of-heart Marie Antoinette; fans that she carried at the great balls and fêtes at Versailles—fans with which she played the coquette—fascinated and flirted—fans behind which she peered at hostile gatherings—fans with which, by a sudden motion, she dismissed traitors and enemies at Court. How eloquently do the fans of Marie Antoinette speak!

The fan is steeped in legend. The Chinese who claim to have invented the fan, trace its origin to the land of legends. One of these tells that Lang-sin, daughter of a wealthy and powerful mandarin, while attending the Feast of Lanterns, was overcome by the heat. Defying convention, she removed her mask, but held it close to her face as she waved it rapidly to and fro. From this caprice, copied by other beauties of the Chinese Court, originated the use of the screen fan— so the Chinese claim.

An old Japanese tale traces the origin of the folding fan to the grief-stricken widow of Atsumori, a noble youth who succumbed to the fierce sense of duty of Kumagai Maozanè. Wishing to retreat from the world and hide her sorrow, she entered the Temple of Miedeo, in Kioto, where as a devoted nun she performed the pious duty of nursing an abbot racked with a terrible fever. Through long weary weeks she fanned him with a folding paper fan, until, miraculously, he was restored to health.

The folding fan is of established Japanese invention. Whether it originated, according to tradition, by a sovereign's observation of the wings of a bat, or was suggested by the unfolding of a palm tree leaf, must be left to the imagination. It is interesting, however, to learn that the Japanese God of Happiness is represented with one in his hand.

In Japan there is a fan for every purpose and occasion: the court fan, dancing fan, tea fan, kitchen or water fan, fan used as bellows, and war fan. In ancient times the war fan was made of leather, with iron handles of considerable length and weight. This particular fan served a dual purpose: to give directions to the army, as well as being a formidable weapon.

Another fan legend of the Japanese relates to the rivet which binds the blades or sticks of the fan together. This old story tells that Kashima, a Japanese god, was charged to subdue the eastern part of the world. Running his sword straight through the earth, he accomplished the feat; however, in time the sword hardened into stone, and was given the name of Kana-meishi, which translated means rivet. The earth being thus riveted and steadied, the people enjoyed a sense of security, and so the rivet came to suggest to them one of the principal parts of the folding fan.

Research into the history of the fan reveals fascinating facts concerning its introduction into various parts of the world. The fan reached Greece from Asia Minor, doubtless through commercial intercourse with the Phoenicians. Greek ladies are said to have always evinced a preference for fans made from peacock feathers, the peacock, as the "bird of Juno," being the symbol of refinement, splendor, and luxury. Must not Euripides have alluded to a fan of peacock feathers, when in *Orestes* the Phrygian slave tells of having "fanned Helen's cheeks and airy curls with a winged fan of round and graceful shape"?

During the Roman Empire at ceremonial banquets, slaves stood behind guests, waving in rythmic motion to and fro, gorgeous fans of enormous size, some of which were of peacock and ostrich feathers fashioned in the shape of a disc or semi-circle, while others were painted in brilliant colors. No patrician was seen without her fan-bearer, who carried a fan attached to a long handle. That a high-born lady could be suspected of fanning herself was unthinkable. There were also smaller fans made of scented wood and ivory, which gallants used when fanning their ladies fair.

From time immemorial, the fan has been symbolic. In ancient Egypt, the fan was a royal emblem of authority, happiness, and repose. The fan or flabellum-bearer was generally of royal birth; he held dignified service about the person of the monarch, and was inducted into office amid much pomp and ceremony.

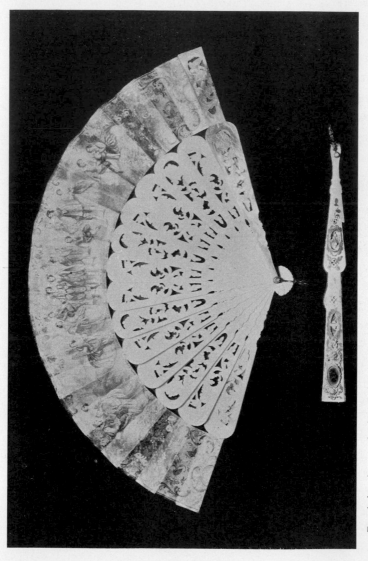

Fan belonging to the late Miss Jennie Ellett of Richmond. Hand-painted lithographed mount, center sticks of carved ivory, guard sticks of carved mother-of-pearl. Below, fan belonging to Elizabeth Anne Valentine of Richmond, showing mirror at the top of the elaborately decorated guard stick. Courtesy of the Valentine Museum.

In Mexico, the fan was a symbol of authority. Contemporaries of Cortez described in their writings the costly flyflaps of exotic feathers, the handles of which were incrusted with precious stones, which were given as diplomatic presents. Carlotta, the beautiful and ill-fated wife of Maximilian, is shown in many of her pictures as Empress of Mexico, holding in her slender hands a wondrous fan of Mexican handicraft.

In Japan, the fan is looked upon as the emblem of life: "as the rays of the fan spread out from the rivet, so the road of life widens into a happy future." From this Oriental symbol, the fan gradually became popular the world over as a gift to a bride. In the Hawaiian Islands, from ancient times to the present day, fabulous flyflaps have been the insignia of royal authority. In India, the fan is known as *punkah,* its original shape being similar to the leaf of a palm tree.

From remotest times, round, square, octagon, and elliptic fan screens were adorned with curious designs and inscriptions, or elaborately embroidered or beaded. Until the introduction of silks, the materials commonly used in fan making were bamboo, palm leaf, wood, leather, paper, and metals.

As time passed, the fan graduated from a symbol of royalty, to a necessary appendage of the aristocracy and the wealthy. Opinion is divided as to just when the fan became in France "that engine of magic charm," but it is believed to have been in general use by the fourteenth century, for various court inventories list the fan under the name of *esmouchoir.* Miniatures of this period also attest the popular use of fans, for many beauties of the French Court are shown with long handled round fans, made of feathers or rice straw. The inventory of Charles V of France, made in 1380, mentions a folding fan made of ivory with an ebony handle, bearing the arms of France and Navarre.

Soon the fan became *de rigueur* in fashionable French circles; no high-born lady's costume was complete without one, and they were designed for all occasions. The materials used were dazzling and costly: gorgeous "gold and silver laces, brilliant feathers, elaborate embroideries, and all that the jewelers of the day could contrive," was expended on this exquisite trinket. Wrote Gay, the English poet:

"Gay France shall make the fan her artists care,
    And with the costly trinket, arm the fair."

With the entrance of Catherine de Medici into France, came the round screen Italian fan which she introduced. This innovation, which was manufactured and sold by perfumers who had followed the Queen to France, enjoyed widespread vogue.

In Italy, Spain, and Portugal, the fashion of carrying fans was adopted around the same time as in France. Shortly before 1600 the Oriental pleated fan had been introduced into Europe, as well as feather fans, and those with skin-screens, which were highly perfumed. During the fifteenth and sixteenth centuries, ladies of rank in Milan, Florence, and Venice, carried feather fans in which small mirrors were set. The handles were jeweled, while the fan usually hung suspended from a gold or silver chain. One of the loveliest of old Italian fans was one of dazzling white, known in Venice as the "betrothal fan." This especial fan was greatly favored by families of the Venetian nobility, and is described as having been made of pure white parchment cut in an open-work design, and trimmed with Venetian lace of the sixteenth century.

What of the fan in England? Here the earliest records date from 1307. As has been noted, Queen Elizabeth owned magnificent fans of great value. It was she who favored the custom that a fan should be the only present which a sovereign should receive from her subjects, and her courtiers lavished upon her fans of every description. Sir Francis Drake is said to have presented her Majesty with one of red and white feathers, the gold handle enameled with a half moon encircled with diamonds and pearls, forming a jeweled frame for a portrait of herself.

Robert Dudley, Earl of Leicester, one of the Queen's most celebrated favorites, presented her with a fan described as being made of "white feathers, the gold handle, thickly jeweled, bearing a lion rampant with a muzzled white bear beneath his foot." Still another of Elizabeth's fabulous fans was one of swansdown with green velvet embroidered with rubies, emeralds, and pearls, the handle being in the shape of a golden monster with head and breast of mother-of-pearl. In all, the Virgin Queen was the proud and vain owner of twenty-seven fans at her death in 1603; fans as dazzling and as costly as many of her noted jewels.

Elizabeth's "fancy for fans" was not solely responsible for their vogue in England. During the reign of her famous father, Henry VIII, two styles of fans were in general use: one for full dress, the other for walking. The latter were quite large, with handles a half yard long, and served as parasols as well. Shakespeare also makes frequent mention of the fan in many of his immortal lines.

Early in the reign of Charles II, a petition known as the "Fan-Makers Grievance, by the importation of Fans from the East Indies," was submitted to the

House of Commons. The petitioners asked that a stop be put to the importation of Indian fans, closing their complaint with the appealing sentence that "great numbers of poor people, continually employed in the work, must otherwise inevitably perish." As a result of this petition, a protective duty of forty shillings a dozen was placed upon imported fans, and if they were painted, their importation was prohibited.

During the latter half of the seventeeth century, a Spanish painter by the name of Cano de Arevalo is said to have gained fame and fortune by painting fans which he sold as French creations. He was luckier than most impostors, for his paintings were recognized throughout Spain, and he was made court painter to the queen. The preference for costly and exquisite French fans continued to prevail in spite of Spanish talent, and especial designs suited to the Spanish taste, were manufactured in large numbers in France. Spanish fans are easily distinguished from French ones by their brilliant colors, large size, and strong materials, while their designs invariably suggest Spanish scenes and customs.

If old Spain was not remarkable for the manufacture of fans, it was the one country in Europe pre-eminent in the gentle art of "fan maneouver." Here as in France, the "mania for fans" knew no bounds. No señorita would have appeared in public, *sans* her mantilla and fan.

"A Spanish lady with her fan" says Disraeli in *Contarini Fleming,* "might shame the tactics of a troop of horse. Now she unfurls it with the slow pomp and conscious elegance of the bird of Juno, now she flutters it with all the languor of the listless beauty, now with all of the liveliness of a vivacious one. Now in the midst of a very tornado she closes it with a whirr, which makes you start.

"Pop! in the midst of your confusion, Dolores taps you on the elbow; you turn round to listen, and Catalina pokes you in your side. Magical instrument! In this land it speaks a particular language, and gallantry requires no other mode to express its most subtle conceits or its most unreasonable demands than this delicate machine."

In 1685, after the Revocation of the Edict of Nantes, scores of French fan makers sought refuge in London, introducing their industry there. During the reign of Queen Anne, London manufacturers obtained a charter of incorporation, after which the trade of fans within the city was limited to members of the corporation.

At "Wilton," the headquarters of the Society of Colonial Dames in the State of Virginia, one may see a beautiful old fan, which was one of the wedding fans of Elizabeth Catesby, who married Doctor William Cocke, sent by Queen Anne as Secretary to her Colony of Virginia in 1712. This commission was renewed by George I after Queen Anne's death, and many descendants of Elizabeth Catesby and William Cocke are living in Virginia today.

There is an aura of romance and history about this lovely old fan. Has it not witnessed the nuptials of countless sons and daughters of the Catesby-Cocke families, as well as the transition of a wilderness-colony into a great nation? Does not its exquisite workmanship, its delicate inlay, reflect the high standard which men achieved two and a quarter centuries ago? There is much to be learned from an old fan.

The original mount of Elizabeth Catesby's fan was of paper, with a hand-painted design on both sides.

One side revealed a "dancing scene," while there was a "musical scene" on the other showing the principal musical instruments that were popular during Queen Anne's reign. Courtiers and their ladies appeared in the costumes of their period—a fanciful and colorful picture we may be sure.

As time passed, the mount became worn and badly torn. At last when it was beyond repair, a new one took its place, which is the one seen today. The present mount is of silk, with an elaborate hand-painted scroll-work design in brilliant colors which surrounds the Catesby coat-of-arms on one side, and the Graham coat-of-arms on the other. This excellent example of armorial painting was done in 1891, and seems destined to endure for a long time to come. The most beautiful feature of the fan are the sticks which are the originals, made of mother-of-pearl with gold inlay. This priceless old fan was given to the Colonial Dames in Virginia by Hartley Graham, the great-great granddaughter of Elizabeth Catesby Cocke, its original owner.

At one time, the fan was so popular in England that Addison proposed to set up a "fan Academy" in which the gallants and ladies of the fashionable world might study the usages of this "weapon of coquetry." Nor was this all. So fan-conscious did Addison become, while writing for the *Spectator* (1711-1719), he contributed his well known and amusing satire on this favored weapon of the fashionable, and we read:

"Women are armed with fans as men with swords, and sometimes do more execution with them. To the end, therefore, that ladies may be entire mistresses of the weapon which they bear, I have erected an Academy for the training up of young women in the exercise of the fan, according to the most fashionable airs and motions that are now practised at court. The ladies who carry fans under me are exercised by the following words of command:

"Handle your fans, Unfurl your fans, Discharge your fans, Ground your fans, Recover your fans, Flutter your fans. By the right observation of the few plain words of command, a woman of tolerable genius who will apply herself diligently to her exercise for the space of but one year, shall be able to give her fan all the graces that can possibly enter into that modish little machine.

"There is an infinite variety of motions to be made use of in the flutter of a fan. There is the angry flutter, the modern flutter, the modest flutter, the merry flutter, and the amorous flutter. There is scarce any emotion in the mind which does not produce a suitable agitation in the fan—insomuch that if I only see the fan of a discip lined lady, I know well whether she laughs, frowns, or blushes.

"I have seen a fan so very angry that it would have been dangerous for the absent lover who provoked it to come within the wind of it; and at other times so languishing, that I have been glad, for the lady's sake, that the lover was at a certain distance from it."

How well the celebrated Addison understood the potentialities of this "modish little machine" no one would presume to question, nor his keen insight into the mind and heart of the capricious lady who in those days, must indeed have felt herself powerless without it.

There are a number of very beautiful old fans in Virginia today, at least one of which belongs to the period of Addison's "Fan Academy." This is the exquisite fan which the fair Evelyn Byrd of "Westover" carried when she was presented at the Court of George II of England, in 1723. She was but sixteen at the time, and as the daughter of William Byrd II, one of the wealthiest and most aristocratic of Virginians, and granddaughter of Colonel Daniel Parke, aide-de-camp to the great Duke of Marlborough, her presentation at Court created quite a stir in London.

Evelyn Byrd was one of the most beautiful and

exquisite flowers of Virginia womanhood. Despite her charm and beauty, wealth and breeding, her life was not a happy one, and it is perhaps the note of tragedy in her life and her untimely death, more than anything else, which has kept her romantic story ever alive in the minds of Virginians.

Colonel William Byrd had been in England on business several years when he sent for his sweet young wife Lucy Parke, and their little daughter Evelyn, to join him in London. This was early in the year 1716, when "Mistress Evelyn" was not quite nine year old, for during the summer of that year William Byrd wrote to his brother-in-law, Colonel John Custis of the Eastern Shore of Virginia, as follows:

"My daughter Evelyn has arrived safe, thank God, and I hope I shall manage her in such a manner that she may be no discredit to her country." That the proud and aristocratic, charming and cultured "Black Swan of Westover" more than realized his fond wish, the social history of the early eighteenth century proves, for after having received the best possible schooling abroad, she was presented to the reigning monarch, George II of England.

For a lass in her early teens, Evelyn Byrd possessed unusual poise and charm, and a certain *hauteur* which Sir Godfrey Kneller seems to have caught in his portrait of this lovely girl. Her flower-like beauty was noted by all who saw her at court, and she captured the hearts of those who met her later at social functions elsewhere in London.

Some say it was the Hanoverian George II of England, who exclaimed in amazement as she made her modest bow before him, "Are there many other as beautiful birds in the forests of America?" Still an-

other story tells us that Lord Chatham, when presented
to William ¡Byrd's young Evelyn remarked that "he
no longer wondered why young gentlemen were so
fond of going to Virginia to study ornithology, since
such beautiful Byrds were there."

The exquisite dress which Evelyn Byrd wore when
she was presented at Court, and the fan which she carried in her slender hands on this momentous occasion,
are both the treasured possessions of her descendants.
The dress is owned by Mrs. Stephen Decatur Mayo, of
Gloucester County, Virginia — the former Isabella
Harrison of "Brandon," while the lovely fan belongs
to her niece, Mrs. Louis E. Fagan of Philadelphia,
who before her marriage was Evelyn Byrd Harrison
of Virginia.

Mrs. W. W. LaPrade of Richmond, *née* Evelyn
Byrd Warwick, also a descendant, fondly recalls having been allowed to "put on" her famous ancestress'
court dress, when she was a little girl of eleven years.
The material is of a heavy cream colored silk, embroidered in pink rosebuds, while the dress is fashioned
along the lines so in vogue at the time of Evelyn
Byrd's presentation at the English Court.

The fan has carved ivory sticks, and the mount is
of parchment on which is hand-painted an enchanting
garden scene. Despite the fact that the fan is over two
hundred years old, one may still follow the artist's design. The gowns of the ladies have full skirts and
tight bodices, while the men are costumed in knee
breeches and coats with lace ruffs. White wigs prevail in the head-dress. The setting for this colorful
gathering appears to be a terraced spot in a French
or English garden; the *mise en scène* seems cool and
inviting—with trees, flowers, a Grecian urn, and stone

steps, while a note of gaiety is injected into the picture by a little dog frisking about.

The fan was left to Mrs. Fagan when she was a wee little miss of three years, by her great-aunt Isabella Harrison of "Brandon," because, as Mrs. Fagan explains it, "I was named Evelyn Byrd after the original owner of the fan." Today, this priceless and treasured heirloom is mounted on black velvet and framed beneath glass—an enduring valentine, to be sure, of Virginia's most romantic lady!

At the Virginia Museum of Fine Arts in Richmond, one may see the celebrated portrait of Evelyn Byrd, painted by Sir Godfrey Kneller, which has been loaned to the Museum by Mrs. Stephen Decatur Mayo. This superb likeness of America's foremost Colonial belle and beauty was first hung at "Westover," but later adorned the walls of historic "Brandon," the exchange being made, doubtless, through the marriage of Richard Evelyn Byrd and Anne, daughter of Benjamin Harrison of "Brandon," in 1826.

In Sir Godfrey Kneller's portrait, the lovely Evelyn is shown sitting on a mossy bank, while to the left of the canvas, on a bow just above her head, sits a cardinal—perhaps a facetious allusion to the family name. Her gown is blue-green in color, void of adornment and cut very low, accentuating her beautiful neckline and shoulders. The sleeves are of three-quarter length, and focus attention on her exquisite hands which rest so naturally on a large straw hat wreathed with morning glories, which she holds in her lap. In her hair a spray of star jasmine glistens like a jeweled pin, while a single soft brown curl falls over one shoulder.

When Evelyn Byrd posed for this portrait, there

Evelyn Byrd of "Westover." From the portrait by Sir Godfrey Kneller, owned by Mrs. Stephen Decatur Mayo, of Gloucester County, Virginia. Photograph by Cook.

was no pain in her young heart. She was treading a rose-strewn path, with never a thorn to prick the joy and tranquility of her days. Her frustrated romance with Charles Mordaunt, grandson and heir of the old Lord Peterborough, was yet to come; as a biographer of her father writes:

"Her hand was kissed by my Lords Oxford and Chesterfield; of whom sneering Harvey deigned to approve; who supped with Pope at his Twickenham villa, while yet the town was ringing with the success of his Odyssey; who was noticed by Beau Nash, the autocrat of Bath; who saw Cibber and Mrs. Oldfield play; who read *Gulliver's Travels* as they were first presented to the public by his Reverence the dean of St. Patrick's, then resident in Dublin; who from the presence-chamber of unroyal royalty, through a society reeking with the wine and musk and snuff of scandal, passed back to her plantation home in the new country as unblemished as she came."

To stand before Sir Godfrey Kneller's portrait of this fair flower of Virginia, is to recall the lines of Tennyson:

"A damsel of high lineage, and a brow
May-blossom, and a cheek of apple-blossom,
Hawk-eyes; and lightly was her slender nose
Tip-tilted like the petal of a flower."

Both in France and England the fan became the mirror of life; the events of the day—social and political, as well as the fashions and frivolities, were depicted upon them. When *Gulliver's Travels* appeared in 1726, scenes representing its grotesque satires on society and politics of the period appeared on fans. Other fans, similar in design, flaunted colorful scenes from popular plays; carried the words and bars from operas; or the rules of popular games within borders of playing cards. Some are said to have even borne records of royal marriages, births, christenings, and deaths—while wars and current events, even the bad manners of the times, found expression on the popular fans of the day.

During the reign of Louis XIII, fans opened to a full half circle, the supple materials of silk, satin, gauze, and vellum, being painted in elaborate designs. One very rare specimen of this period describes the King playing "hide and seek" with the four corners of the globe. During the reign of Louis XIV, a Fan-Makers Guild was established in Paris, and the business of making these exquisite and costly "trifles" became quite an extensive one. The variety of lovely materials which went into fan making at this time are described in the following pretty lines, sent me by a friend who collects fans; the author's name is unknown.

> "Leather, lambskin and taffety,
> Paper, wood, and ivory,
> Bamboo, feathers, and filigree,
> All make fans for you and me."

The different styles of fans mentioned as enjoying a wide vogue in England are said to have either been imported, or copied from French ideas and designs, by French workmen who had found refuge in England. Tortoise-shell, mother-of-pearl, and ivory were elaborately carved—frequently enriched with silver, gold, or enamel, and studded with gems which framed paintings by famous artists.

Fans of this period are attributed to Lebrun, Mignards, and Lemoine. In *The History of the Fan,* M. A. Flory states: "There is little doubt that Raymon de Lafage, Stella, and later Boucher, Watteau, Lancret, Greuze, and other great artists painted their charming pastorals, idyls, *fêtes-champêtres,* and cupids sometimes on fans; but how many of the subjects attributed to their brush are authentic is a difficult matter even for eminent art critics to decide. Young, needy artists, skilful but unknown, led by the demand of fashion to imitate the style originated by artists of renown, have probably painted most of the fine specimens attributed to great painters."

Quite the loveliest fan I have seen, outside of the Louvre and the Metropolitan Museum, is one privately owned in Virginia today, which belonged to the late Mrs. Charlotte Wheeler DeCourcy of Richmond, but passed to her sister, Miss Claribel A. Wheeler of New York and Richmond, after her death. The fan was sent to Mrs. DeCourcy eight years ago as a wedding gift by the late Mrs. Frank W. Pratt, also of Richmond. Accompanying the fan was a note telling something of its romantic and tragic past. These lines I copied, with the gracious consent of Miss Wheeler:

"I am sending you as a wedding gift, this very old fan which has rather an interesting history. It belonged for several generations to a family in New Orleans, and was *always* carried at their weddings. A few years ago, hard times forced the family to sell its treasures, and this fan came into my hands. One queer thing about the sale was, that no one in New Orleans was to have any of the articles offered for sale. *Pride dies hard!"*

To behold this fan of fairy-like beauty is to realize that it undoubtedly is the creation of a great artist, be he a Boucher, a Greuze, or an unknown. Here gauze, hand-painted in the most delicate pastels with tracery of gold—rare old *point* lace, and mother-of-pearl, have combined to make an object of such fragile beauty, that the fan in its entirety, beggars description. When opened it has a full spread of twenty-seven inches, and measures thirteen inches in depth. The

sticks are of mother-of-pearl— the outside, or guard
sticks, tapering to a width of an inch and a half at the
top. Seldom does one see such play of rainbow tints
as these exquisite sticks of mother-of-pearl emit.
The mount is as sheer as gossamer—a transparent
cream-colored gauze on which mythological characters
appear in all their enchanting beauty. In the center
a goddess is shown in her chariot of gold, as if riding
through coral-tinted clouds. At either end, a beautiful
mermaid emerges in all her seductive splendor, while
gorgeous peacocks and birds-of-paradise add their
beauty to an already enchanting scene. Across the
entire top of the fan there is a border of rare old *point*
lace. Here is an exquisite butterfly, blown far from its
native land—by the winds of fortune—or of fate.

How this fan found its way to the New France that
was Louisiana, and the gay and cosmopolitan little
capital of New Orleans, we shall never know. Perhaps it came with other exquisite finery belonging
to some French noblewoman who had settled in the
new province. Or perhaps the key to its mystery lies
in the words of the author of *The History of the Fan*:
"Most of the French fans found in other countries had
been sold at the call of poverty, or given as keepsakes
by the aristocracy who had emigrated."

Still another lovely old fan in Virginia is one which
originally belonged to Mary, the Mother of Washington, and was given by her as a token of friendship, to
Mrs. Robert Wellford of Fredericksburg, the former
"Widow Thornton," *née* Catherine Yates. This treasured antique has never passed out of the family to
whom it was given, and is today owned by Mrs. Arthur
Peyton McCarty of Washington, D. C.—the former
Ellen Spotswood Dickinson of Fredericksburg, Vir-

ginia, a direct descendant of Dr. Robert Wellford and his wife, Catherine Yates Thornton.

Mary Washington's last will and testament was made on May 20, 1778, and since it mentions no fan, she must have personally given the fan to her friend prior to her death. The "Widow Thornton's" second husband was Dr. Robert Wellford, first of his name in Virginia, who had come to America during the early years of the Revolutionary War with the English Medical Staff. Complaints arose because of his kindness to wounded colonial soldiers, so he resigned his position as surgeon in the English Army, and came to Fredericksburg with his good friend John Spotswood, bringing with him a letter of introduction from General Washington.

The eldest son of Robert Wellford and Catherine Yates Thornton was named John Spotswood Wellford, for his father's friend. He married Fannie Page Nelson, to whom the fan was given. Their daughter, Jane Catherine Wellford, married James Parke Corbin of "Laneville" in King and Queen County, and "Moss Neck" in Caroline, and on the death of her mother, inherited the fan.

The eldest daughter of Jane Catherine Wellford and James Parke Corbin was Fannie Nelson Corbin, who married William Henry Dickinson of "Moon's Mount" in Caroline. Fannie Nelson Corbin Dickinson bequeathed the fan to her fourth daughter, Ellen Spotswood Dickinson. This lady married Arthur Peyton McCarty, of Baltimore and New York, a descendant of an old Virginia family.

The fan is made entirely of sandalwood, decorated on both sides with a delicate tracery of gold. There are twenty-eight sticks, each of which is highly polished and measures ten inches in length. Near the top of the fan the sticks are interlaced with ribbon— the color of which seems to have originally been lavender. The color of the sandalwood is a rich, deep tan, and about it still clings a subtle fragrance, as of dying incense. The decorative treatment of the sticks is suggestive of Oriental artistry, for touches of black and gold have been applied to the wood in much the same manner that the Chinese use it on lacquer.

It would be interesting to know how the Spartan Mother of Washington came to possess this dainty article of feminine finery. Early Virginians are known to have imported their "best blue china" from Canton and Nanking, delivered to their nearest ports by ships engaged in the "China trade." So it is possible that the fan came with her set of "best blue and white tea china" mentioned in her will. Mary Cadwalader Jones, in an interesting sketch on fan-collecting, says: "When our grandfathers sent out for the charming old china, which in most families was broken up before people knew how fine it was, they were used also to order for their womankind fans. . ."

In 1785, the City of Dieppe, famous for its carvings, sent to the ill-fated Marie Antoinette on the birth of the Dauphin, a fan of the style known as *brisé*. This famous fan is described as having ivory blades decorated with figures and ornaments designed by Vien. A great number of exquisite fans belonging to Marie Antoinette are in private collections, with several notable examples in the Louvre.

Before the dark and dreadful days of the French Revolution, the fan reflected the lighthearted mood of society, but, ever adapting itself to the exigences of the hour, appeared during the days of the Republic bearing devices instead of decorations, all of which were in strict accordance with "republican ideas." Figures of Liberty, triangles, the letters F. R. for *République Française,* and similar insignia appeared on all French fans of this terrible period. Even the disappearance of allegories and rustic scenes, idyls and *fêtes-champêtres,* cupids and roses—so loved by the young Queen and her followers, did not appease the *bourgeoisie* and fierce patriots.

Beauty and fragility gave way to coarseness and durability; silk, gauze, and spangles were "suspicious materials, being the last vestiges of the aristocratic taste"—thus they were supplanted by crude materials, on which were printed "Vive la Nation," "Mort ou Liberté." Tragic scenes were by no means considered inappropriate. Flory says the "fan á la Marat represents Charlotte Corday carrying her fan in one hand while with the other she deals the citizen Marat his death blow."

Who would suspect that the "Siege of Richmond" and the "Battle of the *Merrimac* and the *Monitor*" were considered fitting subjects to adorn costly fans manufactured almost three quarters of a century ago? Yet these historic scenes of Virginia's tragic era were emblazoned on pictorial fans, believed to have been manufactured in this country to meet the specifications of a Cuban firm engaged in trade with the West Indies, Mexico, and Central America, at the close of the War Between the States.

Such a fan, owned by a Frenchman residing in Cairo, Egypt, was pictured in the magazine *Antiques* several years ago. The fan, a distinct Latin tribute to President Lincoln, was thought to have been given to the owner's grandmother, a titled Frenchwoman, as a souvenir by one of the staff officers associated with the French Army of Occupation in Mexico at the time of President Lincoln's assassination.

The design of the mount was evidently intended to appeal to Mexican tastes of that period. The right guard was equipped with a sharp stiletto, which was released by a spring, and near the center of the shaft there was a small secret compartment for poison. The blades were interwoven with the familiar Mexican arms—an eagle in conflict with a serpent. Above the eagle, a series of small oval frames surrounded daguerreotype inserts portraying five European empresses and queens, balanced by the likenesses of four American warriors, among whom General Grant and General McClellan were clearly recognizable.

The fan's framework was of stamped and gilded metal. On the obverse appeared the head of President Lincoln within a star, surmounted by winged victories, and flanked by a cherubic choir. On the reverse were lithographic depictions of the assassination plot, shooting of the President, the stage scene which President Lincoln was watching when he was attacked by Booth, the assassin's escape, and finally his wounding and capture. The end panels graphically depicted the "Battle of the *Merrimac* and the *Monitor,*" and the "Siege of Richmond." Crowning the entire fan were nine gold stars.

Happily, most of the old fans preserved today are delicate objects of great beauty, few of which serve as grim reminders of tragic eras. The Empress Eugénie, Queen Victoria, Queen Isabella II of Spain, and the late Empress of Russia, all had notable fan collections. Pictures of fans belonging to the Empress Eugénie show them to be magnificent creations, while the wedding fan of the Princess of Wales, later Queen Alexandra, wife of King Edward VII of England, which was made in Copenhagen, is a fairylike creation of all white which looks like frozen lace. The sticks are of elaborately carved ivory, while the mount is entirely of lace with insets of cameo-like medallions, and the Princess' crest and initials worked in an oval in the center.

The wealthy Virginia planters frequently ordered fans, when writing to their London agents for the "latest in fashions." Frequent mention is made in old wills and inventories of "mourning fans," "best fans" and "next best fans"—while the Virginia gentry usually specified a "genteel fan" when ordering these costly trifles for the ladies of their household.

A very beautiful fan which was hand-painted in Paris, and has sticks of hand-carved Chinese ivory, is owned by Mr. F. Otway Byrd, of "Upper Brandon" on the James. This treasured heirloom originally belonged to Mr. Byrd's grandmother, Anne Harrison of "Brandon." The present generation of young ladies in this distinguished family may say, as did Ninette, in Austin Dobson's delightful bit of verse *apropos* of the fan:

> "I swear upon this fan,
> My grandmother's!"

The oldest fan in the large and interesting collection belonging to the Valentine Museum, is a commemorative fan made in 1782 in honor of Admiral Rodney's victory over Comte de Grasse. The fan is rather small, with hand-carved ivory sticks, and is inscribed: "To the immortal Rodney." The mount is of a gold and buff colored paper, with a sprinkling of gold spangles across the top and on the sides. In the center, an acquatint shows Admiral Rodney standing triumphant, with the Spirit of Victory beside him, while surrounding both are flags, cannon, drums, and in the distance, a ship. This interesting and unusual old fan is from the estate of the late Mrs. J. H. Chamberlayne, of Virginia.

One of the loveliest fans in the entire Museum collection is the wedding fan which belonged to Mrs. William Frederick Gray, *née* Elizabeth Ann Valentine, sister of Mann Valentine, of Richmond. This exquisite "weapon of coquetry" belongs to the 1840-1850 period, and reflects all of the beauty and ingenuity which characterized fans of this and an earlier period. The sticks are of mother-of-pearl—the large guard sticks being inlaid with silver, while in one, flashing like a diamond, is a small mirror, so that "my lady" was able to behold her fair image as often as she pleased. The mount is of embroidered satin, and altogether, here is an object of feminine finery to evoke many "oh's" and "ah's."

Perhaps the most beautiful fan in the Valentine Museum is the large white fan, which Katherine E. Cropper of Virginia carried when she was presented at the Court of King Edward VII and Queen Alexandra of England. As one beholds its fragile beauty—sticks of mother-of-pearl with gold inlay—a mount of sheer white silk bordered with Alençon lace, and hand-painted so that, as the fan unfolds, an entrancing landscape is revealed with a beautiful lady in pink as the central *motif*—one does not marvel that Queen Alexandra is said to have commented to the young lady who owned it, "Your fan is prettier than my own."

Other lovely fans in the Museum collection include one which belonged to the late and beloved Miss Jennie Ellett of Richmond. Here again one sees beautiful

Hand-painted silk fan trimmed with Alencon lace, with sticks of mother-of-pearl and gold inlay, carried by Katherine E. Cropper of Virginia when she was presented at the Court of King Edward VII and Queen Alexandra. The Queen is said to have greatly admired this fan, and to have said to its owner, "Your fan is prettier than my own." Courtesy of the Valentine Museum.

sticks of mother-of-pearl, hand-carved rather than with inlay, and an exquisite silver clasp. The mount is of paper, hand-tinted, with a lovely lithographed scene.

A bequest of the late Miss Mattie Bolling of Richmond to the Museum, is a very fine Chinese fan made entirely of hand-carved sandalwood sticks, with an elaborately painted mount showing Chinese characters in different settings and postures, in brilliant costumes of blue, green, black and gold. This fan instinctively conjures up visions of Chinese temples and tea gardens, mandarins and fair ladies.

An unusual and exotic feather fan, given by Mrs. James Caskie of Richmond, has ebony handles and sticks, the mount being made entirely from black breast feathers as soft as down, interspersed with the curly green and blue feathers of the quetzal. This rare bird, known as a Guatemalan trogon, is the national symbol of Guatemala, and anciently was regarded as a deity by the Mayas, whose chiefs alone were permitted to wear its plumes.

The mourning fans of our grandmother's and great-grandmother's day, followed no particular style. Some were folding fans, others were the round or oblong type. Those used for "deep mourning" were severely plain, and as depressing in appearance as an undertaker's garb—dull ebony handles, with mounts of dull black paper or silk. "Light mourning" fans had a touch of color—usually purple. In the Valentine Museum collection one may see a very lovely "light mourning" folding fan, quite large in size, with carved ebony handles, and a mount of sheer black gauze-like material, with a border of hand-painted purple violets across the top.

From the sentimental angle, the most interesting fan

in the Museum collection is the one which Mildred
Lee, daughter of General Robert E. Lee sent to her
"dear Mattie." This fan is a recent accession to the
Museum group, and was given by Miss Gabriella Page.
The fan is an arresting object—made of exotic feathers
with a carved gold and black handle, and is the size of
an average palmetto fan. Its most unusual feature is
the mounted head and breast of a bird which is placed
in the exact center of the fan, against a background of
a variety of dark blue and white feathers, interspersed
with peacock feathers. To assign this impressive ornament to any particular country or period is difficult;
even the card which accompanied it gives no clue as to
its age or nationality. The card, bearing the engraved
name of "Miss Mildred Lee" is inscribed by this lady's
hand as follows:

"For dear Mattie, a Southern fan to waft away all
troubles!" According to the records of the Valentine
Museum, Miss Lee presented the fan to her friend in
1892, and "dear Mattie" was Mrs. Ralph Cross Johnson.

Gaze upon an old fan—handle an old fan—unfold
an old fan—and it is surprising how much is revealed
to us. From these lovely old keepsakes we learn how
our ancestors lived, how they dressed, something of
their tastes and achievements, extravagances and
caprices, fashions and frivolities; their artistic appreciation of the patient and exquisite workmanship of
artisans whose names are now forgotten; something of
the beauty and the horror of their age.

Like an old book upon whose yellowed pages is
written the story of centuries, we see in an old fan the
triumphs and tragedies of a vanished era. Many a
lady lives again in her fan, and speaks to us of great
moments in history.

Old Fabrics and Fashions

"Two things I love, two usual things they are;
The Firste, New-Fashioned cloaths I love to wear,
Newe Tires, newe Ruffes; aye, and newe Gestures too
In all newe Fashions I do love to goe.
    The Second Thing I love is this, I weene
    To ride aboute to have the Newe Cloaths seene."

—"The Gossipping Wives Complaint." *Circa*, 1611.

CHAPTER VI

OLD FABRICS AND FASHIONS

"THE most devoted follower of fashion in the present day gives no more heed to dress and the modes than did the early American colonist," writes Alice Morse Earle in her delightful and informative book, *Costume of Colonial Times*. In Virginia, especially, dress was looked upon as an important "badge of rank," a fact attested by the many orders sent to England by the wealthy planters for the latest in fabrics and fashions. Many of Virginia's early settlers were Cavaliers, with no "Puritanical horror of fine dress"—hence few attempts were made to curb their extravagances in attire—or that of their children—whose garb was almost as elaborate as that of their parents.

Captain John Smith has preserved for us a list of the articles of clothing which the Virginia Company considered necessary for the comfort of the early emigrants. They were advised to equip themselves with a Monmouth cap, three shirts, one waistcoat, one suit of canvas, one suit of frieze, one suit of broadcloth, three pairs of Irish stockings, a pair of garters, four pairs of shoes, three falling bands, and a dozen pairs of points. These purchases entailed a total expenditure of fifty-nine shillings. (*Works of Captain John Smith,* page 607.) It is interesting to note that at least some small provision was made for "dress occasions." If the men wore suits of coarse canvas and frieze on workdays, they also wore broadcloth on Sundays, and some few "luxuries" such as falling bands, waistcoats, and points, were included in their well-balanced wardrobe.

Students of colonial costumes and materials are the debtors of Alice Morse Earle for her definitions of these early, and now almost unheard-of articles of clothing, and the goods from which they were made. Monmouth caps, worth two shillings each, were made to resist bad weather, and had long been worn by sea-faring men. One can visualize the doughty Captain John Smith and his fellow adventurers, stepping ashore at Jamestown

> "With Monmouth cap and cutlass at my side,
> Striding at least a yard at every stride."

Frieze was a coarse woolen stuff, used since the four-teenth century; canvas was a strong cloth made of hemp or flax; broadcloth was of fine wool, and usually black in color. Falling bands were broad, plain linen collars, turned down over the neck of the doublet or jerkin (jacket), while points were ties of leather or woolen yarn decorated with tags or aiglets at one end. They were used instead of buttons in securing clothes, almost exclusively by the early colonists.

When the first settlers stepped ashore at Jamestown on a May day in 1607, their eyes rested upon a virgin forest, dense with trees and foliage, but in it they were to find a fair flower in the Princess Pocahontas—a young Indian maid, who, though she had never seen London, had her own ideas as to "fashionable dress." The historian Strachey, in his *Historie of Travaile into Virginia,* describes an impromptu visit he made to the village of the werowance Pipisco, and of his unexpected meeting with Pipisco's favorite wife. He found her "under the shadowe of a broad-leaved tree, upon a pallett of osiers . . . herself covered with a faire white drest deare skynne or two." She rose to greet him, summoning her maid to fetch her "a frontall of white currall (coral), and pendants of great but imperfect couloured and worse drilled pearles, which she put into her eares, and a chayne, with long lyncks of copper, which came twice or thrice about her neck."

"A jolly ornament" he found her, adding, that with a variety of feathers and flowers stuck in her haire, she seemed "as *debonaire,* quaint, and well pleased as a daughter of the howse of Austria behune with all her jewels." Nor did the sedate Strachey overlook the details of her costume. He goes on to say that "likewise her mayd fetcht her a mantell, which is like a side cloake, made of blew feathers, so arteficyally and thick sowed togither, that it seemed like a deep purple satten . . . very smooth and sleeke." Her "shewe of greatness" impressed Strachey, as well as the formality of their meeting, for he says, "these were ceremonyes which I did not look for, carrying so much presentment of civility . . ." (Strachey, pages 57-58.)

In *Colonial Virginia, Its People and Customs,* Mary Newton Stanard notes: "The American habit of keeping up with European fashions began at Jamestown"—a fact borne out by the following letter which John Pory, Speaker of the famous First Legislature in America— convened by Governor Yeardley in 1619—wrote to a friend in England:

"Our cowe-keeper here of James Citty on Sundays goes accoutred all in ffreshe fflaminge silke, and a wife of one that had in England professed the blacke arte not of a Scholler but a Collier weares her rough bever hatt with a faire perle hatband, and a silken sute thereto correspondent."

In 1621, the Governor, Sir Francis Wyatt, was ordered by the authorities in England "not to permit any but the council and the heads of hundreds to wear gold in their cloaths or to wear silk till they made it themselves." This was intended to encourage the silk industry in Virginia, rather than to discourage the wearing of silk, and the order apparently was given small notice.

Thomas Warnet, a prominent merchant of Jamestown, who died in 1629, bequeathed in his will many articles of costly clothing to various friends and relatives, among them "a coif, a cross-cloth of wrought gold, a pair of silk stockings, a pair of black hose, a pair of red slippers, a sea-green scarf edged with gold lace, six dozen buttons of silk and thread, a felt hat, a black bever hat, a Polish fur cap, a doublet of black camlet, a vest, a sword, and a gold belt." (*Economic History of Virginia in the Seventeenth Century,* Volume II, page 187, by Philip Alexander Bruce.)

"The incongruity of such shining apparel" writes Mr. Bruce "with the rude surroundings of new settlements in the wilderness does not seem to have jarred upon the perceptions of the population except so far as it implied an unnecessary expenditure; and this view was only taken when the resources of the Colony for one cause or another were seriously impaired."

Still later—in 1660—the Virginia colonists were ordered to import "no silk stuffe in garments or in peeces (except for whoods and scarfs), nor silver or gold lace, nor bone lace of silke or threads, nor ribbands wrought with gold or silver in them." The penalty for so doing was prosecution and confiscation, but the act was erased in the original record of the laws, and most likely was vetoed by the Governor.

Sir William Berkeley was Virginia's Governor at this time; a gentleman exceedingly fond of fine dress, so much so that he was incapable of setting an example to those about him of conservatism in one's attire. In 1660—the very year the colonists were ordered to import no finery in silks or laces, Sir William ordered from London "three Yards ffine Lace for ffrills and ffals" which cost £2 8s. This fanciful sounding bit of finery was well named, for frills and falls were sleeve ruffles and collars, very elegant additions to one's wardrobe in those days, especially when made of gold and silver lace, or other fine laces.

In the same year, Governor Berkeley ordered from London "one yard of fine lace for a piner" which was to cost £1 10s. The definition of pinner is "a woman's head-dress, having long flaps hanging down the sides of the cheeks, worn during the early part of the eighteenth century." Pinners were evidently in vogue much earlier, as Sir William's order would indicate. The term was generally used in the plural—hence a "pair of pinners." In 1728 Mrs. Mary Stith of Virginia wrote to her friend Mrs. Thomas Jones then abroad:

"When you come to London pray favour me in your choice of a suit of pinners suitably dressed with a cross-knot roll of whatever the fashion requires, with a suitable ruffle and handkerchief. I like a lace of some breadth, and of a beautiful pattern, that may be plainly seen, fine enough to look well, but not a superfine costly lace. And likewise beg your choice of a very genteel fan." (*Colonial Virginia, Its People and Customs,* page 196.)

From an early date wigs were worn in the colonies, and by 1716 the fashion of wearing them had become universal. Numerous portraits of prominent Virginians bear witness to the popularity of wigs in the colony, and the *Virginia Gazette* carried frequent advertisements *apropos* of this indispensable headgear. Various materials were used for making wigs: mohair, thread, silk, human hair and horse hair, and they were known by a dozen and one different names, including "the tie, the brigadier, the spencer, the major, the albemarle, the ramillies, the grave full-bottom, the giddy feather-top, the campaign, the neck-lock, the bob, the minor bob, the bob major, the lavant, the drop-wig, the buckle-wig, the Grecian fly, the peruke, the beau-peruke, the long-tail, the bob-tail, the fox-tail, the cut-wig, the tuck-wig, the twist wig, the scratch, and the macaroni toupee."

Alice Morse Earle says "Wigs were of varied shapes. They swelled at the sides, and turned under in great rolls, and rose in many puffs, and hung in braids or curls or clubbed tails, and then shrank to a small close tie-wig that vanished at the Revolutionary times in powdered natural hair and a queue of ribbon, a bag, or an eel skin." The young Princetonian tutor, Philip Fithian, writing at "Nomini Hall" in 1774, gives us the following amusing picture of himself, and the importance attached to one's hair-dress at this time:

"I was waked by Sam, the barber, thumping at my door. I was dressed, in powder too; for I propose to see and dine with Miss Jenny Washington today."

What was considered "fashionable and proper attire" for a young Virginia miss of gentle birth and breeding, forty years before the outbreak of the Revolutionary War? Let us turn to the order given by Colonel John Lewis for his young ward in the year

1737. This gentlemen of high estate was the son of Colonel John Lewis and Elizabeth Warner, and the father of Colonel Fielding Lewis of "Kenmore" who married Betty Washington, only sister of George Washington. Colonel John Lewis was married first to Frances Fielding, daughter of Henry Fielding of King and Queen County. She died in 1731, and he married secondly, Priscilla Churchill, daughter of Colonel William Churchill, and widow of Robert Carter of "Nomini Hall," who was the son of "King" Carter, and father of "Councillor Carter." The young Virginia miss for whom Colonel John Lewis placed the elaborate order, was in all probability the daughter of his second wife by her first marriage, for no children were born to John Lewis and Priscilla Churchill. The fortunate young lady was to have, according to the specifications of Colonel Lewis' order:

"A cap, ruffle, and tucker, the lace 5 s. per yard; one pair White Stays; eight pair White kid gloves; two pair Colour'd kid gloves; two pair worsted hose; three pair thread hose; one pair silk shoes laced; one pair morocco shoes; four pair plain Spanish shoes; two pair calf shoes; one mask; one fan; one necklace; one Girdle and Buckle; one piece fashionable Calico; four yards Ribbon for knots; one Hoop Coat; one Hat; one and one half yard of Cambric; one Mantua and Coat of Slite Lustring."

Originally, calico was an East Indian fabric, and its importation into Europe seems to have begun in the early seventeenth century. In England, any plain or unprinted white cotton cloth was called calico. "Fine sprigged calico" or a piece of "fashionable calico" such as Colonel Lewis ordered for his young ward, was a flowered material suitable for dresses and petticoats. Old advertisements both in England and Virginia speak of "Demy Chinted Callico Borders for

Womens Petticoats," while the different fanciful designs to be found in this material were variously known as "Liberty Peak, Basket Work, Covent Garden crossbar, Ranelagh half-moon, Prussian stormont, harlequin moth, and 'a fine check enclosing four Lions Rampant and three flours de Luce.'" Mrs. Earle mentions having seen later calicoes stamped with portraits of Benjamin Franklin and George Washington, and another design of some British officer.

Girdles and buckles of gold and silver were among the articles of dress forbidden by the Massachusetts General Court in 1634, but they were generally worn by the wealthy and fashionable Virginians, even by children, as Colonel Lewis' order for little Miss Carter shows. Silk and leather were also used to make girdles, but gold and silver more frequently went into the "rich ornaments" worn by older women. To these were hung the housewife's bunch of keys, her silver-clasped Bible, and an "equipage," which was an ornamental case to hold scissors, thimble, knife, pencil, tooth-pick case, tweezers, "ear-pick," bodkin, and nail-cleaner.

Lustring was a favored material for coats and dresses during the seventeenth and eighteenth centuries. It was a plain soft silk, which Mrs. Earle says was "universally worn." A mantua, such as Colonel Lewis ordered for his young ward, was a gown or sacque open to display the petticoat; and the coat to accompany it was also to be made of slite lustring. In the *Journal of a Young Lady of Virginia* (1782) we read:

"Hannah was dressed in a lead-coulered habbit open, with a lylack lutestring scirt. Sister wore a blue habbit with a white satin scirt."

The fashionable colors in lustrings in 1783 were,

"Plumb, Pink, Flystale, Cinnamon, and Laylock," so Miss Hannah's "lylack lustestring scirt" was among the most favored shades then in vogue.

If we may judge from the following letter dated April 15, 1752, which the Reverend Thomas Dawson, rector of Bruton Parish Church, sent to his London agents—Messrs. J. Hanbury and Company—*no restrictions whatsoever* were placed upon the dress of the wives of Virginia clergymen two hundred years ago. A minister's wife flaunting such feminine finery as a fashionable brocaded suit, a blue satin petticoat, blue silk stockings and blue silk shoes, would doubtless have been tarred and feathered in Puritan New England, but not in the Old Dominion.

In 1752, during a visit to England, Lady Gooch, wife of Governor Sir William Gooch, was asked to "shop" for her friend Priscilla Bassett Dawson of Virginia. The following letter, found among the Bassett papers at "Eltham" is interesting for its disclosures. To his London agents, the Reverend Dawson wrote as follows:

"Gentlemen: I have writ to Lady Gooch by this opportunity and desired the Favour of her to buy a few articles for Mrs. Dawson, the amount of which I imagine may be about £30. But whatever it is I desire the Favour of you to honour her order. The *Osgood* is arrived, & we are preparing for her or your other ships all the Tobaccoe we possibly can."

The attached order was for

"one fashionable Lace Cap, Handkerchiefs, Ruffles and Tuckers; one fashionable brocade suit; one Pair Stays; one blue Sattin Petticoat, £1; Scarlet Cloth under Petticoat, £2; one pair Blue Sattin Shoes, full trimmed; one hoop, £1; one pair Blue Stockings £0—12s; one fashionable Silver Girdle; one fan, £1." (*William and Mary Quarterly*, Volume VI, page 124.)

From the days of his early manhood, George Washington was perhaps the most fastidiously dressed gentleman in all Virginia. On the eve of the date that he was to call upon the fair Betsy Fauntleroy, "in hope of a revocation of the former cruel sentence," he wrote the following memorandum:

"To have my coat made by the following Directions, to be made a Frock with a Lapel Breast. The Lapel to contain on each side six Button Holes & to be about five or six inches wide all the way equal, & to turn as the Breast on the Coat does, to have it made very long Waisted and in Length to come down to or below the bent of the knee, the Waist from the Armpit to the Fold to be exactly as long or Longer than from thence to the Bottom, not to have more than one fold in the Skirt and the top to be made just to turn in and three Button Holes, the Lapel at the top to turn as the Cape of the Coat and Button to come Parallel with the Button Holes and the Last Button Hole on the Breast to be right opposite the Button on the Hip."

Evidently the future "General Washington" believed that clothes made the man—at least in affairs of the heart.

After his marriage to the rich "Widow Custis," Washington became more and more fastidious in matters of dress, and showed an equal interest in the fine attire of his wife and little step-son and step-daughter. For "Master Custis"—aged six years—Washington ordered from London:

"Six pocket handkerchiefs, small and fine; six pairs gloves; two laced hats; two pieces India Nankeen; six pairs fine thread stockings; four pairs coarse thread stockings; six pairs worsted stockings; four pairs strong shoes; four pairs pumps; one summer suit of clothes to be made of something light and thin; one piece black hair ribbon; one pair handsome Silver shoe and knee buckles; one light duffel cloak with Silver Frogs."

Nankeen was a buff-colored Chinese cotton fabric,

made in Nanking, China. It was used by "all classes
and both sexes, for all variety of outer gear, for both
winter and summer wear," writes Alice Morse Earle.
Shoe buckles were widely worn in the colonies by 1750,
and were extensively advertised by shopkeepers both
at home and abroad. In all important inventories,
and lists of goods ordered from London (for children's
as well as grown persons' wear), we read of silver or
plated shoe and kneebuckles. The latter were considered an important article of dress, many of them
made of gold and silver, and set with paste jewels.

When Lord Dunmore was entertained in Norfolk in
1774, it was necessary to send "an express" to New
Town for Colonel Moseley "to come to town with his
famous wig and shining buckles—he being recognized
the finest gentleman we had"—in order that he might
dance the minuet with Lady Dunmore — Captain
Abyvon, the Mayor of Norfolk, "not being equal to
the occasion."

"The light duffel cloak with Silver Frogs," which
Washington ordered for his small step-son, was made
of a popular material called duffle, which was a
"woolen stuff" originally made in Duffle, a town in
Flanders. It had a thick tufted nap, and was made at
Whitney, England, purposely for winter wear in
America, according to De Foe, an authority frequently
quoted by Alice Morse Earle. Writing in 1683, William Byrd of Virginia said, "The Duffields is the
worst I ever saw ... Coler too light, a Darker blue
pleases better." Frogs were ornamental cloak, coat, or
hat buttons; in 1736 "Spangled Scalloped & Brocaded
Frogs" were advertised in New England, and were no
doubt popular as an ornament of dress in the South,
as well as other elaborate varieties.

Little Miss Martha Custis came in for her share of finery, too, Washington placing the following costly order with his London agent at the same time that he ordered the foregoing fine apparel for her older brother. The little lady was to have:

"Eight pairs kid mitts; four pairs gloves; two pairs silk shoes; four pairs Calamanco shoes; four pairs leather pumps; six pairs fine thread stockings; four pairs fine worsted stockings; two caps; two pairs ruffles; two tuckers, bibs, and aprons if Fashionable; two fans, two masks; two bonnets; one cloth cloak; one stiffened coat of Fashionable silk made to pack-thread stays; six yards Ribbons; two necklaces; one pair Silver sleeve Buttons with Stones; six pocket handkerchiefs."

A little four-year old girl in kid mitts, mask, stiffened coat with "pack-thread stays," a bib and tucker, necklace, apron, and calamanco shoes, must indeed have been a quaint and captivating picture, bedecked in so many "frills and furbelows." Mrs. Earle says an elaborate order such as Washington's, "was indeed a typical example of the fashionable follies of the day."

Mitts were little fingerless gloves, made of kid or silk, and frequently of open lace-work. They were especially favored for summer wear. For many years the fair ladies and small daughters of fashionable Virginia families wore "sun-expelling masks" as a protection against the sun, wind, and cold. They were made of black velvet, white and colored silk, and sometimes held in the hand; but riding masks were usually fitted with a silver mouthpiece, since the hands of the wearer were usually occupied with the reins, or holding herself on the pillion.

Fithian, the young Princetonian tutor in the household of "Councillor" Carter of "Nomini Hall" in Westmoreland County, records in his sprightly diary in the year 1774—

". . . After Service is over, three quarters of an hour is spent in strolling around the Church among the Crowd, in which time you will be invited by several Gentlemen home with them to dinner. The Balls, the Fish-Feasts, the Dancing-Schools, the Christenings, the Cock-fights, the Horse-races, the Chariots, and *Ladies Masked,* for it is a custom among the Westmoreland Ladies whenever they go from home, to muffle up their heads & necks, leaving only a narrow passage for the eyes, in cotton or silk handkerchiefs."

Callimanco was a substantial and fashionable woolen stuff of fine gloss, either ribbed or plain, and frequently flowered, much used during the late seventeenth and eighteenth century for fashionable shoes. James Fontaine, a French Huguenot who settled in Virginia, memtions in his memoirs having attempted to manufacture callimanco in 1694. One constantly finds reference to "calamanco shoes" and "calamanco gowns" in early Virginia orders sent to England. During the visit of George Washington to historic Lexington in 1789, to do him full honor, we read that "Lucindy, pert minx, had a most lovely Gown of Green Callamanco with Plumes to her hatt."

"My best bib and tucker" is a facetious allusion to feminine finery familiar since the days of our childhood. The bib ordered for little Martha Custis was doubtless of linen, designed for use at meals, to be gently placed under the little girl's chin as a protection to her dress. Bibs were also a waist-piece attached to a woman's apron. A tucker was an ornamental frilling of lace or muslin used around the top of a woman's dress, and descending to cover part of the bosom. Little ladies who dressed much the same as their mothers, wore them also.

Aprons enjoyed a widespread vogue. Mrs. Earle writes, "I doubt not many an apron came over in the

Mayflower." Queen Anne favored them, and her example was promptly followed by all loyal and fashionable women in England—and Virginia. Many of
them were costly additions to a lady's wardrobe, and
were made of various materials, even of heavy silver and
gold brocade. Striped gauze, "drest picket" and lawn
embroidered aprons, were among the most popular
kinds, but were too delicate to serve as a useful adjunct
to the toilet. Mrs. Sarah Taylor, of Lower Norfolk
County, left at her death in 1640, a "sea green apron"
(evidently silk) valued at one pound four shillings.
In 1774, Fithian describes Miss Jenny Washington,
aged seventeen; a very comely young lady, judging
from his detailed description.

"Her dress is rich and well chosen, but not tawdry, nor yet too
plain. She appears today in a chintz cotton gown with an elegant
blue stamp, a sky blue silk quilt, *spotted apron,* and her light brown
hair craped up with two rolls at each side, and on top a small cap of
beautiful gauze and rich lace, with an artificial flower interwoven."

Miss Jenny's "sky blue silk quilt" was a quilted
petticoat, and her small cap of "beautiful gauze and
rich lace" was doubtless a "Ranelagh Mob" or a
Queen's "Night Cap," both of which were the height
of fashion during the middle and latter part of the
eighteenth century. "Fly caps with Egrets," "Drest
Gauze Caps" and "Mob Caps" were also popular and
widely worn. Mob caps are described as a caul with
two lappets; Ranelagh mobs were made of gauze or
net, puffed about the head, with two ends crossed under
the chin and then tied at the back, and left hanging
in "floating ends"; the Queen's night-cap was similar
in shape, but made of a finer gauze and more trim and
compact. It is familiar to us as having been worn by

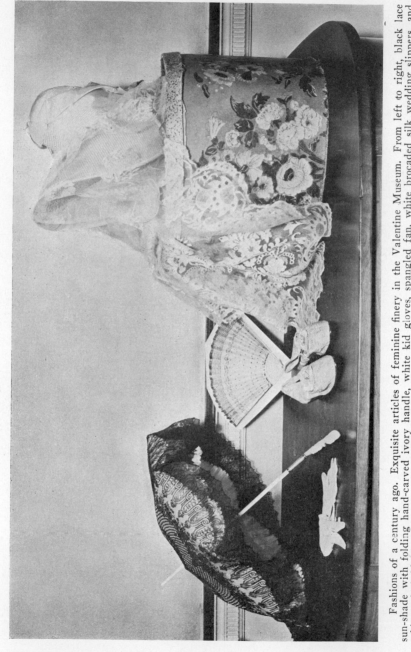

Fashions of a century ago. Exquisite articles of feminine finery in the Valentine Museum. From left to right, black lace sun-shade with folding hand-carved ivory handle, white kid gloves, spangled fan, white brocaded silk wedding slippers, and white satin bridal bonnet and veil and the lovely old flowered bandbox in which the bonnet came. This fetching bridal bonnet and lace veil were worn by Anna Robinson of Richmond when she married Mr. John Shields in Monumental Church, Richmond, in 1836. Courtesy Valentine Museum.

Martha Washington, and shown in so many of her portraits.

Ten years before the American Revolution, there were other towns in Virginia besides the gay little capital of Williamsburg that could boast of "a milliner lately arrived from London," and a shop carrying the latest in fashions. In 1766, "Katherine Randall, milliner, lately arrived from London," opened a shop in Fredericksburg, and advertised in the *Virginia Gazette:*

"Best flowered and plain satins, flowered and plain modes, sarcenets and Persians; flowered, striped, and plain English gauze, a great variety of blonde, minionet, thread and black lace, joining blondes for ladies caps and handkerchiefs, wedding and other fans, a great variety of ribands, French beads and earrings, ladies caps, fly caps and lappets, egrets of all sorts, silk and leather gloves and mits, summer hats and cloaks, cardinals, French tippets, black gauze and catgut love ribands for mourning, silk, thread and cotton stockings for ladies and gentlemen, gentlemen's laced ruffles, bags for wigs and solitaires, Irish linens and tapes in variety, garnet, Bristol stone and pearl sleeve buttons set in silver, garnet and gold brooches, a variety of silver shoe-buckles in the newest fashion for ladies and gentlemen, with knee-buckles for the latter . . . and sundry other articles too tedious to mention."

Sarcanet was a thin firm silk, much used for cloak linings and for hoods; Persian was also a thin silk used chiefly for linings and facings, or for summer wear. In old inventories one frequently sees mention of "a gown of Sprig'd Persian." The word "lace" in early days frequently applied to a lacing cord that held garments in place. Bone lace was used by the earliest colonists—both the Jamestown settlers and the Pilgrims. Lace was of course used to trim gowns and petticoats, aprons and capes, ruffles and caps, as old inventories show, while waistcoats of gold and silver lace were not uncommon in Virginia.

Ribbons were indispensable to the fashionable wardrobe of men, women, and children, well into the eighteenth century. "Silken ribens" were of sufficient importance in early days to be left by will, and "denounced as superfluities" by New England magistrates. For centuries, ribbons were a favorite gift on St. Valentine's Day, and in 1762, "Staunton in the Valley" held a highfly successful fair, during which "Elizabeth Hog and Priscilla Christian went to Crow's Store and got as 'a fairing' a present of ribbon from the clerk." Various ribbons advertised during the eighteenth century were "paduasoy ribbons, love ribbons, Dettingen ribbons, Prussian ribbons, silvered ribbons," and prior to the outbreak of the Revolution, "Liberty ribbons."

A lappett was a lace pendant of a lady's cap or headdress; a tippett was a narrow covering for the neck. Old advertisements carry quaint lines such as "Mecklenburg Tippets for Women and Children;" "very Gentell Tippets Silver'd at 22s 6d." Rattlesnake tippets—a designation sufficiently horrifying to send a member of the gentler sex into a swoon—were really very dainty and lovely additions to a lady's toilet. They were usually made of fine blonde (a French lace originally made of unbleached silk) and adorned with flowers. In winter, tippets served a really useful purpose, when they were made of various furs and worn for warmth.

Cardinals were hooded cloaks, in general use during the first half of the eighteenth century. Originally, they were made of scarlet cloth, like the mozetta of a cardinal. "Bag wig, laced ruffles and black solitaire,"

says Mrs. Earle, "were the marks of a man of fashion
in 1760." A solitaire was a broad black ribbon, worn
loosely around the throat to protect the coat from the
powdered wig.

One of the most interesting orders for costly and
fashionable apparel which Washington sent to England was in the year 1759, when he ordered finery for
himself as well as Lady Washington. The master of
"Mount Vernon" specified "a light Summer Suit made
of Duroy by the measure" (a material similar to cor-
duroy) ; "two best plain bever Hats at 21s," and "one
Sword belt red morocco or buff, no buckles or rings."
Few men were so meticulous in matters of dress as
was Washington. In Shakespeare's immortal lines we
see his counterpart:

> "The expectancy and rose of the fair state,
>   The glass of fashion and the mould of form,
>   The observed of all observers!"

His lady was to have, among other things, "a salmon
coloured Tabby of the enclosed pattern to be made in
a sack and a coat; a Cap, Handkerchief, Tucker &
Ruffles to be made of Brussels Lace or point proper to
be worn with the above negligee, to cost £20.; two
fine Flowered Aprons; one dozen fashionable Cambric
Pockethandkerchiefs; one half dozen Knots and
Breastknots." Breastknots and bosomknots were the
same. They came in brilliant colors, and were made
of satin ribbons.

Martha Washington must have favored the rich
shade of salmon in many of her costliest costumes, for
her manikin in the United States National Museum
in Washington wears a salmon colored hand-painted
silk dress which belonged to the First Lady of America.

Rose Gouveneur Hoes, who has edited a delightful
booklet entitled, *The Costumes of the Mistresses of the
White House as shown in the United States National
Museum,* expresses the opinion that the dress worn by
Mrs. Washington's manikin dates back to colonial days,
and judging from the magnificence of the fabric, must
have been purchased in London.

The skirt of the dress is made of many straight
widths, sewed with considerable fullness to a basque
pointed front and back. The entire dress is hand-
painted in a fanciful design of flowers and insects,
caught up at intervals with green jewels. In the larger
spaces are many of the loveliest of wild flowers—
morning glories, buttercups, violets, daisies, arbutus,
etc., while in the smaller spaces are numerous North
American insects — grasshoppers, flies, lady-bugs,
wasps, indicating that the artist was a lover of nature.
The manikin wears a regal looking lace cap, tied at
the top with a bow of ribbon, while in her hands she
holds a brown satin work-bag elaborately embroidered
in ribbon-work, said to have been made by Martha
Washington's own nimble fingers.

The elegance of "Mount Vernon" wardrobes was by
no means confined to ballroom and drawing-room attire. It is difficult to imagine a more life-like and
colorful picture of the first President than one in which
he is dressed in his drab broadcloth riding suit and
scarlet waistcoat, mounted on his favorite hunter
"Blueskin" riding to the hounds over the rolling and
beautiful countryside surrounding "Mount Vernon."
The ladies of his family and guests frequently followed
the hunt, some in crimson riding habits, keeping to
the hounds, and Mrs. Washington in chariot and four;
the coachman and black postilion astride a forward

horse dressed in the Washington livery of scarlet, white, and gold—forming a colorful picture against the grey background of a winter's day.

Typical of the true sportsman that he was, Washington liked well-fitting, handsomely tailored riding clothes, and the latest and finest equipment for his stables. In the following order to his London agent, he writes with his usual stress of detail:

"Send me a riding frock of a handsome drab broadcloth, with plain double gilt buttons. A riding waistcoat of superfine scarlet cloth and gold lace, with buttons like those of the coat. A blue surtout coat. A neat switch whip with silver cap. One man's riding saddle, one hogskin seat, large plated stirrups, and everything complete. Double reigned bridle and Pelham bit, plated. A very neat and fashionable Newmarket saddle cloth. A large and best portmanteau, saddle, bridle and pillion. Cloak-bag, surcingle, checked saddle cloth, holsters, etc."

In this same order was a black velvet riding cap for Billy, the negro huntsman, in charge of Washington's stables. Billy, in his specially imported hunting suit, always rode "Chinkling," built low and sturdy like his rider. It was invariably Billy who would sound the French horn, and with a cry of "Come Music, come Truelove, ho! Sweetlips," send the hounds dashing headlong to bring Reynard to cover.

The blue "surtout" ordered by Washington was a close-fitting overcoat, long favored by Virginia gentlemen for more than a century. In one of the war letters of General George E. Pickett, C. S. A. to his wife—sent from "Headquarters" and dated June, 1864—he writes in a reminiscent vein of his boyhood days at "Turkey Island" on the James, and of his father acquainting him with the great men of that day. Of his father, General Pickett writes:

"I can hear him now say, 'My son, there was Madison, a very, very small man with introverted eyes and ample forehead. He dressed always in a *surtout of brown,* which was generally dusty and oftener than otherwise faded and shabby. Judge Marshall was very tall and commanding and revolutionary and patriarchal in appearance. He had fine expressive eyes and dressed always in a well-fitting *surtout of blue.* Mr. John Randolph was puny and frail and most uncommon looking. He was swarthy and wrinkled, with eyes as brilliant as stars of the first magnitude. Watkins Leigh was unusually distinguished in appearance. Tazewell was tall and fine looking; but Mr. Monroe was very wrinkled and weather-beaten and so exceedingly awkward that he stumbled over his own feet and walked on everyone else's. Governor Giles used a crutch always and talked like Molasses in July.' " (*Soldier of the South,* pages 108-9.)

A "Newmarket" coat was a close-fitting coat for out-door wear, and like the Newmarket saddle-cloth, probably took its name from the market town in the eastern part of England, a noted horse-racing center. Capuchins were hooded cloaks for women, often costly and elaborate, made of black and colored silks, and trimmed with fringe and laces. Calash bonnets were worn by many of the fashionably dressed women in Virginia from 1765 throughout the century. They are said to have been first introduced by the Duchess of Bedford, and were enormous head-coverings—"a veritable sunshade" says Mrs. Earle, "which could scarcely be called a bonnet."

What of the dress worn by the settlers in the Valley of Virginia? How did it compare with that worn by the planters and their families in Tidewater? Samuel Kercheval in his *History of the Valley of Virginia* says "the linsey petticoat and bed gown" were the universal dress of the women of the Valley in early times, and adds, "a small home-made handkerchief, in point of elegance, would illy supply the place of that profusion of ruffles with which the necks of our ladies are now mantled." Such luxuries and adornments in dress as leghorns, ruffles, curls, combs, rings, and jewels, were not only unknown to the women who with their husbands and fathers first settled the Valley, but says Kercheval, "were not then to be had."

Of the typical men's dress, he gives us this interesting pen-picture:

"The hunting shirt was universally worn. . . This was a kind of loose frock reaching half-way down to the thighs with large sleeves. The cape was large, and sometimes handsomely fringed. The belt, which was always tied behind, answered for several purposes besides that of holding the dress together. . . The hunting shirt was generally made of linsey—sometimes of coarse linen, and a few of dressed deerskins. A pair of drawers, or breeches, and leggings were the dress of the thighs and legs. A pair of moccasins answered for the feet much better than shoes. These were made of dressed deerskin."

At the outbreak of the Revolutionary War, Richmond was a smaller town than either Norfolk or Fredericksburg, yet the same importance was attached to fashionable attire here, as elsewhere in Virginia, and judging from old accounts the gentry indulged in the same prodigality in dress that had prevailed in the Colonial Capital. In 1775 the gentlemen of Richmond appeared in magnificent waistcoats "covered with flowers in gold threads," full coats, breeches, knee-buckles, stockings, high-heeled shoes and a cocked hat. A snowy storm of powdered hair terminated in a queue in the back, and was tied with silk ribbon.

By the beginning of the nineteenth century, the cravat had become indispensable to a gentleman's toilet, and the Richmond gallants, as well as their elders, adorned themselves with these newest gorgets as only a "Richmond exquisite" knew how. In an old issue of *Harper's New Monthly Magazine* there appears a most entertaining sketch entitled "Some Richmond Portraits," and the author, Eugene L. Didier gives us a graphic pen-picture of the fashionably dressed Richmonder around 1800. He writes:

"A Richmond exquisite of the first decade of this century vested himself like a silkworm in the ample folds of his cravat. His valet held one end and he the other of the long thin texture, the former walking round his master till both ends met, when they were tied in a large bow. If the gentleman did not enjoy the luxury of a valet, one end of the cravat was tied to the bed-post, and he walked toward the latter, turning all the while, and wrapping his neck in his cravat till he was wound up like an Egyptian mummy. The stiff collar of the dress-coat stood as high as the ears, and was kept back several inches from the head to enable the wearer to turn to the right or the left. Buckskin breeches and top boots completed the gentleman's apparel, the perfection of both depending on the tightness of the fit."

In the Valentine Museum in Richmond there are a number of remarkably preserved and beautiful old costumes, dating from the late eighteenth through the middle nineteenth century. Here are velvet and brocaded suits, sun-shades and bonnets, "second day" dresses and bridal finery, to delight the student of old costumes, as well as the lover of the old and the quaint in Virginia. Two very lovely suits—one of pale green cut velvet, and the other of light blue taffeta with lace jabot, belonged to Dr. John Peter LeMayeur, who came to Virginia from France in 1785. Dr. LeMayeur took the oath which made him a citizen of Virginia in 1789, and he is said to have been one of Washington's dentists. Another very handsome suit, of black velvet with elaborate trimmings of gold braid, was worn by Peter Chevallie Warwick of Richmond, at the Court of Napoleon III, in 1855.

There are adorable sun-shades with elaborately carved ivory and ebony handles, and bonnets galore.

Mrs. John W. Franklin, the former Miss Betsey Gibson of Richmond, shown wearing the brocaded silk wedding gown of her ancestress, Mrs. George Gibson of Rotterdam. This beautiful old dress is of a heavy cream colored silk, elaborately brocaded, and was purchased in 1767. Richmond *News-Leader* photograph. Courtesy of the Valentine Museum and Dr. Churchill J. Gibson.

The loveliest of these is the bridal bonnet and veil, worn in 1836 by Anna Jane Robinson who married John Shields in Monumental Church, Richmond. It is made of white brocaded silk with streamers of white lute ribbon. Another beautiful bonnet, belonging to her trousseau, is of aquamarine brocaded silk, with a facing of white satin. The oldest and quaintest hat box I have seen in Virginia, is the one these bonnets came in. The background is of peacock blue, with a colorful design of pale and deep pink roses and dahlias, with blue morning glories and their tender green stems entwined in the whole.

The "Old South" speaks again in a group of three fetching bonnets. One, a sun-bonnet, is of caromel colored straw edged with narrow black silk ruffles, with a quaint shoulder ruffle (designed to protect the neck and curls of a young lady from dust during long drives) falling from behind. The other two—one a leghorn and the other a lacy straw—were displayed in the window of a millinery shop in Berryville, Virginia, at the outbreak of the War Between the States. When hostilities began, the shop was closed, and so these lovely bonnets were never sold. They were given to the Museum by Miss Marie Crowe of "Crowe's Nest," Berryville, a daughter of the owner of the shop. Both bonnets are trimmed with gay colored flowers and ribbons, and it is easy to imagine a lass of sweet sixteen, smiling at her Confederate lover from beneath the brim of either of these adorable *chapeaux*.

The oldest dress in the Museum collection (and there are ever so many lovely ones!) is the brocaded silk wedding gown worn by Mrs. George Gibson on June 24, 1767, in Rotterdam. This exquisite old dress is made of a stiff, cream-colored silk, covered with myriads of tiny brocaded flowers in a soft shade of pink. It is fashioned along Watteau lines, and is trimmed with pink silk ruffles.

Mrs. Gibson is the ancestress of a long line of distinguished Virginians, so her beautiful old gown is interesting from many angles. Her husband was a London merchant engaged in business in the Netherlands seaport, and very likely the dress was ordered from a fashionable house in London or Paris. A descendant of Mrs. Gibson's is the Reverend Churchill J. Gibson of Richmond. Dr. Gibson's daughter, Mrs. John W. Franklin, *née* Elizabeth Gibson, who is shown in the accompanying illustration wearing her ancestress' wedding gown, is the sixth generation of "Gibson girls" to have worn it.

The following note, written in 1892 by the late Reverend Churchill J. Gibson, grandson of Mrs. George Gibson, to his cousin Mrs. W. F. Spotswood, speaks eloquently of the pride and interest the members of this distinguished family have manifested in this treasured and lovely old wedding gown. Writes Dr. Gibson:

"Dear Belle,

You expressed a desire to see the Wedding Dress of my Grandmother Mrs. George Gibson of Rotterdam. As my wife wishes to send it to Cincinnati to our other half of grandchildren to look at, she sends it to you, Our Cousin and Miss Lizzie—to inspect—that you may have some idea how our *Ancestresses* used to *prink up* on Wedding Occasions. She was married this very month of June—the 24th, in 1767—in Rotterdam. The dress is 125 years old. None of us would look *as fresh* at that age. Kind regards to the Governor and the children and Miss Lizzie from us both.

Your affectionate Cousin,

Churchill J. Gibson."

There are other wedding gowns of a later date, in satin and tulle, taffeta and lace, with all of the accompanying finery: veil, orange blossoms, gloves, slippers, and hose. To look upon these lovely old dresses, lying between folds of tissue in the long deep drawers of Victorian bureaus in the Museum bedrooms, is to have that inexpressible feeling that comes from seeing a pressed and faded rose between the pages of some treasured book. What tender memories are aroused by the first glimpse of the soft folds of satin and yellowed tulle, the waxen blossoms, and tiny lace-trimmed satin slippers!

As these lovely old bridal gowns are displayed in full view, one's suppressed admiration finds expression in many an "oh" and "ah"—

> "While fancy, like the finger of a clock,
> Runs the great circuit, and is still at home."

Here are the dresses of half a dozen Virginia brides: Judith Michaux, Fannie Williamson, Mary Dorothy Withers, Fannie Archer Anderson, Elizabeth Ann Valentine, and others. The oldest of these belonged to Judith Michaux, of the distinguished French Huguenot family who settled in Goochland and Powhatan. She married Jefferson Swann in 1810. Her wedding dress is of white satin, with an elaborate treatment of satin ruffles and fine tucking around the bottom of the full skirt.

Next, in point of age, is the wedding gown of Fannie Williamson, who married Robert Archer of Richmond, on March 28, 1816. Sheer in texture, and yellowed from age, this dainty dress is made of India muslin embroidered in a delicate and lovely design. The wedding gown of Mary Dorothy Withers, who married John Withers of Dinwiddie, in 1833, is of lustrous white satin with an elaborate treatment of corded folds on both waist and skirt, and full puff sleeves. With it are her white silk wedding slip, long white kid gloves—now a deep ivory—and diminutive bride's slippers, square toed, with tiny bows, and *no heels*.

The wedding dress of Elizabeth Ann Valentine, who married William Frederick Gray on July 18, 1850, is of heavy white taffeta. It is made with a high neck, long sleeves, and a basque waist. The front of the skirt and waist are embroidered in silk thread outlined with silk braid, and the sash has fringed ends. One can visualize the sister of Mann Valentine in this handsome gown. She must indeed have been a regal figure.

The fires of old loves are kindled anew at the sight of old bridal finery. Who can touch a gown of soft silk, yellowed from age and fragrant with lavender or potpourri; or fragile tulle and rose-point lace that clings to waxen blossoms, and not feel a wave of emotion—a tugging at one's heartstrings—a blinding mist in one's eyes?

Look upon the complete bridal outfit that belonged to Fannie Archer Anderson, who married Edwin Lafayette Hobson in St. Paul's Church, Richmond, in 1865, and the lines of Lord Byron, inspired by Belgium's capital, come forcibly to mind—lines that well might have been dedicated to old Richmond—Capital of the Confederacy, and Fannie Archer Anderson's marriage to a Confederate soldier.

> "There was a sound of revelry by night, (the)
> Capital had gathered then
> Her beauty and her chivalry, and bright
> The lamps shone o'er fair women and brave men.

A thousand hearts beat happily; and when
Music arose with its voluptuous swell,
Soft eyes look'd love to eyes which spake again,
And all went merry as a marriage bell."

Fannie Archer Anderson's wedding gown is of white *moiré,* with considerable fullness in the back of the skirt which ends in a train. An exquisite lace bertha, elaborately beaded, almost conceals the high tight-fitting waist. A wreath of orange blossoms crowns the long tulle veil, and her dainty white satin slippers, beaded and trimmed with lace and flowers, have incipient French heels.

"Age cannot wither ... nor custom stale" the infinite variety and charm of old costumes, fabrics, and fashions. The vision of centuries-old bridal finery, court dresses and suits, bonnets and sun-shades, slippers and knee-buckles, will not soon fade; nor the memory of those who wore them, die. Old letters, orders, wills, inventories, and advertisements have a fascination all their own. In their quaint orthography and diction, we find a magic mirror in which our ancestors appear before us, bedecked in all of their fashionable finery.

Fine Furniture

"With furniture superfluously fair."
—SIR WILLIAM ALEXANDER, 1615.

CHAPTER VII

Fine Furniture

Beds

EAR to the heart of the early Virginian were the sturdy pieces of furniture—first of oak, and later of mahogany and walnut, just "out from England" to give comfort and adornment to his wilderness home. In his eye there was a glint of pride and pleasure as he examined each newly arrived piece: the "great bedde," tables, chairs, and cupboards. Had he not paid for them with his good crop of tobacco, and had not his London agent carried out his instructions to the letter, and shipped him only those pieces that were the "latest mode" abroad?

The quality and quantity of the early Virginian's furniture depended, of course, upon his position in the Colony. If he was a wealthy planter, river baron, or merchant, then the rooms of his Georgian mansion were soon filled with the finest furniture obtainable; if he was a man of lesser means, his dormer-windowed cottage was at least furnished with comfortable necessities, for life was abundant in Tidewater.

The arrival in Virginia of ships from England, docking at innumerable river wharfs, was a gala day in the life of the prominent Virginia planter and his family, for their cargo consisted of those luxuries in dress and household furnishings for which the Virginian had waited patiently and prayerfully. So much depended upon his tobacco crop—its shipment from Virginia and safe arrival in England; the "exchange" of the precious brown leaf into currency; how much, or how many good things it would buy for him; and lastly, the return voyage—so seeming slow, and the memorable unloading—at Norfolk, Yorktown, Tappahannock, Port Royal, Leedstown, Fredericksburg, or Falmouth, of the "polished furniture, the beautiful china, the massive silver, the elegant dresses" that adorned the homes and persons of the well-to-do Virginian of that day.

"It was natural that in a new country where life was hard at best, a good bed upon which to lay one's weary bones was a possession of first importance," writes Mary Newton Stanard in *Colonial Virginia, Its People and Customs.* Thus, as she reminds her readers, "my feather bed, or my feather bed and furniture— meaning the bedstead, bed-clothing, tester, curtains, valance and all the paraphernalia then supposed to belong to a proper bed—was not only among the most frequent bequests, but a prized heirloom."

N. Hudson Moore, in her superb reference work *The Collector's Manual,* says in her delightful chapter on "Old-Fashioned Bedsteads":

"Even in the earliest times some attempts were made to have the resting-place soft and warm. The warrior, coming home from war or chase, threw his wearied frame on a simple couch laid upon the floor and covered himself with furs. Little by little the frame of the bed was raised from the floor, coverings grew more elaborate, greater ease was required, and gradually the elaborate structure we require today was evolved. As late as the fourteenth century beds were objects of luxury in England. Many a castle had but one, in which the lord and his lady rested, the remainder of the household sleeping on settles, chests, tables, or on the floor."

In France, the beds in use at this time were enormous, and their hangings both elaborate and costly. Beds that were six feet square were called *couchettes,* or little beds. Only when they were built along enormous lines, measuring anywhere from eight to twelve feet by eleven, were they called couches or beds. Such great beds were mounted on wide steps, and hung with exquisite materials.

The famous "Great Bed of Ware" mentioned by Shakespeare in *Twelfth Night,* is twelve feet square, and is still preserved at Rye House, near the famous old Saracen's Head Inn, where it formerly was. According to the records of Hampton Court, Cardinal Wolsey owned two hundred and eighty beds, most of them hung with silk. Not until the fifteenth and sixteenth centuries was much attention given to the woodwork of beds, since the hangings concealed all of the exposed parts, and were considered the most important part of the bed.

The materials used for the curtains and elaborate coverings of these early beds varied, the most favored materials being velvet, silk, sateen, camblet, India and Patma chintz, French and Pompadour chintz, "fine laylock and fancy callicocs," mohair, fustian, seersucker, perpetuana, kidderminster, serge, darnic, silk darnic, camac, bancour, paly, printed calico, checked and striped linen, corded dimities, harrateen, muslin, and lute-string.

My reliable Webster lists only a few of these interesting-sounding old materials, so whether they were of cotton or silk, wool or linen, I am unable to say. Camblet was a material originally made of camels' hair; fustian was a stout cloth made of cotton or flax; lute-string (lustring) was a glossy, plain heavy silk;

calico (in England) was a white cotton cloth, and printed calico the same material only with a colored design, while kidderminster is defined by Webster as being "a two-ply carpet made at Kidderminster, England." N. Hudson Moore states in her *Manual* that there were scores of other goods brought from the East Indies, "with unfamiliar names and high prices." Harrateen she describes as a "favorite stuff" which as late as 1750 cost four dollars a yard, and adds, "a set of curtains all made was worth two hundred dollars."

The wealthy Virginian was not long in learning that a full-dress bed with "petticoat valance" and window curtains to match, trimmed with fringe and tied back with cords, was the mode of the hour in England. He relied on his London agent to keep him informed of the trends in fashion, so it is not surprising that early Virginia inventories list innumerable "great beddes" with all of their fine and costly trappings.

The inventory of Ambrose Fielding of "Wicko-comoco Hall" in Northumberland County, made in 1674, lists among other valuable possessions, "a great bedde with curtains and valance lined with silk, damask tester, silk counterpane, linen sheets, a feather-bed and blankets."

In 1678, Colonel Francis Eppes of Henrico County, Virginia, inventoried "One large new feather-bed with camblett curtains and double vallins (valance) lined with yellow silk, bolster, pillows, counterpane, rodds and hooks, tops and stands, one curtaine and some ffringe damnified—twenty four pounds, five shillings."

James Sampson of Isle of Wight County left, in 1689, sheets trimmed with "Elgin lace;" Thomas Jefferson, great-grandfather of the "Sage of Monticello" owned valuable bed-trappings of chintz and kidderminster, while Joseph Ball, in 1711, bequeathed his wife his "feather-bed, bolsters, and all furniture thereto belonging," and to his daughter Mary, the mother of Washington, "all the feathers in the kitchen loft to be put in a bed for her." In 1719, Orlando Jones of Williamsburg, likewise bequeathed to his wife, "his best feather-bed and furniture" and to his daughter, "his *next* best feather-bed and furniture." Both of these Virginia gentlemen made better husbands than the immortal Shakespeare, who it will be remembered, left his *"second* best bed" to his wife!

George Washington it appears, gave much more time and thought to acquiring household possessions than did the Mistress of "Mount Vernon." There are continuous records of his orders abroad as well as purchases at home, and he was one of the largest buyers and highest bidders at the *vendue* at "Belvoir," the home of the Fairfax family. The closing of this famous Virginia estate, and sale of the entire household effects (due to the continued residence of the family in England) probably represents the first prominent auction sale in Virginia of its kind, and it is interesting to think of the great Washington as one of the most spirited of buyers: bidding for mahogany, brass, and copper ware—even such quaint trifles as a toasting-fork, pickle-pots, pewter plates, pillows; and more valuable articles such as Persian carpets, a shaving table and desk. At this sale alone, which was held in 1774, Colonel Washington's purchases totaled two hundred pounds sterling, and among them was a "mahogany settee-bed with Saxon green covers for same, thirteen pounds."

The most famous bed in Virginia today is the one on which "The Father of his Country" breathed his last. When the Mount Vernon Ladies Association acquired "Mount Vernon" they found an empty house. Fortunately some one thought of the inventory of the original contents of the mansion-house, made by the appraisers of George Washington's estate shortly after his death, which had been filed with other of his court records. It specified in minute detail the articles of furniture in each room, as well as their make and material, so by this means the re-furnishing of "Mount Vernon" was undertaken in an accurate and authentic manner.

Among the first to contribute original pieces were the descendants of Nellie Custis. Mrs. Robert E. Lee sent from "Arlington" the handsome Hepplewhite sideboard; her son, General George Washington Custis Lee gave back a mirror, wall-brackets, and the hallowed *death-bed,* while Miss Mary Custis Lee donated the old hall lantern, also chairs, bed-curtains and other articles.

The bed on which the great Washington died is a large four-poster, dressed as it was in Washington's day, with a broad canopy, curtains, and large bolster. Paul Horgan, in his deeply touching chapter, "The Death of a Man," in the *American Historical Scene,* gives us this pen-picture of the room in which the greatest American breathed his last:

"The bedroom at Mount Vernon as it was on the night of December 14, 1799 was depicted many times thereafter in engravings. These were pictures which took the people to the death-bed of their father. For what he had done for them in his lifetime, they repaid him with their grief. There can be no other coin for the pay of greatness. . .

"One of these engravings of the final hour at Mount Vernon showed where he lay, and where the others were by him: Mrs. Washington at the foot of the bed in a chair; Colonel Lear and

Doctor Craik near the head; Christopher, the body-servant standing beyond them; the women, Charlotte, Caroline, and Molly near the door; a candle burning on a bed-table against the window between which and another window the bedstead stood in the room; none of the faces having likeness to their subjects; an unreal atmosphere in the drawing and the medium of the engraved lines; nothing of the humanity and the trial that met at such a moment; only symbols, really, for an event which lived within people's knowledge by means of imagination and experience of life and death here lifted above limning into legendary character.

"Presently the grief which the engraving signalized died away, and the name and knowledge of General Washington became more impersonal the widelier they spread; until like a sort of gracious weather, they dwelled over the nation and were as blessedly taken for granted as any force which is accepted for the bounty it yields to things that grow."

Where, in all America, is there so hallowed a piece of furniture as this great bed on which Virginia's immortal son found the sleep of eternal peace?

There are a surprising number of other historic beds still to be found in the Old Dominion, most of them notable examples of fine woodwork and beautiful carving, and *all* of them "dressed" in the finery that belonged to their period. In the Carlyle House in Alexandria, in the northeast upper bed-chamber known as "General Braddock's Room" there is an enormous tester bed, with the quaint side steps originally used for climbing into it. According to tradition, this great bed was frequently occupied by General Braddock during the French and Indian Wars. At "Arlington," not far distant, there is a handsomely carved four-poster in the bedroom once occupied by General Lee.

In Williamsburg there are numerous fine old canopied beds, among them the one in the Peachy House which "overlooks the turfed expanse of the Court House Green and has before it the ever-present reminder of Sir Christopher Wren in the Court House walls." The upper bedroom in which the great four-poster stands is the center of romantic interest in the house, with LaFayette as the focal point. It is furnished with a mahogany bureau of "age unknown," a small chest of drawers, and a spinning wheel upon which many a gentlewoman spun in times of necessity. But the great bed is at once the cynosure of all eyes, for its huge legs have never been cut down, and its top almost reaches the ceiling. How indispensable were the quaint little side steps to such a bed as this; not alone to the occupant, but to the maid servant who must change the fine linens, and "dress" it daily in all of its paraphernalia!

Another famous old Williamsburg bed, and quite the largest and most beautiful of the "great beddes" I have seen in Virginia, is the one in the Richard Bland Tavern on the Duke of Gloucester Street. This quaint old house with its eight front dormer windows was built in 1710. It was the home of Richard Bland, who, in 1766, announced in a pamphlet that America was no part of the Kingdom of Great Britain, and was only united with it by the common tie of the Crown. He was a member of the First Continental Congress, and one of the great patriots of his day.

His long, two-storied house, with its great rooms individually named, such as "The Great Chamber," "Mr. Page's Room," and the "Bull's Head Room" was handsomely furnished with massive pieces of mahogany, of which fact the great four-poster bed bears eloquent testimony. The massive reeded posts suggest Sheraton, while other intricate and delicate details of workmanship clearly stamp it as the creation of a great cabinet-maker, and a *chef-d'œuvre* of noble proportions.

At historic "Berkeley," the home of that illustrious family — the Harrisons — there is another beautiful Colonial four-post canopied bed, which is reputed to have once belonged to the beautiful Evelyn Byrd of "Westover." Not only were the Harrisons and the Byrds neighbors, but friends as well, and as might be expected, were eventually united by ties of marriage, for on April 6, 1826, Richard Evelyn Byrd, son of Thomas Taylor Byrd and Mary Armistead his wife, married Anne Harrison, daughter of Benjamin Harrison of "Brandon."

Early in the eighteenth century "Berkeley" became the colonial seat of the Harrison family. Here lived at various times, Benjamin Harrison, Attorney General and Treasurer of the Colony; Major Benjamin Harrison, member of the House of Burgesses; Benjamin Harrison, member of the Continental Congress and Signer of the Declaration of Independence, and William Henry Harrison of "Tippecanoe" fame and ninth President of the United States and the grandfather of Benjamin Harrison, twenty-third president. The imposing old brick mansion at "Berkeley" stands today, a significant reminder of its colonial and historic associations, and the generations of great men it has sheltered.

At beautiful "Wilton" on-the-James, built by William Randolph II of Turkey Island in 1753, which has been restored by the Society of Colonial Dames in Virginia and is used as the Society's headquarters, there is a lovely old four-post mahogany bed, which was imported from England before the Revolutionary War. The "Three Trees" *motif* is carved on the slender, graceful posts, and the entire bed is "dressed" in brilliant chintz—wall curtain, canopy, bolster, spread, and "petticoat valance."

Another "great bed" with historic associations, adorns one of the guest-chambers at old "Marmion" in King George County, not far from the blue Potomac. According to tradition, there was a house on the vast tract of Marmion land—some two thousand two hundred and seventy-three acres—in 1674, erected by John Fitzhugh, son of the original owner.

For four successive generations "Marmion" was owned by members of the Fitzhugh family, but in 1785 came into the possession of Major George Washington Lewis, son of Colonel Fielding Lewis of "Kenmore" and his wife Betty Washington, only sister of General George Washington. Today, the direct descendants of Major George Washington Lewis boast an unbroken tenure of over a century and a half.

"Marmion" has many claims to distinction, not least among them its intimate association with the Washington and Lewis families, as well as its connection through other ties of marriage, with many of the most prominent families of the Northern Neck of Virginia, including the Daingerfields, Willises, Brockenbroughs, Tayloes, Dickinsons, and Grymeses, and the distinguished Plater and Forrest families of Maryland.

Architecturally, "Marmion" has a plain and unpretentious exterior, yet can boast of having had perhaps the most beautiful interior (in one of its rooms) of any great house in Virginia. Today, the entire paneling and pilasters that once adorned the walls of the "Marmion" parlor—paneling richly decorated with paintings done by a Hessian soldier—forms one of the "period" rooms in the Early American Wing of the Metropolitan Museum in New York.

For a time, four Lewis sisters reigned over "Marmion," dispensing hospitality to a seeming never-ending gathering of guests, for throughout Virginia the hospitality of this old house has been proverbial. Ann, Attaway, Zola, and Lucy were the daughters of Fielding Lewis III and his wife Mary Imogen Green, whose grandfather, Colonel Uriah Forrest of Revolutionary fame married Rebecca Plater, the daughter of Governor George Plater of Maryland. Fielding Lewis III was the son of Daingerfield Lewis, grandson of Major George Washington Lewis, and great-grandson of Colonel Fielding Lewis and Betty Washington.

Ann Lewis, the eldest of the sisters, married William Dickinson of "Wheatland" in Essex County; Attaway married John Dickinson of "Berry Plain" in King George County, a brother of William. After her death, John Dickinson married her younger sister, Zola, while Lucy Lewis, the youngest of the sisters, married Carter Grymes, and resides at "Marmion."

Edith Tunis Sale, in her notable book *Interiors of Virginia Houses of Colonial Times,* uses as one of her illustrations, a charming picture of Lucy Lewis Grymes, sitting beside the great bed at "Marmion" which once belonged to Virginia's illustrious John Marshall, also a kinsman of the house.

Another beautiful four-poster bed which vies in size and exquisite workmanship with the Sheraton bed in the Richard Bland Tavern, is the one which belonged to Lady Jean Skipwith, and is still preserved at "Prestwould" the handsome estate of Sir Peyton Skipwith, in Mecklenburg County.

This truly "great bedde" is hung with exquisite rose silk, the canopy of which is drawn through a brass empire wreath which almost touches the ceiling. Nearby is an antique child's tent-bed of beautiful workmanship, while in the small dressing room adjoining Lady Jean's "Pink Room" there is a rare old mahogany field-bed of unusual lines.

Sir Peyton was descended from a long line of notable and wealthy Skipwiths, and it is not surprising that he should have chosen the name of his ancestral English home for his vast Virginia estate, or that he should have furnished it with priceless pieces of mahogany, such as his Lady's great bed, and the rare and exquisite little tent-bed for the youngest member of the family.

In contrast to the several "great beddes" that lent comfort and beauty to the large bed-chambers of the wealthier houses of Virginia, there was the *one* bed that belonged to the humble cottage of the poor planter: a bed that was cheerfully given over to a wayside traveller or stranger-guest. The historian, Robert Beverley, writing of Virginia about 1700, says of the hospitality of that day:

"The inhabitants are very courteous to travellers, who need no other recommendation but they being human creatures. A stranger has no more to do but to enquire upon the road where any gentleman or good housekeeper lives, and there he may depend upon being received with hospitality. This good nature is so general among these people that the gentry when they go abroad order their principal servant to entertain all visitors with everything the plantation offers. And the poor planters who have but one bed will often sit up or lie upon a form or couch all night to make room for a weary traveller to repose himself after his journey."

What of that quaint contrivance, the trundle-bed? The earliest name for this diminutive bed on casters was truckle-bed, truckle meaning "to trundle," and trundle simply implying "to roll along freely; to roll on casters." Long before Eugene Field penned his poem *Little Boy Blue,* and painted for us that poignant picture of the little boy who, having placed his toy dog and tin soldier in their accustomed place, toddled off "to his trundle-bed, and dreamed of his pretty toys"— this quaint ancestor of the present-day bassinet and crib was well-nigh a necessity in every early American home.

In a recent issue of the magazine *Antiques,* in an article captioned "The Editor's Attic," interesting and enlightening reference is made to the early trundle-bed. To quote:

"Such contrivances were child-size, box-like affairs with sides not more than fifteen inches above the floor. They were mounted on casters to permit their being easily trundled or moved about. By day the trundle-bed lay doggo beneath an adult four-poster, whose valance hid the diminutive intruder. When darkness fell, the small chariot of sleep was dragged forth for the occupancy of one or two youngsters of appropriate length and breadth.

"This custom explains why the grown-ups of the time built their great bedsteads so high above the floor as to be accessible only by the exercise of superhuman agility or the employment of a stepping bench. . . The trundle-bed is no late invention. Its advent probably coincides with that of overwhelming families, and dissatisfaction with the repose afforded by a heap of straw."

As the wills and inventories of our ancestors bear witness, the term *bed* implied the feather mattress, or else a ticking filled with wool or other soft material, while *bedstead* referred to the supporting frame. Thus, in her will, Mary Washington bequeathes to her son, General George Washington her "best bed, bedstead, and Virginia cloth curtains, quilted blue and white quilt, and best dressing-glass."

Chairs

In the British Museum in London, one may behold the oldest piece of cabinet-makers' work known to man: Queen Hatasu's chair, of the Eighteenth Egyptian Dynasty, sixteen hundred years before the Christian Era. It is made of ivory, ebony, and various metals, yet for all of its antiquity, holds not half the appeal that does the great Coronation Chair of England, in which all English sovereigns have been crowned since 1273.

There is still preserved in old Boston the chair used by the first Governor of Massachusetts. Next to being taken to see the house of Paul Revere, one of the greatest thrills of my childhood was being allowed to sit in this historic chair.

In the Parish House of Old St. Paul's Church, Norfolk, there is an impressive looking chair that once belonged to the great American patriot, John Hancock. How this chair came to be in Virginia I have been unable to learn; perhaps it was purchased at one of the numerous auction sales which followed so close upon the passing of this great American.

It was John Hancock's wish that his mansion and the magnificent furnishings as well, go to the Commonwealth of Massachusetts, and in accordance with his wishes both were offered by his heirs, first to the State, and next to the City of Boston. Incredible as it may seem, both refused them, and, as a result, the valuable portraits and handsome furnishings were put up for sale, and scattered far and wide.

Today, as one stands beside John Hancock's old chair, one is reminded that the Declaration of Independence—as it first stood—bore only his name; a

Magnificent mirror said to have been bought in France by Thomas Jefferson at a cost of $1,500.00 and brought by him to America. According to tradition, the mirror once hung in the White House, and later in the Army and Navy Club. It was purchased at an auction sale by the late J. F. Biggs of Richmond, and placed in Pratt's Castle, where it now hangs. On either side of the mirror are shown two beautiful rosewood Cathedral back chairs of unusual weight. Courtesy of Mrs. J. F. Biggs.

name written so large, and firm, and clear, that even George III of England is said to have been able to read it without his spectacles!

According to Mary Newton Stanard, the first chair in America of which there is any record, is the green velvet one in which Lord Delaware sat in Jamestown Church. "Probably the next" she writes "is the 'Wainscott chaire' bequeathed in 1623 by John Atkins of Jamestown, to his friend Christopher Davison, Secretary of the Colony."

There were, of course, few or no chairs in Virginia during the early years of the first settlement. Ships chests, standards, and stools were made to serve the purpose of chairs for a number of years. Even in England, chairs were rare until the beginning of the seventeenth century. Prior to this time, only the master of the house was given a chair, while the less important members of the household used benches, settles, and stools. N. Hudson Moore in her valuable *Collector's Manual* says that "Stools were in common use at table till well into the seventeenth century."

When the Virginia wilderness was cleared—when settlements and towns sprang up and began to grow, and the Virginia planter grew rich from his great shipments of tobacco to England, his inventories and wills listed numerous types of chairs, among them: "great chairs, small chairs, high-back chairs, low-back chairs, arm chairs, elbow chairs, plain wooden chairs, Russian leather chairs, Turkey-work chairs, willow chairs, cane chairs, Dutch chairs, silk chairs, silver-stuff chairs, but *no* rocking chairs." The elbow chair was frequently called "roundabout" and was very popular in Virginia, one of its known *devotees* being none other

than that impassioned patriot and orator, Patrick
Henry.

Virginia's Royal Governors were not long in im-
porting from England those luxurious furnishings in
keeping with the dignity of their exalted office, and as
early as 1710, orders for furnishing the "Pallace" in
Williamsburg sound very splendid indeed. Various
orders specified, among other things, "three dozen
strong fashionable chairs, three large looking glasses,
four chimney glasses for the lower apartments, and
one marble buffette or sideboard with a cistern and
fountain."

Beverley, the historian, whose early writings of Virginia manners and customs furnish the student with
such delightful pictures of life in our ancestors' day,
pens this critical comment concerning the leisurely-
disposed, luxury-loving Virginians around 1700:

"They are such abominable ill husbands that though their country
be filled with wood, yet they have all their woodenware from England, their cabinets, chairs, tables, stools, chests, cart-wheels, and all
other things, even so much as their bowls and birchen brooms to the
eternal reproach of their laziness."

In the *Gazette* of 1739, Virginians read that the sloop
Ruth, of Rhode Island, had entered York River with
"four cases of drawers, four desks, and other things."
This is one of the earliest references of New England
cabinet-makers marketing their craft in the South.
By 1766 Williamsburg boasted of several cabinet-
makers established in that fair little city, among them
one "B. Bucktrout, cabinet-maker from London" who
advertised in the *Gazette,* that in his shop he was making "all kinds of cabinet-work in the newest fashions,"
and could supply to all desirous of having same "the
mathematical gouty chair."

In "Pratt's Castle" on Gamble's Hill in Richmond, there are two beautiful old Cathedral-back chairs of solid rosewood, elaborately carved, whose graceful appearance would never indicate their surprising heavy weight. In the Virginia Historical Society there are several lovely examples of Chippendale chairs, with cabriole legs and claw-and-ball feet, that once adorned a famous Virginia home.

For sheer *quaintness* I can think of no chair I have seen in Virginia that takes precedence over the early American "Sleigh Rocker" which is but one of many interesting pieces in the collection of Early American furniture belonging to Miss Catherine Gordon of Richmond. This unusual old piece is so named because of the long front and back rockers that resemble the runners of a sleigh. For the most part, the wood is of pine and poplar, with the rounds made of hickory. The age of this facinating old chair is estimated to be one hundred and fifty years, and as one examines the time-worn rockers, arm-rests, and head-rest, one feels that here indeed is a perfect example of the old and the quaint.

Thackeray was a collector-of-sorts, and became so attached to an old cane-bottomed chair he had acquired on one of his quests of the quaint, that he wrote a charming ballad about it, entitled "The Cane-bottomed Chair" which runs like this:

"In tattered old slippers that toast at the bars,
And a ragged old jacket perfumed with cigars
Away from the world and its toils and its cares,
I've a snug little kingdom up four pair of stairs.

"To mount to this realm is a toil, to be sure,
But the fire there is bright and the air rather pure;

And the view I behold on a sunshiny day
Is grand through the chimney-pots over the way.

"This snug little chamber is cramm'd in all nooks
With worthless old knick-knacks and silly old books,
And foolish old odds and foolish old ends,
Crack'd bargains from brokers and keepsakes from friends.

"Old armor, prints, pictures, pipes, china, (all crack'd),
Old rickety tables, and chairs broken-backed;
A two-penny treasury, wondrous to see;
What matter? 't is pleasant to you friend, and me.

"But of all the cheap treasures that garnish my nest,
There's one that I love and I cherish the best;
For the finest of couches that's padded with hair,
I never would change thee, my cane-bottomed chair.

"'T is a bandy-legg'd, high-shouldered, worm-eaten seat
With a creaking old back, and twist'd old feet;
But since the fair morning when Fanny sat there
I bless thee and love thee, old cane-bottom'd chair!"

Tables

The oldest form of a table was a board on trestles. Later the board or boards were permanently attached to the trestle bases, the workmanship and design was less crude, and this convenient contrivance for eating purposes became known as a trestle-table. Its companion piece was a long bench or form, which was placed on one side only, the other being unoccupied. As early as 1530 the trestle-table was in use in England, and the first Virginia settlers used them as well.

In the Virginia Museum of Fine Arts in Richmond, there is a seventeenth century English trestle-table, made of oak, which conjures up visions of old English halls—long and cold—where the master of the house and his guests sat down to a meal of venison, or a chine of boiled beef or mutton, ale or beer, and as many "manchets" as the company required. A "manchet" was a loaf of fine white bread, not to be confused with "household bread" which was coarser and more commonplace. The interesting old trestle-table in the Virginia Museum of Fine Arts is from the Strause collection. The long narrow "board" consists of three oak planks put together with battens at either end. These joined planks of sturdy oak rest on a trestle with X-shaped legs, and altogether this ancient table is a sight to warm the heart of the antiquarian.

One of the interesting illustrations in *Interiors of Virginia Houses of Colonial Times,* by Edith Tunis Sale, shows an early trestle-table with matching chairs in the old kitchen at "Shirley," the ancestral home of the Hills and Carters, and one of the most magnificent Colonial estates in Virginia. This old table is said to be such a perfect specimen of Colonial kitchen furniture, that when "Mount Vernon" was being restored, an appeal was made to the owners of "Shirley" for sketches of it.

The second step in table growth was the long narrow table, generally much larger than the trestle-table, which was popular at inns and taverns from 1600 to 1650, and was familiarly known as the "cavalier table." Like all early tables it was placed against the wall, and the accompanying piece of furniture was a long bench. A smaller table of the same date, designed primarily for family purposes, was the narrow oak table with joint stool. This type table was supported by four sturdy carved legs which were joined at the bottom by oak rails, which served the two-fold purpose of support and foot-rest.

By 1650, the "baluster" table had come into vogue,

and in length and breadth resembled its predecessors, as well as being made of oak. The average length of the baluster table was ten feet, its chief claim to distinction being its elaborate leg treatment resembling a baluster. The delicately wrought, hand-turned, beautifully carved spindle-legs of these tables bore a striking resemblance to a set of small pillars supporting a handrail, hence the name "baluster."

The dining table that came into being between 1650 and 1700 was variously known as the "hundred-legged" or "gate-legged" table, and as can be imagined, is the ancestor of our present day gate-legged table. A similar table was the "spider-legged" table, only this was a more fragile table in all respects. One of these early gate-legged tables, made of oak, adorned the dining room of William Penn.

Among several outstanding pieces of early American furniture belonging to Miss Catherine Gordon of Richmond, is a rare pine gate-legged table, estimated to be close to two hundred years old. Here is truly an old piece to delight the antiquarian—the original hardware, the sturdy legs, the thick boards, and yet, a table of unusually beautiful and graceful lines.

Another very early table of which one seldom hears today, was known as a "credence" table. These were small, but sturdy corner tables where food was tested before serving (not for their savory flavor, but for possible poison), the very name credence implying the purpose the table was intended to serve. In a recent issue of the magazine *Antiques,* a London firm advertised: "A noble old oake credence table made in about 1650, price one hundred and fifty dollars, delivered to your port." The accompanying illustration showed the table with a back raised leaf and three very sturdy carved legs. Such tables are today used in England to hold silver plate.

By 1700 the "side table" with drawers was a conspicuous piece in the dining rooms and halls of wealthy homes. These were massive affairs, and the undisputed ancestor of the sideboard and buffet which followed years later.

Pictures of early "tea tables" show them to closely resemble the small graceful tables which we designate today as "coffee tables." Only the beverage seems to have changed with the passing centuries. Then as now, these dainty tables—light in weight and small in size—were conveniently and comfortably placed before the hostess, whether she sat in a chair or on a settee. It would be interesting to have a picture of the tea table over which Governor Spotswood's gracious lady presided when Colonel William Byrd, adventurer and chronicler extraordinary, visited them at their "palace" at Germanna in 1732. But in his delightful diary recording his journey, called *A Progress to the Mines,* the "Black Swan of Westover"—charming, witty, and wise—penned this delightful picture of the now forgotten settlement at Germanna and the Spotswood's sociability:

"September 27, 1732. This famous town consists of Col. Spotswood's enchanted castle on one side of the street, and a baker's dozen of ruinous tenements on the other, where so many German families had dwelt some years ago; but now removed ten miles higher, in the fork of Rappahannock, to land of their own. There had also been a chapel about a bow-shot from the colonel's house, at the end of an avenue of cherry trees, but some pious people had lately burnt it down, with intent to get another built nearer to their own homes.

"Here I arrived about three o'clock, and found only Mrs. Spotswood at home, who received her old acquaintance with many a gracious smile. I was carried into a room elegantly set off with pier glasses, the largest of which came soon after to an odd misfortune. Amongst other favorite animals that cheered this lady's solitude, a brace of tame deer ran familiarly about the house, and one of them came to stare at me as a stranger. But unluckily spying his own figure in the glass, he made a spring over the tea table that stood under it, and shattered the glass to pieces, and falling back upon the tea table, made a terrible fracas among the china.

"This exploit was so sudden, and accompanied with such a noise, that it surprised me, and perfectly frightened Mrs. Spotswood. But it was worth all the damage, to show the moderation and good humor with which she bore the disaster. In the evening the noble Colonel came home from his mines, who saluted me very civilly, and Mrs. Spotswood's sister, Miss Theky, who had been to meet him *en cavalier,* was so kind too as to bid me welcome. We talked over a legend of old stories, supped about nine, and then prattled with the ladies, till it was time for a traveller to retire."

By the middle of the eighteenth century "serving tables" were much in use, some of them having two leaves—one at either end, so that when necessary, its capacity could be increased. These tables were long and narrow, had four legs, and were often ornate and beautiful objects, with a carved gilt frieze rail, and a carved gilt rosette at the top of each leg. The wood was mahogany, which was fast coming into vogue, and muchly desired in fine furniture of this period.

There is an interesting legend concerning mahogany and its introduction into England. Queen Elizabeth had an eye for beautiful woods it seems, and she is credited with having owned the first piece of mahogany furniture known to have been in use in England. This was a gift of the gallant Sir Walter Raleigh, and was made from the wood of some West Indies mahogany he had procured for ship repairs—a strange new wood which the Queen much admired.

By 1750 England was leading the world in the

beauty and worth of her furniture, whereas in the previous century France had produced furniture of such beauty and elegance that it was freely copied everywhere. At last there arose a great artist, Thomas Chippendale, and after "feeling his way through copied work" as one writer describes it, originated a style of his own that has endured to this day.

It was Chippendale who realized the beautiful effects to be gained from the close-grained wood of mahogany, and who first used it extensively in his creations. Rivals arose in the field: the Adam brothers, Hepplewhite, and Sheraton, the most notable of them all being Thomas Sheraton. Original pieces, as well as beautifully executed copies of these great cabinet-makers early adorned the homes of the wealthier Virginians.

In 1774, at the sale of furniture at "Belvoir," the Virginia seat of the Fairfax family, George Washington bought many fine and costly pieces, among them a mahogany Hepplewhite sideboard and a mahogany Pembroke table, named for the lady who first desired one made for her. Both pieces have been returned to "Mount Vernon" and are placed just as they were during General Washington's occupancy.

Tables, tables, tables! There is no end to them. Practically all of the tables in that delightful group we term today, "occasional tables," were first introduced during the middle of the eighteenth and the beginning of the nineteenth century. One of the loveliest of these—the Tier table, was originally called a "Dumb Waiter," and dates from 1760-65.

"Pie-crust" tables—the old ones—clearly show the marks of the carving tool along the edges of the crust, while modern ones are sand-papered down so as to be perfectly smooth. Tilt-top tables were sometimes handpainted in the center, or had a border of inlay, usually mother-of-pearl.

Night or bed-tables are likewise copied from the mid-eighteenth century "occasional group." One of the quaintest of these which is rarely seen today is the "bird cage stand," also known as a "wig stand," but as a rule dedicated to the support of a Colonial candlestick with its dipped candle. These odd little tables derive their name from their resemblance to a barred bird cage. The small circular "dish" top rests on four delicately rounded pillars or legs, which are so placed that they form a square about the size of a bird cage. This is supported by a short, round base, from which extend three slender curving legs.

"Gallery" tables probably originated with Chippendale. Some of the loveliest and oldest of these are definitely attributed to him. These small, square, graceful tables with their delicately wrought railing, served as tea tables originally, and are similar in size and appearance to the popular "Coffee" tables of today.

Hepplewhite designed exquisite fitted dressing tables, with under-slide and covered compartment, and both he and Sheraton were noted for their lovely card tables. While more graceful and delicate in design, these card tables were inspired by earlier "Gaming" tables, all of which had cabriole legs, usually terminating in pad or claw-and-ball feet. These fascinating tables had a back drop-leaf which could be extended during the time of play; there was a single front drawer, and in each of the four corners were smooth carved hollows, presumably to hold dice, chips, or coins.

Washington is known to have been a card enthusiast, and was an expert both at whist and that intriguing game called "Loo." One of the most interesting pieces in the sitting room at "Mount Vernon" is the "Loo table" at which the General was accustomed to play the card game of which he was so fond, while another card table at "Mount Vernon" is one at which he and LaFayette are said to have whiled away many an idle moment at whist.

Loo reached the peak of its popularity in Virginia just before the outbreak of the Revolution. In a half-century old issue of *Harper's New Monthly Magazine* in an article captioned "Some Richmond Portraits" the following amusing account of the game is given:

"The favorite amusement of the most stylish Richmond ladies at that time was a game of cards called loo. The ladies met at each other's houses, and after discussing a dish of tea and another of gossip, the card-table was brought out. Gentlemen were admitted to this entertaining circle, and he who played the most careless and dashing game was the most welcome, provided he was not too successful in his winnings. The stakes were small, but by forfeits, etc., the money in the pool would sometimes accumulate until it amounted to fifty, seventy-five, and a hundred dollars. Then the game became intensely interesting. . ."

Thomas Jefferson was a lover of beautiful tables, and numerous kinds graced the stately rooms at "Monticello," several of which may still be seen occupying their accustomed places in this stately house. It would indeed be interesting to know what type of table Washington was recalling in fond memory, when he wrote to William Fitzhugh, that celebrated host of "Chatham": "I have put my legs oftener under your mahogany at 'Chatham' than anywhere else in the world, and have enjoyed your good dinners, your good wines, and your good company more than any other."

By 1800 the list of "occasional" tables for practical as well as decorative purposes was steadily growing. To the already long list of those in use were added Sheraton "Sofa" tables, Marlborough tables which were placed beneath Chippendale mirrors, elaborate "Pier" tables which were intended to occupy the space between two wall openings, and the several interesting types made by Duncan Phyfe.

Duncan Phyfe was born in Scotland in 1768, and came to America in 1783. He was apprenticed to a cabinet maker in Albany, but ten years later opened a shop of his own in New York for the making of furniture. He made chairs, settees, tables, and sideboards, using mostly solid mahogany, some mahogany veneer, satin-wood and maple, and later rosewood. Phyfe's standard of workmanship was high, his woods were selected with care, and his best pieces made prior to 1820, when his work lost much of its original charm and began to show the influence of Adam and Sheraton.

A handsome pedestal table, attributed to Duncan Phyfe (and the only one of its kind I have seen in Virginia) is owned by Mrs. Bernard H. Baylor of Richmond, the former Anne Robertson Barksdale. How this beautiful piece of furniture (perhaps I should say pieces, for there are really two tables, with deep drop sides, which when joined make one great table almost three yards in length) came into Mrs. Baylor's possession is a singular and interesting story.

Three years ago, on the death of Miss Mattie Bolling, one of Richmond's oldest and most beloved residents, the table passed to Mrs. Baylor, whose father, Mr. Robert J. Barksdale of Richmond, was a cousin of Miss Bolling's, and through his maternal great-grandparents—William Robertson and Elizabeth Bolling, a descendant of Pocahontas.

Miss Bolling was past eighty when she died in 1936, and but a few months before her death had told a relative living with her that she wished the table "to go to the Barksdale who married a Baylor." For strangely enough, the table (or tables) had originally come from one of the Baylor estates in Caroline, probably "New Market" near Bowling Green, the home of Colonel John Baylor, and had been bought by Miss Bolling fifty years before, in Fredericksburg. Thus, by a singular coincidence, there adorns the present home of Major Bernard H. Baylor, a beautiful piece of old mahogany that originally belonged to one of his forbears, but as has happened many times in Virginia, passed out of the family long ago.

The table is of a deep red mahogany, each of the two sections (which may be used separately, as a drop-leaf table) having four reeded urn-shaped legs. These support the top, and rest on a base. From this base four tapering reeded legs, two at either end, spread gracefully in the traditional Duncan Phyfe manner, and have brass claw tips. Each table is fifty-three and seven-eighths inches wide, twenty-eight and three-fourths inches high, and forty-seven and three-fourths inches long with the leaf outspread. Placed together, as intended, the pair form a table of majestic lines, with a total length of ninety four and one half inches. At "Arlington," the beautiful home of the Lee family, there is a handsome pedestal table said to have originally belonged to John Randolph of "Roanoke," which, from many angles, is similar to the Baylor table.

Two of the most historic tables in the country are in

Virginia today: the beautiful Queen Anne drop-leaf table on which the terms of the surrender at Yorktown are said to have been drawn up, and the small, graceful, one-drawer table on which George Mason of "Gunston Hall" wrote the Virginia Bill of Rights. The Queen Anne table is privately owned and graces one of the beautiful lower rooms of "Pratt's Castle" in Richmond; George Mason's table was presented to the Virginia Historical Society by his great-grandson, and is displayed in the large fire-proof gallery of the Society's headquarters.

Many years ago, the "Surrender" table was purchased by the late J. F. Biggs of Richmond, from the owners of the Moore House in Yorktown, where the terms of the surrender were drawn up October 18, 1781. In a charmingly written and illustrated booklet entitled *Historic Shrines of Virginia,* by William E. Carson, one finds a vivid description of this historic scene:

"On October eighteenth, the commissioners met to settle the terms. They met in the Moore House as being convenient to both lines. The British Army was represented by Lieutenant-Colonel Dundas and Major Ross, and the French by Viscount de Noailles, and the Americans by Lieutenant-Colonel Laurens. The commissioners drew up fourteen articles governing the surrender of the British army. On the morning of October nineteenth, these articles were submitted to Cornwallis, with the demand that they be signed by eleven o'clock. Cornwallis submitted, and at noon allied troops marched into Yorktown to take possession.

"Then came the drama of the surrender. The British column moved out of Yorktown along the Hampton road, which was lined on one side by Americans, on the other by the French. The Americans, in their ragged garb, made a poor showing except that they looked like the veteran soldiers they were. The French, in their fine white uniforms and plumed hats, were the most imposing troops in the world.

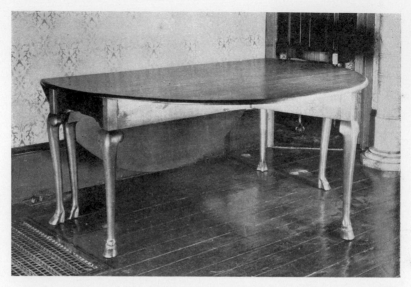

Queen Anne drop-leaf table with unusual colt's feet. The terms of the surrender of Yorktown are said to have been drawn up on this table October 18, 1781. Purchased years ago by the late J. F. Biggs of Richmond, from the owners of the Moore House at Yorktown. Courtesy of Mrs. J. F. Biggs.

On this simple table George Mason of "Gunston Hall" is said to have written the Virginia Bill of Rights. A silver plaque is on the top, bearing the Mason crest and inscription. Courtesy of the Virginia Historical Society.

A "Great Bedde" with Sheraton reeded posts, which adorns one of the famous bedrooms of the Richard Bland Tavern in Williamsburg.

"The British fifers, with a touch of satire, played an old tune, 'The World Turned Upside Down,' as the redcoats moved along the road to the field where they laid down their arms. A new age had, indeed, dawned on the world."

Yes, and perhaps a new age of Anglo-American friendship, when in October, 1931, a descendant of Lord Cornwallis was among the distinguished guests present at the celebration of the Yorktown Sesqui-Centennial.

When Mr. Biggs purchased the prized table, papers relating to its history and ownership went with it, but, according to Mrs. Biggs who now owns it, these and other important documents were stolen from her husband's office-safe years ago. Thus much information that today would be of interest and value to the historian as well as the antiquarian, was destroyed or lost.

This beautiful table fairly beggars description. It is unusually large for an oval drop-leaf table, and yet of such delicate and graceful proportions one can visualize it, resplendent in candle light and rare old lace, fine china and glistening silver, far better than as a barren board upon which one of the greatest documents in history was written.

The wood is of rich dark brown walnut, with a surprising satin-smoothness for a piece of its age. There are six graceful cabriole legs that terminate in a delicate colt's foot; legs that can be moved at will, in much the same manner as a gate-legged table. The oval drop-sides when extended give the table a length of seventy inches, but one inch more than the width, which measures sixty-nine inches. The "colt's" feet indicate an earlier date than either the "web" or "pad"

feet, which were common on Early American Queen
Anne tables around 1750.

The writing-table upon which that sterling figure
in Colonial Virginia—George Mason of "Gunston
Hall" wrote the Virginia Bill of Rights, might, on
first glance, be mistaken for a bedside table, so severely
plain and seemingly small is this historic piece. Perhaps it did stand beside George Mason's bed, or in a
quiet, inconspicuous corner of his library, always
"handy" when this quiet country gentleman of old Virginia wished to pen some brilliant thought which
flashed across his mind.

George Mason's great intellect found its fullest expression in his peerless Virginia Bill of Rights and
the First Constitution of Virginia, two incomparable
documents whose words and wisdom served to guide
Thomas Jefferson in his final draft of the Declaration
of Independence. Today, there hangs framed over the
mantle in the library at "Gunston Hall," between
George Mason's own blue ginger jars (did he, too, love
the old and the quaint?) a photostatic copy of his immortal Bill of Rights.

The chaste little mahogany table, with its one small
drawer and slender curving legs seems characteristic
of its great owner—a piece of simple dignity, made to
endure. In the center of the table there is a handsome
silver plaque, at the top of which is an engraved crest
and beneath it, *Pro Patria Semper*. The remainder of
the inscription reads:

"The Writing Table of George Mason of 'Gunston Hall,'
Fairfax County, Virginia, upon which he wrote the
Virginia Bill of Rights adopted in Convention June 12, 1776.
Presented to the Virginia Historical Society by his
great-grandson, George Mason, of Alexandria, Virginia."

Spinets and Harpsichords

It was the gay and music-loving little town of Williamsburg that set the precedent for musicales in Virginia, as well as being more or less responsible for the Virginia gentry becoming "music-minded." President John Blair's quaint diary (1751) makes frequent mention of the musical entertainments given at the College, as well as in private homes, and himself owned a spinet on which the ladies of his family played with great dexterity. What was true of Mrs. Blair and her daughters was also true of many other charming and talented ladies in the Colony.

A surprising number of orders were sent to London for fine spinets and harpsichords. Many of these quaint old instruments, in mellowed rosewood and mahogany cases, grace Virginia homes today, their ivory keyboards yellowed with age; their strings once sweetly tuned, now rattly and discordant from a century of disuse.

The spinet resembled the harpsichord, and like that instrument, was superseded by the pianoforte. Each note had but one string, which was struck by a quilled jack acted on by one of the finger keys. The strings were placed horizontally, and nearly at right angles to the keys; the general outline of the instrument resembled that of a harp laid in a horizontal position; for this reason the spinet, when first introduced, was called a "couched harp."

The harpsichord was also a stringed instrument with a keyboard, similar in form to a modern grand pianoforte. As the pressure of the fingers upon the keys, when heavy or light, made no difference in the quality of tone produced, the harpsichord sometimes had two

keyboards—one for the loud, the other for the soft
tones. The keys were attached to levers, which at their
ends had slips of wood called jacks, furnished with
plectra of crow-quill or hard leather; these struck or
twanged the strings, and produced the tone which has
been likened to "a scratch with a sound at the end of it."

In spite of this unappealing and odd-sounding definition which encyclopedias give to these quaint instruments, spinets and harpsichords were considered ac-
quisitions to the most splendidly furnished and equipped Virginia homes of almost two centuries ago, and
afforded many hours of pleasure and entertainment to
those able to enjoy them.

The inventory of Cuthbert Ogle, of Williamsburg,
lists in 1755, "a fiddle and case, a harpsichord and large
collection of music," which included the works of
Händel and other famous composers.

The *Virginia Gazette* carried frequent advertisements of musical instruments for sale, and in 1767, the
following was given prominent space:

"To be sold for prime cost, a complete Harpsichord with three
stops, just imported from London, made by Kirpman, the Queen's
instrument maker, and supposed by good judges to be the best in the
Colony. Inquire of the printer."

One may venture to predict that "the printer" received many inquiries, and that the harpsichord soon
adorned one of the more fortunate houses in Virginia.

Many of the most prominent men in the colony
preferred to order direct from London, intrusting the
selection of their musical instruments to their agents,
who, as a rule, could be relied upon to send them only
the "latest mode."

In 1760, Colonel John Baylor of "New Market" in
Caroline, ordered from his London agents, Messrs.

Cary and Company, "a spinnett and close stool," also an accordian for "A. Hoomes." In a letter to another agent, Mr. Samuel Athawes of London, dated September 30, 1762, Colonel Baylor writes:

"Lucy likewise desires you will be kind enough to choose her a dozen new songs and with the notes for the Spinnett. The agreeable manner in which we spent one evening makes me very heartily wish there was a possibility of a repetition, but that is not to be expected at our distance. . ." (From the Baylor Family Papers, in the possession of Major Bernard H. Baylor, of Richmond.)

Philip Vickers Fithian—to give him the dignity of his full name, was the young Princetonian tutor at "Nomini Hall" in Westmoreland County, the great estate of "Councillor" Robert Carter. It was here, and in the neighboring homes, that Fithian found so much of import and interest to record in his sprightly diary— a quaint record of Colonial life in Virginia that is a never-ending delight to the reader.

Fithian frequently alludes to the many harpsichords and spinets in the neighborhood of "Nomini Hall," adding that most of the girls of the Carter's circle played on them. All of the young ladies at "Mount Airey," the beautiful estate of the Tayloes in Richmond County, "played well" according to Fithian, and of the muchly admired young Jenny Washington he records:

"She plays well on the harpsichord and spinet, understands the principles of music and therefore performs her tunes in perfect time. . . She sings likewise to her instrument."

Acrostics and poetical effusions frequently appeared in the *Gazette,* most of them composed by ardent swains who preferred to remain anonymous. One such romantic bit of verse, which had as its *raison d'être* Miss Anne Geddy and her spinet, and which appeared in the

year 1768 was captioned, "On Miss Anne Geddy sing-
ing and playing on the Spinet." The first stanza ran
thus:

> "When Nancy on the spinnet plays
> I fondly on the virgin gaze
> And wish that she was mine;
> Her air, her voice, her lovely face
> Unite with such excessive grace,
> The Nymph appears divine."

The following year—1769—there appeared in the
Virginia Gazette a similar romantic rhyme entitled,
"Lines on Hearing a Young Lady Play on the Harpsi-
chord," one of the stanzas reading:

> "When Sukey to her harpsichord repairs
> And, smiling bids me give attentive ears,
> With bliss supreme the lovely maid I view.
> But with reluctance forced to bid adieu,
> Her charms, I find, are on my heart impress'd,
> Nor time nor absence can regain the rest."

In 1771, Thomas Jefferson, long recognized as a
music enthusiast, ordered from his London merchant a
clavichord. This order, however, was quickly rescind-
ed, and the following explanatory letter sent to his
agent:

> "I have since seen a Forte piano and am charmed with it. Send me
> this instrument then, instead of the clavichord; let the case be fine
> mahogany, solid, not veneered. The compass from Double G to F
> in alt. A plenty of spare strings and the workmanship on the whole
> very handsome and worthy the acceptance of a lady for whom I
> intend it."

Here we have Jefferson the *connoisseur,* as well as
Jefferson the wooer.

In the East Parlor, as the Music Room at "Mount
Vernon" is called, one may see the original harpsichord

which was imported from London in 1793, and given by General Washington to his young stepdaughter, Nellie Custis. In the Mary Washington Cottage at Fredericksburg there is a beautiful old pianoforte of Viennese make, which belonged to one of the members of the Washington family, and in the Valentine Museum in Richmond, there is a handsome and unusually ornate rosewood spinet which came from "Prestwould" and is believed to have belonged to the wife of Sir Peyton Skipwith.

One of the earliest pianos in Virginia to be imported direct from Germany, is the beautiful small rosewood upright, which today graces the drawing room of the spacious Fredericksburg home of Mrs. J. Minor Holloway, the former Fannie Corbin Gordon, of "Santee" in Caroline County.

This quaint little instrument was ordered direct from Dresden early in the nineteenth century, by James Parke Corbin of "Moss Neck" in Caroline, for his wife who was Jane Catherine Wellford. James Parke Corbin was one of the wealthiest young landowners in *ante-bellum* Virginia, and was a grandson of Richard Corbin of "Laneville" in King and Queen, Receiver-General in the Colony of Virginia for His Majesty George III, at the time of the outbreak of the Revolution.

On the death of Jane Wellford Corbin, the piano passed to her daughter Fannie Nelson Corbin, who, in 1857 was married to William Henry Dickinson amid the last scene of splendor old "Moss Neck" was to witness before the outbreak of the War Between the States. Of the many children born to this union, a daughter, Evelyn May Dickinson, inherited the treasured small piano, and on her marriage to Robert Voss

Gordon, carried it with her to "Santee" the beautiful old Gordon estate in Caroline to which she went as a bride.

Mrs. Gordon gave the piano to her daughter many years ago, and today it occupies an honored place in her lovely home, while nearby hangs a portrait in oils of its first owner. The beautifully grained casing is of rosewood; on each side of the piano, midway, there is a quaint handle, while in the center of the front, near the top, is a keyhole where presumably the long lost key was inserted to unlock the case when necessary. The most notable feature of this lovely old piece is the leg treatment, for at each end there is a delicate rope-leg, hand carved. The piano measures forty-six inches in height, forty-nine inches in width, and in the accustomed place carries in gilt letters the name of

E. Rosenkrantz

Goldene   Medaille

Dresden.

Like the great houses which sheltered them, these old pieces of "fine furniture" were truly

> "Built in the old Colonial day,
> When men lived in a grander way
> With ampler hospitality."

The Contents of an Old Chest

"In ivory coffers have I stuff'd my crowns;
In cypress chests my arras counterpoints,
Costly apparel, tents and canopies,
Fine linen, Turkey cushions boss'd with pearl,
Valance of Venice gold in needlework—"

—SHAKESPEARE.

CHAPTER VIII
THE CONTENTS OF AN OLD CHEST

OLD chests invariably conjure up visions of buccaneers and buried treasure, secret charts and desert isles, and ships that once roamed the seven seas. Yet long before the day when pirates infested the Spanish Main and made of it a terrain of terror, and the names of "Captain Kidd" and the notorious "Blackbeard" brought fear to many a stout-hearted seaman, chests occupied an honored and important place in every household—from feudal castle to the humblest cottage.

During the Middle Ages, and for centuries thereafter, the chest ranked next to the bed as the most important article of household furniture. In Italy especially, where wealth was general and beauty and elegance flourished for so long a time, chests were considered a virtual necessity in every home. Particularly was this true of the "stout one of iron" which held the family treasure.

Since there were no banks, the wealthy merchant was forced to turn to his great chest with its ponderous lock and strong handles, as the safest means he knew of storing his ducats, and thus we find that the iron chest was the *first* safety deposit box. Not until 1401, at Barcelona, was a bank of deposit instituted for the accommodation of private merchants, so it is readily seen what an important article the chest was.

Among the Venetian and Florentine nobility, very
ornate chests were an essential part of every bride's
dowry. These magnificent receptacles were often
massive, and whether of the Gothic period or of the
Renaissance, were beautifully carved or inlaid. Old
pictures show some of these chests to be of oak,
elaborately carved and supported by four claw feet.
Others were made of cedar and cypress, occasionally
of olive and rich satin-wood, and were painted and
gilded, or inlaid with ivory, ebony, tortoise-shell, lapis-
lazuli, or any other exquisite material the mind of the
cabinet maker conceived to add to its beauty.

Famous artists were sometimes employed to add
their magic touch to these old *cassoni,* and frequently
painted scenes and figures portraying events in the life
of the owner appeared on the most costly and magnificent of these Italian Brides' Chests, though more often
the design was of flowers and cupidons.

Visualize, if you can, the dazzling array of bridal
finery these gorgeous old chests contained: fine linens,
rare point laces, pieces of rich damask and silk brocade, cloth-of-gold, and great lengths of regal velvet
in ruby red, amethyst, and emerald green. Such rich
stuffs were calculated by the pound weight, and the
"great pearls" by the gross. Even jewelled accessories
included in the bride's trousseau, such as girdles of
silver and gold, enamelled and jewelled buttons,
buckles, and garlands, were kept in especially designed
small chests or coffers.

In the early churches coffers were much in use, the
few which are still in existence being housed in
Museums. In Kennett's *Parochial Antiquities* he
gives the following interesting account of the famous
old Warwick Chest:

"Ela, Countess of Warwick, who died very aged, in the year 1300, was so great a friend of Oxford University, that she caused a common chest to be made, and did put into it two hundred and twenty marks; out of which such as were poor scholars might upon security at any time borrow something gratis for their wants; in consideration thereof, the University were obliged to celebrate certain masses every year in Saint Mary's Church. Which chest was in being in Edward IVth's time, and called by the name of Warwick Chest."

The English-made chest was generally of oak throughout. At the Virginia Museum of Fine Arts in Richmond there is an interesting example of a middle-seventeenth century English chest. Made entirely of old English oak, the two front panels are enriched by a design known as the *guilloche,* which is a pattern formed by a continuous line of circles, each enclosing a carved rosette. The top rail is also decorated with carving; the rails and stiles are "mortise-and-tenon" joined, and the lock-plate is believed to be the original. This old chest is from the Strause collection.

When those three storm-tossed little vessels—the *Godspeed,* the *Discovery,* and the *Sarah Constant*—arrived at Jamestown in the spring of 1607 with their small band of weary settlers, there must have been many "standards" and ship chests aboard. Standards were crude, box-like affairs, with locks and no legs, but occasionally handles, while ship chests were especially designed for travelling and took the place of trunks. It is interesting to ponder their contents.

When the Pilgrim Fathers and Mothers sailed on the *Mayflower* for their new home across the sea—the bleak and rock-ribbed coast of Massachusetts—they, too, packed their scant belongings in chests; stout boxes no doubt, and, we may safely assume, void of any ornamentation.

In *Colonial Families of the United States of America,* (Volume I) by Mackenzie, there is an interesting genealogy of the Forrest family, whose members have won such distinction in the annals of American history. Thomas Forrest and his wife "Mistress Forrest," with their only child Peter, aged seven, left England with Captain Christopher Newport on his second voyage to Virginia, arriving at Jamestown in the year 1608.

According to author Mackenzie, "Mistress Forrest" was the *first gentlewoman* to arrive in the Colony. (The italics are his.) The marriage of her maid Ann Burrass, to John Laydon, is said to have been the first marriage to take place in Virginia. The ceremony was performed by the Reverend Robert Hunt who had administered the first communion celebrated at Jamestown, and, writes Mary Newton Stanard, "when the good Master Hunt spoke the solemn words that meant the founding of the first English family in the first English colony in America, they fell on the ears of his hearers with due significance."

On her arrival in the primeval forest that was Virginia, "Mistress Forrest" no doubt was accoutred as befitted a lady of her station, and we may be sure her wardrobe and other possessions were carefully packed in numerous old chests. I confess to an insatiable curiosity as to what impedimenta and articles of clothing a lady of gentility would bring with her on arriving in an Indian-infested wilderness that was to be her future home. Perhaps my inquisitiveness is attributable to a matter of kinship, for in Virginia today I have numerous cousins who are direct descendants of this "genteel lady" and her good husband.

The Forrests, with other Virginia families, removed

to St. Mary's County, Maryland, in 1635. Among their distinguished descendants was Colonel Uriah Forrest of the Continental Army, who served as aide to General Washington at the Battle of Germantown, where he lost a leg. He married Rebecca Plater, daughter of Governor George Plater, third Governor of Maryland.

Mary Newton Stanard, writing in *Colonial Virginia, Its People and Customs,* makes the following interesting statement regarding old chests: "Next in importance to the bed was the chest in all its forms, from the plain or carved wooden box which served the double purpose of seat and receptacle for clothing, to the chest of drawers."

In the inventory of Ambrose Fielding of "Wickocomoco Hall," made in 1674, the "greate room" (which presumably was the hall) was furnished with a "long dining table," serving table, small table, a cupboard, *two chests,* and numerous other articles one might expect to find in a well furnished late seventeenth century home in Virginia. "Ye parlor chamber" contained a "great bedd" with curtains and valance lined with silk, damask tester, silk counterpane, linen sheets, a feather-bed and blankets, a leather chair, a silk chair, a "carved chest with locks and keys," a looking glass, pewter basin, brass candlestick, a warming pad, and other articles of comfort and luxury.

The inventory of Colonel Francis Eppes, of Henrico County, Virginia, dated October 1, 1678, contains numerous items which show him to have been a man of wealth and importance. Among them are listed the following chests: "One old middle-sized chest, with lock and key; one small old chest, with lock and key; two other old chests without keys, and one without hinges."

Mrs. Elizabeth Digges of York County, widow of
Edward Digges, Governor of Virginia, furnished her
home with costly linens, draperies, rugs, and all manner
of fine furniture. The rooms in her house were designated as the "yellow room," the "red room," the "large
room," the "front room," the "back room," the "hall
parlor," and in addition to these there were rooms in
the garret, also a passageway, the kitchen and the
cellar. In the passage between the hall parlor and the
"yellow room" was placed a chest containing "thirty
damask, thirty-six diaper, and sixty flaxen napkins;
three diaper, nine damask, and forty-eight flaxen table-
cloths; eight diaper towels, three pairs of holland sheets
and pillow-biers, eight ells of holland, eight yards of
calico, five ells of linen, and four yards of bunting."
(Records of York County, 1690-1694.)

Governor Alexander Spotswood, who is best remembered as Virginia's greatest Cavalier, and the original
Knight of the Golden Horseshoe, was a *connoisseur* as
well. His home at Germanna, with its terraced gardens
and velvet lawn where gorgeous peacocks paraded in
all their glory, was filled with handsome furnishings,
pier glasses, and silver-plate. In one of his inventories,
made in Orange in 1740, there are listed numerous
handsome novelties that graced the eighteenth century
parlors of the wealthy Virginian of that day, among
them, "two japanned chests on castors."

In the Valley of Virginia there are numerous lovely
old painted *Amana* chests, brought by the early German
settlers. While the men concerned themselves chiefly
with cultivating their land, the women devoted most of
their time to household duties and homespun handicrafts, and many a thrifty housewife filled her chest

with hand-woven coverlets and patchwork quilts, whose bright colors ran the gamut of the rainbow.

These colorful *kists,* as they were called by their immigrant owners, are a universal possession of German, Swiss, and Scandinavian immigrants, and in the village of Amana, Iowa, may be found in great numbers and varieties.

Writing of Amana Chests in a recent issue of the magazine *Antiques,* Grace E. Chaffee says:

"In these surviving chests one catches the vase motive found in Alsatian decoration, as well as the panel division of ornament and sometimes of construction; the rose, common to both Scandinavian and German design; the fruit, favored for boxes and chests in eastern Switzerland; the double rose, frequent on Bavarian chests, and the familiar tulip. In the Amana attics there are, as well, innumerable plain or very simply decorated chests in which the women still keep their store of blankets, carpet rags, and even dried fruits and vegetables."

In Flanders, during the fifteenth and sixteenth century, the fronts of chests were beautifully and elaborately carved, then sent to England to be fitted with other parts. Many of these finished chests crossed the Atlantic in low-lying broad-hulked vessels, destined for the port of New Amsterdam and the comfortable homes of the Dutch burghers, grown suddenly rich from their trading in furs.

The proud old patroons—lords of great manorhouses along the Hudson, brought with them on their arrival in this country, many a handsome old *Kas.* These massive Dutch chests were elaborately carved, and corresponded to handsome European cupboards. Usually there was a long drawer at the bottom; both sets of cupboard doors opened, revealing deep shelves within.

Many a moon must have waxed and waned before these old Dutch *Kas* were filled with the vast quantity of "Hollands" every well-to-do Dutch housewife deemed necessary for her married daughter's household, as well as her own. It required years to grow the flax; comb, bleach, and spin the thread; then weave into linen cloth that was bleached many times before it became the white of perfection which characterized all original "Hollands."

No doubt the good *vrouw's* sturdy and spacious *Kas* was the ancestor of our own grandmother's linen press or cupboard. The original chest of drawers was not at all the piece of furniture which goes by that name today, but was simply a chest *with* drawers. "Trussing Coffers" were clothes-chests which took the place of trunks, and a "hutch" was a chest which stood upon legs. By 1724 numerous other woods were used to make chests, including walnut, cherry, maple, hickory, poplar, pine, ash, and still later, cedar. Is there not something thrilling about a hunt chest, resplendant in ash or oak? And quaint and appealing about an old blanket chest, made of pine?

The oldest, and undoubtedly the most interesting chest in Virginia, is the one which belonged to that picturesque figure of Colonial days—the fabulous Lord Fairfax, Proprietor of the Northern Neck of Virginia. This massive chest, made entirely of iron and weighing several hundred pounds, is on exhibit in the lobby of the Shenandoah National Bank in Winchester. The chest is unusually ornate for one of solid iron, and is enriched by the use of crossed flat bars which form a pattern of geometrical squares. The top of the chest, or lid, extends several inches beyond the front and sides; there is a ponderous lock of a beautiful scroll-

Lord Fairfax Chest.

work design, and the side handles are large and heavy.

The Fairfax chest measures thirty and three-fourths inches in length, is eighteen inches deep, while the top, which is supported by hinges, measures thirty-two and three-fourths inches in length, and nineteen and one-half inches in width. George Washington's old iron chest which is in the National Museum in Washington, is similar to Lord Fairfax's, though not so ornate. Both chests undoubtedly were brought or ordered from England, and were intended for monies and similar valuables.

There is filed in the Circuit Court of Frederick County, Virginia, the estate account of Colonel Thomas Bryan Martin, one of the executors of Lord Fairfax, which itemizes the contents found in this old chest. I am greatly indebted to Mr. Harold G. Brown, Executive Vice-President of the Shenandoah National Bank of Winchester, for the following interesting and highly illuminating account, copied from an old paper which is framed and on display in his bank.

"TREASURE CHEST OF LORD FAIRFAX

"Excerpt from estate account of Colonel Thomas Bryan Martin, one of the executors of Thomas Lord Fairfax, Baron Cameron in that part of Great Britain called Scotland, and Lord Proprietor of the Northern Neck of Virginia, by Doctor Robert Dunbar, Executor of Colonel John S. Woodcock, Executor of Colonel Martin.

"1798

"September 25th. By cash contained in an *Iron Chest* found in the house of Thomas B. Martin, deceased, and which has been delivered by Robert Dunbar to Robert Macky, and was found to contain Seven Hundred and Thirty Crowns; Eighteen Thousand Eight Hundred and Seventy Three Dollars and Eighty Cents; Cut Silver Three Hundred and Seventy and an Half Ounces; English and Portuguese Gold Two Hundred and Fifty Six Ounces Eighteen and an Half Penny-weight; Spanish Cob Gold Sixty Three Ounces and

Two Penny-weight; French and Spanish Gold One Hundred and Thirty Seven Ounces and Eleven and an Half Penny-weight; German Gold Fifty Ounces and Twelve Penny-weight, Amounting to, as Credited by Robert Macky, Eight Thousand Six Hundred and Eighty Two Pounds, Three Shillings, Seven and an Half Pence."

The certified statement of the Deputy Clerk of the Circuit Court of Frederick County, Virginia, follows:

"State of Virginia

"County of Frederick, To-Wit:

"I, J. W. Baker, Deputy Clerk, Circuit Court of Frederick County Virginia, do hereby certify that the foregoing and annexed is a true and correct copy of that part of the settlement of the estate of Thomas Bryan Martin, who was executor of Thomas Lord Fairfax, in account with the estate of John S. Woodcock, who was executor of Thomas Bryan Martin, that itemizes *the contents of the Iron Chest in which Lord Fairfax kept his monies.* Said settlement is of record in Will Book Number Two, pages 305-337 of the Superior Court Records of the County of Frederick.

"Given under my hand and the Seal of my said Court this sixth day of May, one thousand nine hundred and thirty three, and in the one hundred and fifty seventh year of the Commonwealth. Signed

"J. W. Baker

"Deputy Clerk Circuit Court of

"Frederick County Virginia."

What of this fabulous figure—Thomas Lord Fairfax, "Baron Cameron in that part of Great Britain called Scotland, and Lord Proprietor of the Northern Neck of Virginia"? Here indeed, was a monarch of all he surveyed—the master of countless acres of primitive land that stretched from the Potomac to the Rappahannock—an area so vast that today it passes the limits of belief.

In the year 1664, Charles II of England granted to Alexander Lord Culpeper a large territory in Virginia, soon thereafter designated as the Northern Neck, which was defined as "lying between the Potomac and the Rappahannock rivers." Lord Culpeper "acquired by purchase the sole ownership of the territory, which as then understood, comprised fourteen of the present counties of Virginia." Through the marriage of his daughter Catherine, an only heir, to the fifth Lord Fairfax, a descendant of the Commander-in-Chief of the Cromwellian forces in the Civil War in England, this lordly domain passed into the possession of the Fairfax family.

In 1692, there was born to Lady Catherine and the Fifth Lord Fairfax a son who was to fall heir not only to an illustrious title, but to his mother's vast Virginia inheritance, which passed to him by entail when he reached the age of eighteen. The son was Thomas Lord Fairfax, who in time became one of the most colorful characters in Colonial Virginia, and a friend of George Washington's.

Lord Fairfax first visited Virginia in 1736, in order to determine the actual limits of that part of his lands west of the Blue Ridge. Returning to England the following year, he began at once to dispose of his English and Scottish holdings, and in 1742 returned to Virginia where he spent the remainder of his life.

For a time he resided at "Belvoir" with his cousin William Fairfax, whom he had induced to become manager of the Northern Neck. "Belvoir" overlooked the broad blue waters of the Potomac, and was only twelve miles below "Mount Vernon." Here it was that Lord Fairfax first made the acquaintance of George Washington, then a lad of sixteen. The acquaintance ripened into a long and enduring friendship between the two; a friendship that was to survive all differences of political opinion and allegiance, when the storm clouds of the American Revolution broke over Virginia.

The loveliness of the Shenandoah Valley had long appealed to His Lordship, and in 1748 he moved to Frederick County, and on a sloping stretch of land eleven miles southeast of Winchester, had laid off for himself an estate that he chose to call—after the English custom—a "Manor."

It is said that Lord Fairfax's original plan was to erect a castle on his manor, but for some unknown reason, abandoned the idea and built instead a one-story house, with dormer windows, which he named "Greenway Court" after a seat of the Culpepers in Kent County, England. The crowning feature of "Greenway Court" was the wide front veranda, which extended the entire length of the house, commanding a sweeping view of the beautiful Blue Ridge Mountains.

White Post, in Clarke County, came by its name from the original white post erected here by Lord Fairfax, as a guide-post to "Greenway Court." Today, standing in the center of intersecting highways, there is a duplicate of the original white post, which, with its sign-board, pointed the way to the Fairfax estate. Originally in Frederick County, Clarke was made a separate county a century ago.

It was by this route that His Lordship travelled between 1749-1769, when he went to preside over the sessions of the Justices Court which were held in Winchester. An amusing story is told concerning the peppery old Englishman and Colonel James Wood, founder of Winchester and the first clerk of Frederick County Court. It seems that Lord Fairfax much preferred the town of Stephensburg to that of Winchester, and when the seat of justice was about to be decided upon and both places were under consideration, he exerted all of his influence in behalf of Stephensburg.

The result was a bitter disappointment to His Lordship, for Colonel Wood it seems, outwitted his titled contemporary, and according to tradition, "by treating one of the justices to a bowl of toddy" secured his vote in favor of Winchester, which then and there settled the question. So indignant was Lord Fairfax, when he learned of the incident, that he is said to never again have spoken to the magistrate who had allowed himself to be degraded in such a manner.

For almost forty years, "Greenway Court" was the scene of much entertaining, Lord Fairfax continuously surrounding himself with his favorite male acquaintances, often inviting to his hospitable board as many as twenty gentlemen in a single day. His Lordship made no effort to conceal his dislike of the ladies, and it is chronicled that no woman was ever admitted to "Greenway Court."

While he enjoyed the broad veranda and large rooms of his manor-house, he invariably slept in a little "out house" described as being only twelve feet square. Nor was this his only eccentricity. Proclaimed by all who knew him as a fastidious dresser, His Lordship kept on hand an extensive and elaborate wardrobe for daily as well as formal occasions, and seems to have delighted in fine fabrics and bright colors. According to an old account itemizing his wardrobe at "Greenway Court," he had on hand during one season, the following articles of clothing:

"One velvet suit, and other suits in brown, blue, and drab; scarlet and green silk coats; scarlet laced, green damask laced, and gold tissue waistcoats; and scarlet plush and black velvet breeches."

In character, conduct, and appearance, Lord Fairfax remained a typical and traditional English aristocrat to the end of his days. Despite his attachment to Virginia, he remained a Loyalist and a Tory, even in the face of his friendship for George Washington and others who championed the Colonists' cause, but because of his inactivity, remained unmolested during the Revolutionary War.

When the news reached "Greenway Court" of the surrender of Lord Cornwallis at Yorktown, Lord Fairfax told his body servant that it was time for him to be "put to bed." He died soon thereafter at the ripe old age of ninety-one, and is buried in a crypt of Christ Church at Winchester; strangely enough, not far distant from the bank in which his great Iron Chest is today on display.

Old Clocks

"By day its voice is low and light;
But in the silent dead of night,
Distinct as a passing footstep's fall,
It echoes along the vacant hall,
Along the ceiling, along the floor,
And seems to say, at each chamber door—
          For ever—never;
          Never—for ever!"

CHAPTER IX

OLD CLOCKS

WHO can resist the appeal of an old clock? Few relics of the past have come to us so wrapped in veneration as these old time-pieces, which through the passing years have witnessed life and death, love and hate, triumph and disaster, and man's progress in an ever-changing world. We may feel a strong attachment for an old chair, a lustre pitcher, a Chelsea teapot, or a plate of "Old Spode," but more than any other household possession or treasure, the clock "ticks its way into our affections."

From the simple sun-dial of King Ahaz, mentioned in the Old Testament, instruments for marking the hours have passed through countless stages of improvement and development, until today, highly perfected clocks—electrical and otherwise—are in general use throughout the civilized world.

Egyptians, Greeks, Italians, Arabians, and Chinese, all used sun-dials, and in Anglo-Saxon England dials were cut on the walls of churches. These, however, were of no service at night or on cloudy days, so man's inventive genius brought about the second step in telling time: the hour-glass. This quaint device for marking the hour was nothing more than a glass having two bulbs and a connecting opening through which the sand in one bulb ran into the other. The amount of sand and size of the opening were such that a given amount of time was consumed in the passage.

The earliest mechanical contrivance for keeping time was the water clock, which was first used among the Eastern nations and introduced into Greece by Plato. Next came the wheel clock, whose inventor is unknown, though the honor is frequently ascribed to Boethius. N. Hudson Moore, in *The Old Clock Book* says that "the first clocks composed of an assemblage of wheels, of which there is no doubt as to age, is the clock in St. Paul's Cathedral, London, which was put up in 1286; one at Canterbury Cathedral, 1292; one at Exeter, 1300; and one in the palace yard, London, of about the same period."

One of the oldest and most famous clocks in the world is the Strassburg Clock, in the Strassburg Cathedral. The present one is the third to acquire fame. The first was built in 1352, the second in 1570, and the last, early in the nineteenth century. This celebrated old clock is thirty feet high and fifteen feet wide at the base. At the bottom is a large globe of the heavens, which shows the course of the stars and the passing of each important one across the meridian of Strassburg. Behind the globe is a calendar, which shows the day of the month and the occurrence of all the religious festivals.

Above the calendar are automatic figures, one of which is drawn across the platform on each day. Thus Apollo crosses on Sunday, Diana on Monday, etc. Above these figures is the dial, which tells the time of day. Next is a planetarium, and above this is a globe which shows the phases of the moon. On the next floor are several figures, which strike the quarter hours. These represent the different periods of life—infancy,

youth, old age, and death. Above all is a figure of
Christ. At noon on each day, the Twelve Apostles
pass before Him in procession, and at the same time
a cock appears and crows three times.

Another famous clock is the Astronomical Clock of
the Cathedral of Beauvais, France, which though less
than one hundred years old, has much of the "old
world" magic associated with ancient cathedral clocks
in Europe. This marvelous clock is thirty-three feet
tall, seventeen feet wide, and nine and one-half feet
deep. It shows every imaginable type of time on its
fifty-two dials, including sidereal, solar, absolute, ap-
parent, mean, astronomical, international, nautical, mid
and east European, etc. In addition it shows the day,
week, month, and year; a wealth of astronomical detail
such as eclipses, beginning and end of day, position of
moon, comets, declensions and holidays. It was con-
structed by a local clockmaker in 1863 at a cost of one
hundred and thirty thousand francs. Ripley featured
this incredible clock in his equally incredible column,
but failed to tell how long a time was required to complete it. It would be interesting to know.

Countless books have been written about famous
clocks all over the world, for their story is one of never-
ending amazement and delight to the reader. In so
brief a sketch as this, mention of more than two or
three is impossible, but London's famous "Big Ben"
must claim our attention for a few minutes' time.

This world-famous clock, whose sonorous strokes
have been heard by millions, not alone in London but
in all parts of the world, via radio, is one of the great
"bell clocks" of Europe. In fact, "Big Ben" is simply
the name given the bell in the clock whose great face
looks out upon the majestic city of London from its

commanding situation in the Parliament Clock Tower. Its four quarters were cast by Warner in 1856, it weighs thirteen and one-half tons, and is nine feet in diameter.

Before the word "clock" came into general use, an instrument for telling time was called "horologue," and this as late as the reign of James I. "Clock" referred only to the bell upon which the hour was struck. It is surprising, and interesting, the similarity of names given clocks today in many countries. In Germany, clock is *Glocke;* in France, *cloche;* Ireland, *clog;* Scotland, *knock;* Wales, *cloc;* Holland, *klocke;* China, *glog*.

But it is the household clock that "ticks its way into our affections," and, whether we wish it or not, plays an important rôle in our daily living. Perhaps it is just as well that modern clocks have no such mottoes as did the old ones, reminding us of the unalterable hand of Time: "Old Time, the clock-setter, that bald sexton Time," as Shakespeare says.

Hayden, in his delightful book, *Chats on Old Clocks,* says of the domestic clock:

"This may be said to be the clock in use in a great house, apart from the cathedral or church clock, the turret clock, or the more public clock common to the gaze of everybody. The nobility employed, on the continent and in this country (England), great clockmakers to produce these new scientific timekeepers for use in their private apartments. But there came another phase when the clock visible to the dependent was supplanted by more delicate mechanism of greater value and richer ornamentation . . . *The Personal Clock.* This was the watch. It was carried on the person. It was the gift of a lover to his mistress. It was a rich and rare jewel of scientific construction, set in crystal, embellished with enamel and other rich decoration. In a measure it supplanted the clock and drove it to a lower plane."

The earliest household clocks came from England, and by 1600 were being manufactured for such moderate prices that the average household possessed at least one. These clocks were variously known as "birdcage," "lantern" or "bed-post" clocks. That royal "Bluebeard," Henry VIII, gave to the ill-fated Anne Boleyn on her wedding day, a small clock of the style known as "bird-cage"—four inches deep and ten inches high. I never contemplate this clock, or its pathetic first owner, but that the lines of Cowper,

"Slow comes the hour, its passing speed how great!
    Waiting to seize it—Vigilantly wait"

seem prophetic of Anne Boleyn and her fate as the second wife of the unconscionable Henry.

These type clocks were placed on wall-shelves or brackets, and were wound by pulling down the opposite ends of ropes on which the weights were hung. They varied: some struck the hour, others had an alarm, while thirty hours was the maximum length of time any of them ran. The lantern clock was inspired by the lantern of that period; its shape was almost identical, and its usage as well had much to do with its name. The clock, like the lantern, hung from a wall or stood on a bracket, while its chains and weights were suspended beneath it.

When one thinks of the domestic clocks of this period, there is brought vividly to mind the death-bed scene of Charles II, as described by Macauley; the year is 1685.

"The morning light began to peep through the windows of Whitehall; and Charles desired the attendants to pull aside the curtains, that he might have one more look at the day. He remarked that it was time to *wind up the clock* that stood near his bed. These little circumstances were long remembered, because they proved beyond dispute that, when he declared himself a Roman Catholic, he was in full possession of his faculties. He apologized to those who had stood round him all night for the trouble which he caused. He had been, he said, a most unconscionable time dying; but he hoped that they would excuse it. This was the last glimpse of that exquisite urbanity so often found potent to charm away resentment of a justly incensed nation. Soon after dawn the speech of the dying man failed."

A bond of loyalty and sentiment existed between Charles and his "dominion" that was Virginia. Had not the colonists proclaimed him King a full month before he was proclaimed King in England? And not only this, but Sir William Berkeley, hot-headed old Cavalier that he was, had, in his official capacity as Governor of Virginia, invited Charles while in Holland, to come and reign over his faithful subjects in Virginia.

The story is interesting, if not amusing. Sir William went so far as to send abroad Colonel Richard Lee, who was almost as ardent a loyalist as himself, to invite "King Charles II," as he chose to call him, to come over to Virginia. Colonel Lee proceeded to Holland and saw the young prince, to whom he extended the invitation, but the luxury-loving Charles was wary of a wilderness boasting but twenty thousand souls, so the invitation was graciously declined.

When it became evident that Charles would ascend the throne of England, Berkeley hastened to proclaim him King in Virginia. This was in March, 1660, a month before Charles was proclaimed King in England.

For this act of recognition and loyalty, the new Monarch showed his gratitude by issuing coins whose motto referred to Virginia as a fourth section of his kingdom, being named as of equal rank with England,

Scotland, and Ireland. When it became known that Virginia had been the first to recognize and proclaim the new King, the term "Old Dominion," still used and beloved today, was given the colony, claiming precedence for it over other dominions.

Frequent changes in the guise of improvements continued to be noted in mid-seventeenth century clocks. By 1661 the pendulum had been introduced, and superseded the balance. The first form was known as the "bob pendulum," which by 1680 was followed by the "royal" or long pendulum. Hayden states that the advent of the pendulum came at a time when "the art of the clockmaker required the necessary impetus to carry him to newer and more extended fields." It was the invention of the pendulum that revolutionized the domestic clock.

What of early clocks in Virginia? Philip Alexander Bruce in the *Economic History of Virginia in the Seventeenth Century,* says that among the household possessions of the planters there were "clocks of various and often of costly patterns." The earliest reference to a clock in Virginia that I have been able to find is "a clock valued at £4." which belonged to Major Philip Stephens of York County, listed among other articles in the appraisal of his estate, September 2, 1658. Another early reference to a clock in York County, is the "clock with weights" listed in the personal estate of Captain Francis Mathews. The wealthy Mrs. Elizabeth Digges, widow of Edward Digges, Governor of Virginia, also had listed "one clock" in the appraisal of her many valuable possessions, in 1691.

A clock appears in the inventory of Ralph Wormeley of "Rosegill" in Middlesex, in 1701. Other

owners of clocks in different parts of the colony were
Henry Lee, of Westmoreland; James Ball, of Lancaster; Matthew Hubard, of York, and Mrs. Ann
Mason of Stafford. Wills and inventories list these
particular clocks between the years 1746 and 1762.

In the *Virginia Gazette,* March 1768, there was advertised a lottery for disposing of furniture which belonged to James Hamilton. Included in the lot was
an "eight day clock." Through the same medium, in
1766, James Galt "clock and watchmaker, and jeweler"
of Williamsburg, announced his plans to remove to
Shockoe, near Richmond Town, where he "would keep
clocks in repair by the year at reasonable rates."

Old directories show that between 1683 and 1770
many American cities had expert clockmakers advertising their wares, including Boston, New York, Philadelphia, Wilmington, Baltimore, and Charleston.
The ingenious Eli Terry, who was making clocks in
Connecticut by 1800, is generally credited with being
the "father of American clockmaking," yet, almost
half a century before Terry appeared on the clockmakers' horizon, Joshua Lockwood, strangely overlooked by most writers on old timepieces, was advertising in the *South Carolina Gazette.*

We first hear of him on January 20, 1757, when he
publishes his arrival in these quaint words:

"Arrived with Captain Curling, Joshua Lockwood, Watchmaker,
who begs leave to acquaint the Ladies and Gentlemen of this province
that he intends to follow the Art or calling of Watchmaking, mend-
ing, and repairing at Mr. Lee's, Carpenter, in Elliott Street, and
Ladies and Gentlemen will be waited upon in the Country."

By 1761 he had married a daughter of old Charleston and had made quite a success of his clock business. From the outset, Lockwood imported a variety

of clocks, some ornate, depicting contemporaneous scenes, and others of unusual mechanism. In 1761 he sold

"Eight Day Clocks with hours, minutes, seconds, day of the month and the Moon's Age in the Arch: Ditto, with a Face in the Arch, with Eyes moving as natural as Life: Ditto with a Hunt in the Face, where the Buck, Dogs and Sportsmen are to be seen all in the full Chace, as natural as the thing itself, with a Slave planting in the Arch, the Motto, 'success to the planters!' the last his own invention, which he hopes will please his Friends. Some of the cases Mahogany, and others japanned, with pyramidal Heads neatly adorned with flute and frieze Work, the Capitals and Bases of Brass, the Pillars inlaid or fluted, with ditto all guilt the same as a Watch."

But it was the New England States that lead the country in the number of clockmakers they produced, just as they did in the number of early American silversmiths. "Of all the States, Connecticut led the way as to the value and permanence of her works in this line," writes N. Hudson Moore in the *Old Clock Book*. "Her beginnings were small, but her final performance, like the shot fired at Concord, is now heard round the world. Not till after the Revolution, and when peace had allowed men to turn their attention once more to their trades, did the wonderful progress, which in the next thirty years revolutionized the clock-making business, advance with giant strides."

The two Terrys, Eli and Eli Jr., Silas Hoadley, Seth Thomas, and Chauncey Jerome were the foremost clockmakers in the Connecticut group, and many of their quaint and charming old shelf clocks, with their original wooden or brass works, may be found in Virginia today. Eli Terry was born at East Windsor, Connecticut, on April 13, 1772. At the age of twenty he had made his first wooden clock. It is still in "going order," and is owned by Terry's grandsons who made the highest bid for it—one thousand dollars—at an auction many years ago.

Terry's first clocks were made entirely by hand, but since the demand for clocks at that time was relatively small, only three or four were commenced at one time, and most of these ordered beforehand by purchasers. In 1797 Terry took out what is believed to be the first patent he ever applied for, and he suffered the same fate as the great English potter, Wedgewood, whose contemporaries took his inventions with no qualms of conscience, and used them as if their own.

The cases were considered a distinctly separate part of the clock, and were gotten direct from cabinet-makers. When in 1809, Eli Terry, Seth Thomas, and Silas Hoadley began making wooden clocks under the firm name of Terry, Thomas, and Hoadley, Mr. Thomas did what was then called "joiner work." This involved making the cases, "putting together" clocks (fitting the wheels and different parts together) and getting the clocks, one at a time, into running order.

The partnership of Terry, Thomas, and Hoadley lasted but one year, and in 1810 became Thomas and Hoadley, Terry having sold out his interest in the firm. Two years later Seth Thomas sold out to Hoadley and began to manufacture clocks on his own.

One of their contemporaries, Chauncey Jerome, whose "bronze looking glass clock" is one of the loveliest of the New England shelf clocks, did a thriving business in Richmond, and other parts of Virginia between 1835 and 1837, when Jerome established a factory in Richmond. His labels were printed by Thomas White, whose shop was across the street from

Shelf Clock of the "Pillar and Scroll" design, made in 1816. The old label on the inside reads, "Patent Clocks, Invented by Eli Terry. Made and Sold at Plymouth, Connecticut, by Seth Thomas. Warranted if well used." This clock has its original wooden works, and is in perfect running order. Owned by the author.

the Bell Tavern at Fifteenth and Main, and many of these quaint century-old clocks with their yellowed Richmond labels, are to be found in Virginia today.

In his book, *American Clock Making,* published in 1860, Chauncey Jerome says of the first American Shelf Clocks:

"Mr. Eli Terry in the year 1814 invented a beautiful shelf clock made of wood which completely revolutionized the whole business. The making of the old-fashioned hang-up wood clock passed out of existence. This patent article Mr. Terry introduced was called the 'Pillar Scroll-Top Case.' The pillars were about twenty-one inches long, three-eights at the top, resting on a square base, three-quarters of an inch at the base, and the top finished by a handsome cap. It had a large dial eleven inches square, and a tablet below the dial seven by eleven inches."

These clocks sold for fifteen dollars a piece when first manufactured, but of course are worth a great deal more today.

In 1812, when Seth Thomas severed his partnership with Hoadley and went into the clock-making business independently, he began at once to make Shelf Clocks, such as he had helped to make while in partnership with Eli Terry. By 1816, Thomas had again gone into business with Terry, having paid him one thousand dollars for the right to produce his newest shelf clock.

In the author's possession is one of these original old clocks; a beautiful example of the "Pillar and Scroll" design, the case of which is a rich dark red mahogany, with the scroll finished in black and gold-leaf. The delicately carved small claw feet are among the loveliest features of the clock, while on either side, chaste slender columns—or pillars—extend the full length of the case.

The works are Eli Terry's original "wooden works" which he patented, and despite the clock's venerable age, it still tells perfect time, and ticks the hours away with unbroken regularity. The large hand-painted dial, the small brass pendulum, the heavy weights, the quaint brass key used in winding the clock, all are the originals. The clock runs for thirty hours, and chimes the hour. The rhythmic "tick-tock" of the swinging pendulum, the bell-like toll of the passing hours, the strange and sweet companionship of this priceless and venerable old timepiece, make it one of the author's most treasured possessions.

The most famous of all clockmakers in Massachusetts were the Willard brothers—Benjamin, Simon, and Aaron. Of the three, Simon was by far the most noted, and unquestionably the best clockmaker. He remained in Massachusetts all of his life, and at his death in Roxbury in 1848, left a son who perpetuated his business. Simon Willard advertised very little, but relied mainly on his clock papers, one of which reads:

"Clock Manufactory
"Simon Willard

"At his Clock Dial in Roxbury street, manufactures every kind of Clock Work, such as large Clocks for Steeples, made in the best manner, and warranted, price with one dial, 500 dollars; with two dials, 600 dollars; with three dials 700 dollars; with four dials, 900 dollars. Common eight day clocks with very elegant faces and mahogany cases, price from 50 to 60 dollars. Elegant eight-day Time pieces, price thirty dollars. Time pieces which run 30 hours and warranted, price 10 dollars. Spring clocks of all kinds, price from 50 to 60 dollars. Clocks that will run one year with once winding up, with very elegant cases, price 100 dollars. Time pieces for Astronomical purposes, price 70 dollars. Time pieces for meeting houses to place before the gallery, with neat enameled dials, price 55 dollars. Chime clocks that will play 6 tunes, price 120 dollars. Perambulators are also made at said place, which can be affixed to any kind of wheel carriage, and will tell the miles and rods exact, price 15 dollars.

"Gentlemen who wish to purchase any kind of clocks are invited to call at said Willards Clock Manufactory, where they will receive satisfactory evidence, that it is much cheaper to purchase new, than old and second hand clocks; He warrants all his work—and as he is ambitious to give satisfaction—he doubts not of receiving the public approbation and patronage."

Despite the fact that the name of Willard is invariably associated with the type clock that has come to be known as "banjo" the above paper attests to the variety of clocks they made, and foremost among them were the handsome Grandfather Clocks, some of which were very costly and beautiful objects. Recently a well known Boston firm, dealing in jewels, gold, old silverware and fine furniture, advertised for sale an "American grandfather clock in good cherry case, by Benjamin Willard, Roxbury. Height seven feet five inches to top of finials. *Circa* 1775. Priced five hundred and twenty-five dollars."

At "Wilton" on the James, near Richmond, one may see a truly magnificent Grandfather Clock, by Simon Willard, the case of which is mahogany inlaid with marquetry. The beautiful grain of the wood, the peerless workmanship, the handsome dial and brass finials, make this clock truly a *chef d'œuvre* of noble proportions. When "Wilton" was restored by the Colonial Dames in Virginia, and became the Society's headquarters, among those who contributed handsome old pieces to furnish the great hall and large rooms, was Mr. J. Bernard Robb, of "Struan" on the River Road, Richmond.

Mr. Robb's gift to "Wilton" was the Simon Willard Grandfather Clock, whose history he has been kind enough to give me. The clock was first owned by Mr. Luke Tiernan, of Baltimore, in 1798, in whose family it has passed from generation to generation. Mr. Tiernan bequeathed the clock to his son, Charles Tiernan, who in turn bequeathed it to his son, Charles Bernard Tiernan, who in turn bequeathed it to his nephew Charles Tiernan Darling. The clock last passed to Mr. Darling's sister Nancy Darling Robb, wife of J. Bernard Robb of "Gaymont" in Caroline County, and later of "Struan" in Richmond. It was in memory of his wife that Mr. Robb gave the clock to "Wilton."

This magnificent old clock stands sentinel in the great hall of a once great house, seeming proud of its past: a past that must have witnessed countless scenes in that imperishable picture of love and loyalty, life and labor, in the "Old South."

The most historic clock in Virginia, and one of the handsomest, is that impressive timepiece familiarly known as "Dunmore Clock," manufactured by John Jeffray, master clockmaker of Glasgow, Scotland. Its first home in Virginia was the imposing Governor's Palace in Williamsburg, where it was placed by the Earl of Dunmore, last Royal Governor of Virginia, in the year 1771. Today, "Dunmore Clock" ticks the passing hours away from a graceful stair-landing in the home of the late Harrison Trent Nicholas, of Lynchburg, Virginia, in whose family the clock has been a treasured possession for many generations.

It is doubtful if anywhere in America there is a clock with so thrilling and historic a past, as that of "Dunmore Clock." This handsome old timepiece has witnessed elegance and beauty in a setting that today is being reincarnated in Colonial Williamsburg; it has known the proud touch of an autocratic and titled master; then desertion, after that master fled from the Governor's abode when word reached him that a band of incensed American patriots had risen in revolt against him in the Virginia House of Burgesses.

Only a clock possessing invisible strength, and an indefinable something akin to serenity, such as "Dunmore Clock" assuredly has, could have stood the test of what followed. The callous hand of the auctioneer followed the proud touch of John Murray, Earl of Dunmore, while a frenzied cry called for bids, bids, bids—and a buyer. "Dunmore Clock" found a new home and a new master in young John Ambler, owner of Jamestown Island. To Jamestown and the Jaquelin-Ambler mansion went the clock in 1775, where it joined the Revolutionary cause. Here it remained until 1807, when John Ambler moved his family to Richmond. Through the passing years it ticked the minutes and chimed the hours for a devoted family, who had come to look upon it almost as one of their circle.

Before me is a twenty-page typewritten manuscript, giving the complete history of this celebrated clock. Where to begin, and end, that is the question! Try and gaze through imaginative eyes upon this noble old timepiece. "Dunmore Clock" stands seven and one-half feet high, in a "Grandfather Case" of lustrous old mahogany, chaste in design. Three brass finials crown the beautifully curving top, and at the top and base of two gracefully fluted columns that stand on either side of the face, are brass caps.

The clock's face is brass, burnished for the circle of the numbers, with a center of dull stippled brass. Above the dial is a circle for the striker, with a deeply melodious bell. At the top of the inner circle of the dial is the second-hand, and below, on a crescent-shaped marker is the name of the maker, John Jeffray, Glasgow. Under this is a slot through which run the days of the month. Around the face, filling in the square of the glass cover, is a delicate and decorative treatment of filigree brass. The works, pendulum, and weights are of solid brass.

A brass plate, recently placed on the clock as a memorial to its late owner, Harrison Trent Nicholas of Lynchburg, is inscribed:

Owners of this Clock
John Murray, Earl of Dunmore,
Last Royal Governor of Virginia.

John Ambler, II, of Jamestown,
his son
John Jaquelin Ambler,
his widow
Elizabeth Barbour Ambler,
her grandson
Harrison Trent Nicholas
of Lynchburg, Virginia
Born March 9, 1869, in Buckingham County,
Died April 29, 1934.

Colonel John Ambler, after moving from Jamestown in 1807, remained in Richmond until his death in 1836. "Dunmore Clock" followed the family to their new home on Shockoe Hill, and on the death of the master of the house, passed to his widow (and third wife, *née* Catherine Bush), "the beautiful Widow Norton." She survived John Ambler by ten years, and at her death in 1846 willed the clock to her son, John Jaquelin Ambler.

John Jaquelin Ambler is said to have been handsome and clever, and blessed beyond measure with the good things of this life. He had received unusual advantages in education and travel; wrote his memoirs, and married the lovely Elizabeth Barbour, daughter of Philip Pendleton Barbour of "Frescati" in Orange County, an Associate Justice of the Supreme Court, and Speaker of the House.

When John Jaquelin Ambler inherited "Dunmore Clock" he had it brought to his home "Jaquelin Hall" in Madison County. For the eight remaining years of his life he looked with pride and pleasure upon his treasured clock, for though he had inherited many other family heirlooms, including numerous portraits of his Jaquelin-Ambler forbears (recently exhibited *en bloc* at the Virginia Museum of Fine Arts) it remained his most prized possession. As he lay on his death-bed in 1854, the striker on the old clock was set at "silence" lest its chimes disturb the stricken master of the house. When John Jaquelin Ambler closed his eyes in eternal sleep, "Dunmore Clock" struck one.

Troubled times lay ahead. Seven years later when the storm clouds of the War Between the States finally broke over Virginia, John Jaquelin Ambler's widow and children took refuge at "Glen Ambler" in Amherst County, another of the Ambler estates. To be sure, "Dunmore Clock" followed its owner to "Glen Ambler," and there it remained until the close of the tragic conflict.

Joy and peace came once again to Elizabeth Barbour Ambler and her children. Among the Virginia youth of the post-war era who married, unafraid of the lean days which lay ahead, were John Jaquelin Ambler's daughter, Ella Cary Ambler, and John

Scott Nicholas, son of a distinguished Virginia family. When John Scott Nicholas took his bride to the old Nicholas estate, "Seven Islands" on the James, Elizabeth Barbour Ambler followed her daughter to her new home, taking "Dunmore Clock" with her.

In 1874 John Scott Nicholas moved his family to Lynchburg, so that the children could have the advantage of city schooling. "Dunmore Clock" and Grandma Ambler went along too. In all of the Ambler annals, there is no more lively or lovable character than "Grandma Ambler," widow of John Jaquelin Ambler, and daughter of Philip Pendleton Barbour. Often she was the mainstay of the family during "reconstruction days". Once a wealthy woman, her now slender means and forceful personality did much to help her son-in-law's struggling young family meet the exigences of those trying times.

Many tales are told of this lovable old lady, and her firm management of her youthful grandsons. When they became too troublesome, she would tie them to the posts of her great tester-bed, a relic of more splendid days. She was spirited and high-tempered when the occasion demanded, yet gentle and loving as well. She was especially devoted to her second grandson, Harrison Trent Nicholas, who she said, "had the Barbour head." He always slept by her bed, and ate the bread and drank the milk she would bring him in the middle of the night, when he complained of being hungry.

Gloom descended on the Nicholas household when Grandma Ambler was paralyzed and became an invalid. She had been a tower of strength and a fountain of wisdom to the members of her family; now she lay helpless. But Grandma Ambler's mind was

Close-up of "Dunmore Clock" showing the elaborate details of workmanship on the handsome brass face. On a crescent-shaped marker is the name of the maker, John Jeffray of Glasgow, Scotland.

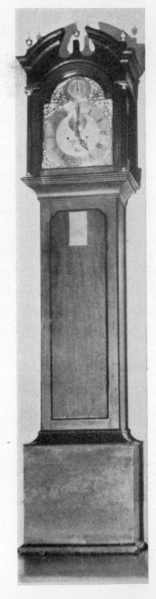

Clock once owned by John Murray, Earl of Dunmore, last Royal Governor of Virginia, and placed by him in the Governor's Palace at Williamsburg. Bought at auction in 1775 by John Ambler, owner of Jamestown Island. This famous old timepiece is still in the possession of descendants of John Ambler. Courtesy of Mrs. Harrison Trent Nicholas of Lynchburg.

as keenly alert as ever, and as she lay bedridden, she thought of the needs of the present, even as she made plans for the future. One day she called her grandson to her—he was now a school boy—and said to him:

"Here, Harry, take this gold plate down and see what you can get for it. I'm more comfortable without those teeth, and I won't need them any more." In those days teeth were set in plates of solid gold. The proud boy brought back a silver sugar dish and tray, engraved with his mother's initials, both of which remain in his family's possession.

Often she told him the story of the clock and how it came into the Amblers' possession. She told him too, many stories of the splendor of the past; of the fine records of his ancestors; of various valuable relics that had come down from some branch of the family. Then one day, when her eyes were so dimmed that everything she saw was as through a mist, she called her favorite grandson to her side. He must come closer—kneel—for she had something very important to say to him. The boy obeyed, and these words fell upon his eager ears: *"Harry, I am going to leave you the clock; take care of it all your life; it has a wonderful history."*

In a touching and beautifully written history of "Dunmore Clock" and the two notable families so intimately linked with it, the wife of the late Harrison Trent Nicholas (*née* Mattie Craighill) has written a fascinating story for contemporary Amblers and Nicholases. Taking up the story, she says:

"The old clock ticked on through the years in the Nicholas home on Seventeenth Street, Diamond Hill; saw children grow to men and women of importance to their community; saw happiness and sorrow —marriages, deaths, births, grandchildren, merry gatherings of friends and relatives, illnesses, difficulties of many kinds, successes and fail-ures—all the sunshine and shadow of a wholesome family life. Then it saw the family's dissolution with the passing, first of the father and soon after the mother. Life is like a kaleidoscope—a turn, and the pattern we see is all new, but as lovely and as intricate as the one that was there before."

Harrison Trent Nicholas was a master worthy of his ancient clock. The dying words of his old grandmother were forever indelibly impressed on his heart, and to the day of his death, "Dunmore Clock" was dearly loved and tenderly cared for by him. When he wound it every Sunday morning, his wife recalls how "his eyes assumed an affectionate expression as he watched the great brass weights ascend—and his touch on the clock was like a caress."

There are those who feel that "Dunmore Clock" should be returned to the restored Governor's Palace in Williamsburg, where once again, it can tick away the passing minutes and chime the hours in its original setting. There, thousands of interested visitors could look upon this ancient timepiece, instead of the few who are privileged to now see it as it stands in a private residence.

Meantime, "Dunmore Clock" ticks on. Like count-less inanimate objects that are old and reverenced, this famous clock has acquired personality, and absorbed the spirit of its many devoted owners. To look upon it is to know that here indeed is a treasured relic of the past—a noble reminder of people and events woven into the colorful fabric that is Virginia's history and heritage.

Chairs for a Royal Wedding

"Ghosts of dead hours, and days that once were fair."

CHAPTER X
CHAIRS FOR A ROYAL WEDDING

STORIED Antiques! What tales of love and laughter, music and merriment, beauty and grandeur yes, even pride and prejudice, sorrow and sacrifice, these old pieces might tell, could they but speak! Among the countless lovely old heirlooms of many a Virginia family, none perhaps are so steeped in glamour and romance as the two Empire chairs that today adorn a Richmond home: chairs that were made in 1803 for the wedding of the beautiful Betsey Patterson of Baltimore, and Jerome Bonaparte, younger brother of the great Napoleon.

Originally there were twenty-four of these exquisite chairs, which are similar in design and construction to the painted furniture to which Sheraton was much addicted. A Philadelphia cabinet-maker was commissioned to make several dozen of these painted side chairs with cane seats, for there were to be a great many guests at the wedding and supper following; a far greater number than ever before had been entertained in the spacious Patterson home. Four sets of six each, were completed in time for the nuptials.

After the wedding festivities, Mr. and Mrs. Patterson anticipating no further need for the "extra chairs," decided to give them to relatives and friends as mementoes of a Royal Wedding. The chairs were distributed in sets of six, just as they had come from the cabinet-maker, and the two now in Richmond are the companions of four others which were given to Miss Anne Porter of Baltimore, a neighbor and friend of the Pattersons. With each succeeding generation the six chairs have changed hands and homes, but have never left the Porter family, being last inherited by Miss Porter's great-niece, Miss Rebecca Thornton, who first brought them to Virginia.

Miss Emerald Bristow, lecturer on Decorative Arts at the Virginia Museum of Fine Arts in Richmond, has studied at close range the intricate details of workmanship on these lovely old chairs, and gives the following illuminating and interesting version of their historical background. To quote Miss Bristow:

"The cabinet-maker, whose name unfortunately has been forgotten, evidently took special pains to work out a design appropriate to the occasion of the wedding of a brother of the Great Napoleon. The turned legs and stretchers are borrowed from the French Directoire style, the current vogue in Paris at the time. The back with its plain bars, curving slightly to fit the human body, is an early echo of the Grecian classic in design, which was to be so prominent in the furniture of the period of the Napoleonic Empire. The color scheme is very military—deep French blue with bands of black and gold and gold-painted ornament.

"In spite of the stiffly classic griffins, acanthus foliage and conventionalized lotus—symbolic of Napoleon's victories in Italy, Greece, and Egypt, a love motif has been introduced, the torches. The torches here are also rendered in a rather stiff manner and are borrowed from classicism. However, they were undoubtedly introduced as symbols of Hymen, the god of happy marriage. That had been the symbol of the happily wed royal couples used in the early Louis XVI-Marie Antoinette style. Much earlier, in English furniture of the time of William and Mary, the flame finials on the tops of grandfather clocks and on the early crested cabinets were introduced as Hymen-torch flames, symbolic of the marital happiness of the monarchs.

"Although still quite strong and sturdy after one hundred and thirty-six years of service, the chairs had begun to show wear and

looked rather shabby. The painted decoration and even much of the
background paint had been worn off. The caning of the seats had
loosened or broken. Two had even been over-painted with a thick
green and been relegated to the kitchen! Their present owner took
them to be done over at the shop of one of Richmond's well known
antique dealers. Here they were carefully cleaned, each coat of paint
was analyzed for its color, and the detail of the decoration was completely recovered. Now they are restored to their former elegance,
and to a place of honor in the house.

"The chairs were said to have had matching blue velvet cushions
of the flat boxed type, which were attached by tasseled cords of gold
silk. They must have looked as handsome as young Bonaparte's full
dress uniform of a naval officer, on that long ago wedding day!
When the owner finds an authentic model the cushions, too, are to
be replaced."

To touch the satin-like smoothness of these exquisite
old chairs, to sit in them, is to be transplanted momentarily to a large, high-ceilinged room, dazzling with
candle-light and great mirrors that reflect the colorful
costumes of the guests; a room where conversation is
lost in the rhythm of music and laughter. One seems
to see the handsome young Jerome, resplendent in all
his naval regalia, rise from his seat at the glittering
bride's table as he offers a toast to his bride; then someone else rises—perhaps the French Consul or the
Mayor of Baltimore, and again the glasses are raised—
this time to the long life and happiness of both the
bride and groom.

The picture soon fades, for the sequel to the story
of Elizabeth and Jerome Bonaparte's marriage is less
happy than has been that of the "extra chairs" made
especially for that memorable occasion. Eighteen
years before, when Baltimore was a small seaport with
unpaved streets and stage coach communication, Elizabeth Patterson was born to a father of Irish parentage

and an American mother descended from a well-to-do Maryland family. Her father William Patterson, had arrived in America at the age of fourteen, and with typical Irish tenacity had climbed the ladder of fortune, until, at the time of Elizabeth's birth, he was considered the wealthiest man in Baltimore, and next to Charles Carroll, one of the wealthiest men in America.

From this home of wealth and indulgence, Betsey Patterson (for so she was called by her host of friends and admirers) stepped out into the world with parental love, social position, wealth, and beauty as her shield and buckler against the disappointments and tragedies of life. What soothsayer would have dared to predict anything but a life of triumph for this daughter of old Maryland?

Jerome Bonaparte had been educated at Juilly, and afterwards became a naval lieutenant. During the summer of 1803 (he was then nineteen) he was sent out on an expedition to the West Indies, but his vessel was pursued by English cruisers, and he was forced to put in at New York.

As can be imagined, the presence of Napoleon's younger brother in America was an event of more than ordinary social interest, and despite the absence of telephone or telegraph and the scarcity of newspapers, such exciting news travelled fast. Among the first American cities to learn of young Bonaparte's arrival in New York was Baltimore, and by the same stage coach which brought the news, a message was dispatched from Commodore Barney inviting Jerome and his entourage to visit Baltimore. Barney had served with great distinction in the American Revolution, and when but twenty-three years of age had been promoted by Congress to the rank of Commodore, and had received from the State of Pennsylvania a gold-hilted sword. It was an invitation not to be ignored, and Jerome promptly accepted.

Early in September of 1803, the dashing young Frenchman arrived in Baltimore, amid much pomp and ceremony, and flutter of feminine hearts. It was at the Fall Races that he first saw Betsey Patterson, dressed in a suit of buff silk which but accentuated her dark beauty. Jerome is said to have been so impressed by her striking beauty and decided *chic,* that he publicly proclaimed, "there is the lady I am going to marry!"

This impetuous statement but kindled anew the vanity and ambition that was to play so strong a rôle in Betsey Patterson's tragic life, and lent piquancy to their meeting. At this time she was a reigning belle of Baltimore, and while many suitors had asked her hand in marriage, she had chosen to remain heart free. Her beauty of face and form was acknowledged by all who saw her. Writes Mary McLeod in an old issue of *The Southern Magazine:*

"The contour of her head was pure Grecian, exquisitely formed, and covered with a mass of dark curls. Her forehead was fair and shapely, and her eyes were large, dark, and tender. The loveliness of her mouth and chin, the radiant complexion and perfectly moulded figure, all combined with wit, charm, and wealth, made her one of the most desirable young women."

Had Betsey Patterson been as wise as she was beautiful, she would have read Lord Lyttleton's *Advice to a Lady,* and remembered long thereafter the line:

"Your heart's supreme ambition? To be fair."

But beauty alone was not enough. Fame and a title must be hers, and herein lies the romantic and tragic story of this American girl's marriage to the younger brother of the great and relentless Napoleon.

Jerome was of course presented to William Patterson's daughter soon after his arrival in Baltimore, and after their first meeting, they frequently met in such prominent homes as that of Samuel Chase, one of the Signers of the Declaration of Independence, and others of equal note. As can be imagined, Mr. and Mrs. Patterson looked with "growing alarm" upon the budding romance of their daughter and a member of the haughty and ambitious Bonaparte family. From the first they realized with what opposition and disapproval an alliance between their daughter and Napoleon's younger brother would meet, and took immediate steps to separate the couple and bring to an end the *affaire d'amour*.

Betsey was taken to the seclusion of the Patterson's country estate in Virginia, where, with her mother she spent several miserable weeks, all the while entreating her parents to let her return to Baltimore and Jerome. Clearly the enforced separation had failed to achieve the desired results. Absence had only made "the heart grow fonder" and now Jerome and Betsey determined to marry. Seeing the futility of further attempting to reason with two such strong wills, and hoping in some wise to placate Napoleon, William Patterson and his wife proceeded with the plans for their daughter's marriage.

It was on Christmas Eve in the year 1803 that Jerome Bonaparte, later King of Westphalia, and Elizabeth Patterson, daughter of a rich Irish merchant, became man and wife. The ceremony was performed in the Patterson home by the Right Reverend John Carroll, first Archbishop of the Catholic Church in America,

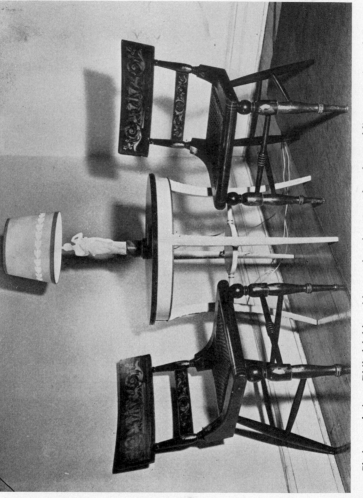

Chairs made by a Philadelphia cabinet-maker in 1803 for the wedding reception of Jerome Bonaparte and Betsey Patterson of Baltimore. Inherited by Miss Rebecca Thornton, who first brought them to Virginia. (Richmond *Times-Dispatch* photograph.) Courtesy of Miss Emerald Bristow.

and was witnessed by a notable gathering of Maryland society, the French Consul, the Mayor of Baltimore, Jerome's Secretary, and other distinguished persons.

Betsey Patterson was never more radiant than on this memorable evening. Her gown was an exquisite importation, fashioned in the mode of the hour, made of white muslin elaborately embroidered, with an extreme *décolletage*. Never before had Baltimore witnessed such a splendid scene. The wedding supper was an occasion long remembered, for it not only afforded William Patterson and his wife an opportunity to display their wealth, but it gave them as well an opportunity to honor their princely son-in-law, which they did unstintingly.

Memorable months followed. During January the happy couple spent their days at "Homestead" the country estate of the Pattersons. In February they visited in Washington where they were entertained by the French Minister and Aaron Burr. During the summer months they travelled leisurely through the enchanting Virginia countryside, spending some time at Old Sweet Springs. These famous Springs were the rendezvous of the Southern gentry of that day, as well as distinguished foreigners and Cabinet members, and here, in that once famous hostelry known as "Jefferson House" Jerome Bonaparte and his bride whiled away many happy hours. Today, the magnificent old ball-room where Jerome and Betsey danced the minuet, echoes only to the music and voices of long ago, for it is deserted and mouldy from disuse. But there are those who declare that on moonlit summer nights two figures can be seen, moving in graceful rhythm across the once polished floors—the figures of Jerome and

Betsey, dancing the graceful and perfectly timed steps of the minuet, as they once did, in the long ago.

This idyllic interlude was but the inevitable lull before the storm. Clouds were fast gathering on the marital horizon of this happy pair, and what William Patterson had long feared, at last came to pass. Pressure was brought to bear upon Jerome to return to France, while all French vessels were warned under no circumstances to give passage to the young person with whom Jerome had allied himself.

Jerome is said to have made several attempts to return to France accompanied by his wife, but without success. Finally, on March 11, 1805, they set sail from Baltimore on the *Erin,* one of Mr. Patterson's merchant ships, landing at Lisbon. Here Jerome parted with Elizabeth (a parting that was destined to be their last) and hastened to Paris alone, hoping, by a personal interview with Napoleon who was now Emperor, to bring about a reconciliation as well as the recognition of his wife.

Napoleon remained unmoved by his younger brother's appeal, and not only refused to recognize his American marriage, but succeeded in forcing Jerome to accept the arrangement he had planned for him. Despite the refusal of Pope Pius VII to declare the marriage null and void, Jerome was united in marriage with Catherine, Princess of Württemberg, and later was crowned King of Westphalia.

Meantime, Betsey, left on board the *Erin* at Lisbon, was informed that all French ports had been forbidden to permit "Madame Patterson" to land. The vessel proceeded to Amsterdam, whence the overland journey to Paris would be shorter and less strenuous, should Jerome's mission prove successful. Clearly seeing her predicament, and face to face with the necessity of soon reaching a port of safety, Elizabeth hastened to England, where on July 7, 1805, she gave birth to a son, whom she named Jerome Napoleon Bonaparte.

For all of her undisguised ambition, one cannot help but feel a wave of pity for this proud and pampered American girl, who so suddenly had come to know the meaning of life's cruelties. Though she had met with rebuffs and rejections, and her pride had suffered many stinging blows, the fires of ambition still burned deep in Elizabeth Patterson's breast, and it is clear that she still hoped to wring some gain from her marriage to the Emperor's younger brother.

Her first desire was to reside in Europe and press her claims against Napoleon, but her father, realizing the futility of any further overtures to members of the Bonaparte family, insisted that his daughter return home. She arrived in America in the early autumn of 1807, a few weeks after Jerome had married Catherine, Princess of Württemberg.

There are various versions of what followed. As King of Westphalia, Jerome is said to have invited Elizabeth to return to Europe and reside within his territory, which offer she is credited with having declined on the grounds that "Westphalia was a large Kingdom, but not large enough for two queens." When Jerome offered her money, she is said to have sent him the bitter retort that she had accepted the offer of Napoleon, (presumably a financial arrangement) and preferred "being sheltered under the wings of an eagle to being suspended from the bill of a goose."

Was this acrimonious remark attributable to her wounded pride, her undying ambition, or to the

smouldering fires of a love which still burned deep
in her heart for the romantic young Jerome? The answer we shall never know. But this and other wit-
ticisms, (as well, perhaps as some of her caustic re-
marks directed against Jerome) are said to have so
amused Napoleon that he once asked what he might
do for so wise and witty a woman. Ever alert to press
her rightful claims, Elizabeth answered: for herself,
the title and privileges of a duchess; for her son, due
recognition on the part of the Bonaparte family. Napoleon is supposed to have promised her the former,
but it was a promise never fulfilled.

The greater part of Elizabeth's tragic life was spent
in Europe, where her son was frequently entertained
by Jerome and cordially received by his consort. It
is said that Elizabeth's son bore such a striking resemblance to Napoleon, and possessed so many of his
natural mannerisms, that the French people objected
to his being seen on the streets of Paris.

Only once did Elizabeth and Jerome ever meet face
to face, after their parting at Lisbon. It was in the
gallery of the Pitti Palace in Florence, when they were
both well past middle age. Jerome was accompanied
by Catherine who had become very portly, while he
too, showed his approaching old age, but Elizabeth still
retained her beauty of face and figure. Jerome appeared as if stunned; neither spoke, and both hastily
left the gallery. It was, they knew, the final scene in
the drama that had been their lives. The curtain must
inevitably fall.

Through the long years of her storm-tossed life,
Elizabeth Patterson witnessed the passing of most of
the members of the Bonaparte family, as well as her
own. What thoughts consumed this once beautiful

woman, as she lay on her dying bed? Seventeen years before, Jerome had died; and more than half a century before the ambitious and relentless Napoleon. Had the sad memory of St. Helena brought her sweet revenge? The answer lay locked in her tired old heart—a heart that now was stilled in death.

She is buried in a small triangular lot in Greenmount Cemetery, Baltimore. A simple head-stone marks her grave, and is inscribed with these all-too applicable words:

"After life's fitful fever she sleeps well."

The Saga of Silver

"He is a great man who uses earthenware dishes as if they were silver; but he is equally great who uses silver as if it were earthenware."

—SENECA (8 B. C.-65 A. D.)

CHAPTER XI

THE SAGA OF SILVER

THE saga of silver forms one of the most brilliant and breath-taking chapters in history. Through its long and glittering career, silver, more than any other of earth's treasures, has swayed the destiny of men and of nations, until today, man's use of this precious metal has spread to the far corners of the globe, and scarcely a man, woman, or child but knows its touch.

The legend of silver tells that the world's first silver mine lay somewhere close to the shores of the Mediterranean, and according to a Greek myth, man's search for it was a moon-madness. Certain it is that the ancients linked silver with Luna, Goddess of the Moon. Luna caustic, or silver nitrate is thus derived.

Through the Dark and Middle Ages men mined silver in many parts of Europe, but the yield paled into insignificance beside the fabulous flow of silver from the New World. Long before the Spanish Conquest, Mexican mines had been worked, producing vast quantities of this lustrous metal, so that not in their wildest and most fantastic dreams could the Spaniards conceive of the glittering golconda they were to find hidden in the hills of the countries they were to conquer.

The story of Cortez, who with but four hundred men, fifteen horses, and seven cannon, conquered the lucrative and highly civilized kingdom of Montezuma, has few parallels in the annals of history. As a classic of amazing adventure and achievement—and of cruelty —it stands supreme.

Even today, when man's creative talents have reached what seems to be the pinnacle of perfection, one marvels at the skill and artistry of the Aztecs in their gold and silver craft; at the almost unbelievable tributes they gave to Cortez and his men, in their zeal to induce him to leave them and their beautiful City of the Floating Islands unharmed.

"Silver fish covered with scales that moved; tiny animals and reptiles beautifully carved; silver helmets, shields, and cuirasses, and trays of solid gold and silver as large as cart-wheels,"—these were among the dazzling array of gifts the young King Montezuma sent the cruel Cortez, but to no avail, for the prophecy of the wise men of the Aztecs came to pass, and Montezuma's great kingdom became the white man's domain. These fabulous tributes given to the Spaniards were as mere trifles compared to what they were ultimately to mine and own, ere they had conquered the land and sent to their doom, thousands of the natives who worked and died as slaves in the mines.

In Peru, as in Mexico, the ancients made exquisite figures of gold and silver. Dazzling tales are told of the Inca, one of the ruling class of Peruvian Indians at the time of the Spanish conquest, who made exotic gardens in which trees and plants were imitated in precious metals, gold being used for the flowers and fruits, and silver for the trunks and leaves of the trees, and for the stems and leaves of the flowers.

From time immemorial, silver, like an argent thread running through the tapestry of life, has, in one form or another, touched the hand of man. Homer speaks of silver wine cups, and Pliny describes dinners served from "purest antique silver." Picture a retinue of slaves filing past the nefarious Nero, bearing massive silver platters, laden with delicacies to tempt the Roman Emperor.

In ancient days silver vessels were frequently buried with dead kings, and silver toilet articles with queens. In Pompeii, before Vesuvius vent its wrath and buried the splendor of that classic city under a mountain of molten lava, food was often cooked in massive silver utensils.

When the wives of the Pharaohs appeared in all their regal and beautiful raiment, silver jewelry was worn extravagantly. And when Cleopatra, with her sinister beauty and seductive splendor captured the heart of Mark Antony, the river Nile was often the scene of their rendezvous, where, drifting down the placid stream, gleaming silver oars splashed softly in the moonlight. Shakespeare alludes to this particular scene in *Antony and Cleopatra:*

> "The barge she sat in, like a burnish'd throne,
> Burn'd on the water; the poop was beaten gold;
> Purple the sails, and so perfumed
> That the winds were love-sick with them; the oars were silver,
> Which to the tune of flutes kept stroke, and made
> The water which they beat to follow faster,
> As amorous of their strokes. For her own person,
> It beggar'd all description."

From Biblical times to the present day, the uses of silver have been manifold. Roman generals frequently carried camp silver on campaigns, but were sometimes compelled to bury it. In England during the War of the Roses, quantities of silver plate was sacrificed that the battle might go on; later, "the zeal of the Reformation kept the melting pots boiling." In 1643, in order to replenish his sadly depleted treasury, Charles I ordered all silverware melted and remade into coins, much in the same manner as Mussolini used the gold wedding rings of Italy's patriotic women, to help finance his war against Ethiopia. France likewise "often piled the sacrificial altar high with silver offerings," and during the War Between the States, both the North and the South melted silverware to meet the demands of the conflict.

In medieval times, covers were locked on massive silver dishes to guard against poisoning. Prominent and wealthy nobles employed official tasters—invariably a trusted aide, who tasted all food before it left the kitchen to make sure it had not been tampered with in any way. This being done, the food was immediately put in a silver dish and the lid locked on, while the silver key was secreted on the person of the "taster." The dish when brought to the table was unlocked before the eyes of its owner, who, let us hope, was able to partake of his food with a feeling of reassurance and calm.

The Normans dressed their roasts with a cover of gold or silver foil for decorative reasons, and in the eighteenth century tea was put in handsomely carved silver caskets, which were locked and put in the parlor for safekeeping. During the Victorian era, silver scissors, thimble, tape-measure, pincushion and other trinkets, were strung on a silver chain attached to a silver brooch known as a chatelaine, and worn by unmarried women to indicate to eligible men their domestic qualities.

Of all silver tableware, the spoon is by far the oldest.

One writer claims that the spoon "is almost as old as man." In any event, it is, as one very witty Frenchman claimed, "certainly as old as soup." In primitive times, shell, wood, flint, and horn materials were used for the purpose of fashioning spoons. Later, the Egyptians formed more ornate types, some being made from ivory, and having elaborately carved handles. Silver and bronze spoons were first used by the Greeks and Romans. Wooden, tin, and horn spoons were in use in the Middle Ages, knobs frequently being on the end of the handles. During the Renaissance, artisans made spoons from brass, pewter, and silver.

C. Louise Avery, in her superb book, *Early American Silver,* says that spoons had been accepted as a desirable and necessary feature of table equipment several centuries before forks came to be so regarded. Enclycopedias tell us that the Greeks, Romans, and other ancient nationalities knew nothing of table forks, "though they had large forks for hay, and also iron forks for taking meat out of pots." The use of any species of forks for table purposes was unknown until the fifteenth century, and then they were only known in Italy.

Not until after the reign of the much-married Henry VIII, did English sovereigns know the luxury of forks; prior to that time both prince and pauper used their fingers! Early in the seventeenth century, an Englishman while visiting in Italy, noted with mingled interest and curiosity (as well, no doubt, as concealed amazement) the use of forks at the table, and on his return home proceeded to imitate the custom. As late as the middle of the seventeenth century, forks were used only by the highest classes in England. At this time their handles as a rule were made of ivory, and they had but two prongs. Similar ivory-handled knives were also made around this time, but in England they were not made in sets until early in the eighteenth century, while the general use of silver forks in Great Britain was even later.

A recent innovation known as the "spork," which was put on the market several years ago by an Edinburgh firm, combines the uses of both spoon and fork, as its name would indicate. The manufacturers claim that it is ideal for curries, minces, and the peripatetic green pea, and in general for all foods "difficult to handle."

At a Quarter Court held at James City, April 15, 1641, there was recorded the inventory of household furnishings reserved for the widow of Captain Adam Thoroughgood, of Lower Norfolk County. From the articles enumerated, one may form some idea of what was considered to be a "fit allowance" for furnishing the chamber of a gentlewoman of means, in the wilderness that was then Virginia. The lady was given: "One bed, with blankets, rug and the furniture thereunto belonging, two pair of sheets and pillow cases; one table with carpet; table cloth and napkins, *knives* and *forks;* one cupboard and cupboard clothes; six chairs, six stools, six cushions, six pictures hanging in the chamber, one pewter basin and ewer, one warming pan, one pair of andirons in the chimney, one pair of tongs, one fire shovel, one chair of wicker for a child."

The plate for the lady's cupboard was to contain: "one salt cellar, one bowl, one tankard, one wine cup, and one dozen spoons." (*Virginia Magazine of History and Biography,* Volume II, Pages 416-17.) In 1642, when the estate of Adam Thoroughgood was

divided, it included among other articles of silver,
"two dozen spoons and two small bowls" and the widow
"did claim them as a gift given her by her brothers
Sir John Thoroughgood, Knt., and Mr. Thomas
Thoroughgood, at her marriage with their brother,
Captain Thoroughgood." Mary Newton Stanard states
that this is doubtless the earliest reference to silver as
a wedding present in America.

As far removed from the world of fashion as Virginians were, the wealthier families in the Colony laid
great stress on the importance of their household furnishings being in the "latest mode." Thus, in 1655
Colonel Richard Lee while on a trip to London, took
with him some of his silver plate to have its "fashion
changed." There was a prevailing law in England
forbidding the export of silver, and as the Colonel
was about to embark for home his "trunk of plate"
was seized by customs officers at Gravesend, who released it only after Colonel Lee made affidavit that it
was all intended for his personal use; that it had been
brought from Virginia a year and a half before, and
that every piece was engraved with his coat-of-arms.

William Fitzhugh of Stafford County, founder of
one of the wealthiest and most distinguished families
in Virginia, possessed a large quantity of handsome
silver bearing his coat-of-arms. He invested heavily
in a variety of costly plate, expressing himself on the
subject as buying it not alone for the sake of enjoyment
and adornment, but because he considered it a sound
investment for his children.

In a letter to his London agents, Mr. John Cooper
and Mr. Nicholas Hayward, dated June 1, 1688, Fitzhugh calls their attention to a previous letter containing an order for some silver-ware, and adds to his pre-

vious list some additional pieces he desires, with the following comment: "Pray let it be plain and strong, being in these particulars following if my money will reach to it, but rather leave some out than bring me a penny in Debt." The latest order includes:

"One dozen Silver hafted knives, one dozen silver forks, one dozen silver spoons large and strong; one set castors, one three quart tankard, a pair silver candlesticks less than them sent last year by Mr Hayward but more substantial. One silver salvator plate, four silver porringers, two small ones; a small silver bason, one dozen silver plates, four silver dishes—two pretty large for a good joint of meat, and two of a smaller sort. If my money falls short let it be wanting in the dishes; if there be any remaining at the overplus, be what it will laid out in silver plates, and let it thus be marked WFS (presumably the S is for Senior, since he had a son, also William Fitzhugh) and coat of arms put upon all pieces that are proper, especially the dishes, plates, and tankards, that I have sent enclosed and blazoned in a letter to Mr Hayward. Pray let it be sent by the first conveniency and by bill loading, delivered at my landing." (*Virginia Magazine of History and Biography,* Volume II, pages 268-269.)

His will, which is recorded at Stafford Courthouse begins, "I, William Fitzhugh, of Stafford County, gentleman, now bound for England," and is dated April 9, 1700. In addition to vast tracts of land, slaves, etc., it disposes of fifty-eight pieces of massive silver, including a silver Monteith bowl and a silver chocolate pot, both of which he states "I brought out of England" (evidently at the time of his emigration to Virginia), as well as numerous tankards, great and small. (*Virginia Magazine of History and Biography,* Volume II, Page 276-278.)

The inventory of the personal estate of Henry Fitzhugh of "Eagle's Nest," grandson of the *émigré* William Fitzhugh, and father of William Fitzhugh III, of "Chatham," which was recorded in Stafford, March

2, 1742, shows a very large and valuable estate. In silver it lists "a silver-hilted cutlass and belt, a single-hilted small dress sword, a set of silver knee buckles, a silver watch, twelve silver spoons, twelve ivory knives, six teaspoons, tongs, a soup ladle, two pair of silver candlesticks, snuffers and pan, six silver plates, a silver teapot, engraved, a parcel of old silver (valued at £6. 15. 11½), new silver plate (valued at £11. 17. 9), six silver plates, one large two-handled silver cup, silver punch ladle, etc." (*Virginia Magazine of History and Biography,* Volume II, Page 278-279).

Edmund Berkeley of Middlesex County, member of the Council, who married Lucy, daughter of Lewis Burwell, was another wealthy colonist whose possessions showed the scope of his culture and intellect. Aside from a notable library, his inventory taken the eighteenth and nineteenth days of June, 1719, lists innumerable pieces of silver, including:

"One silver watch, one pair large silver buckles, one pair silver spurs, eight cases of knives, fifteen fforks, nine small ivory handle knives and fforks, one set crimson velvet holsters laced with silver, one silver ladle, one large salver, one silver tankard, one silver tea kettle, one silver teapot and lamp, two silver chafing dishes, three silver castors, one large caudle cup, ten tea spoons, one pair tea tongs, one strainer, one old silver porringer B(Burwell), six silver spoons marked L, three new silver spoons marked E. B., four salts with his cypher, sixteen silver spoons, forty four silver buttons, etc." (*William and Mary Quarterly,* Volume II, page 251.)

The late Lyon G. Tyler, editor of the above *Quarterly,* in an article on "Coats-of-Arms in Virginia," written in 1894, mentions having "seen the fine old silver of Warner Lewis, now in possession of the Selden family, of Gloucester County, exhibiting numerous quarterings—Lewis, Warner, Bowles, How-ell, and two coats not yet identified." And what was true of the silver of this family, was also true of many others in Virginia. On the tenth of April, 1739, Moore Fauntleroy of Richmond County, bequeathed to his son, Moore, "my silver tankard that has my coat-of-arms upon it."

It is interesting to note that the term "silver plate" so frequently used in early wills and inventories in Virginia, referred only to solid silver, which has always been so termed in England. Tankards, caudle cups, casters, Monteith bowls, porringers, canisters, beakers, salvers, standing salts or "great salts" all had important uses, and a brief description of each of them seems appropriate.

Francis Hill Bigelow, in his important work, *Historic Silver of the Colonies, and Its Makers,* says that "The tankard enjoyed great popularity as a drinking vessel in the beer drinking countries of Northern Europe during the sixteenth, seventeenth and eighteenth centuries." The earliest form of tankard he describes as globular, usually heavily embossed, while the shape was derived from pottery jugs so frequently mounted by Elizabethan silversmiths. In its usual form the tankard had a large, tapering body, a hinged lid with a thumb-piece to facilitate its raising, and a handle.

"A long cherished delusion," writes Mr. Bigelow, "is that the ends of most of the handles of the tankards after 1660 are fitted with 'whistles,' for the purpose of whistling for a further supply of liquor. But these are in reality 'blow-holes,' which insure equality between the internal and external pressure of the air, and, therefore, prevent any deformations of the metal which may be softened as the result of the changes of temperature occurring during the process of soldering."

The caudle cup resembled a small modern sugar bowl with handles. During the reign of Charles II it reached the peak of its popularity, when it was considered, next to the tankard, indispensable to every English household. Small caudle cups varied in size and degree of enrichment with the taste and wealth of their owners, and were intended to serve as domestic wine or beer cups, as well as for special beverages such as caudle, which was to ultimately give them their name. Caudle was a "warm drink made of wine or ale mixed with bread, sugar, spices, and sometimes eggs," and posset was a similar drink of "curdled milk mixed with spiced wine or ale, and very small pieces of bread or oaten cake." (Jackson.)

The caster was a cruet for condiments, and according to Bigelow, received its name from the act of "casting" salt or pepper from a receptacle, hence the pierced tops. Cruet frames of handsomely carved silver appeared in the eighteenth century. These usually held two glass cruets for vinegar and oil, two silver casters for Cayenne and Jamaica pepper, and one for either sugar or salt.

In the seventeenth century, Englishmen developed a fondness for a number of new beverages, including tea, coffee, chocolate, and punch, and the Virginians were not long in following suit. C. Louise Avery, in her book, *Early American Silver,* says that punch drinking became so popular in the late seventeenth and early eighteenth century, that large numbers of punch bowls were made in England during this time, with and without handles. In Virginia, Bumbo and Arrack became such popular drinks, that the *bon vivants* of the Colony thought nothing of paying goodly sums for recipes of these potent concoctions. Thus it was that William Randolph of "Tuckahoe" sold to his friend Peter Jefferson—father of the immortal Thomas—two hundred acres of land in Albemarle, for Henry Wetherburn's "biggest bowl of Arrack punch." Wetherburn was long the host of the celebrated Raleigh Tavern in Williamsburg, and his fame as a mixer of punch soon spread to the remote corners of Virginia.

The most costly and beautiful of old silver punch bowls was the "Monteith" which came into fashion before 1700. This especial bowl had a removable notched rim which held glasses, and came by its name from a "fantastical Scot called Monteigh" who, it seems, was wont to appear in a coat which had a similar notched border. Later on, Monteith bowls became less ornate, although certain silversmiths clung to elaborate designs. New England silversmiths made unusually fine bowls of this type, especially Paul Revere and John Coney of Boston (1655-1722).

A magnificent Monteith by Coney, corresponding to English Monteiths of the 1690-1705 period, and engraved with the arms of the Colman family of Boston, was sold at the American Art Association Anderson Galleries in April, 1937, for the staggering sum of *thirty thousand dollars!* The bowl had a boldly fluted body, a serrated rim, elaborately chased and further adorned with cast masks, while on either side a large drop handle emerged from lion masks. According to the magazine *Antiques,* no other American silver bowl approaching the sumptuousness of this Coney item is known, and when placed on the black-draped stand in front of the huge crowd gathered for this notable *vendue,* the great bowl shone "like a diadem of white fire."

Aside from William Fitzhugh's "Monteith" which he "brought out of England," several other notables in Virginia owned them as well. In 1769 the silver plate at "Westover" was valued at six hundred and sixty two pounds, and included "two large punch bowls." The complete list of silver, which is found in the *Virginia Magazine of History and Biography,* (Volume IX, Page 81-82,) gives some idea of the vast wealth of William Byrd, and his facilities for entertaining. The list includes:

"An epergne, a pitcher and stand, a bread basket, ten candlesticks, a snuffer stand, a large cup, two large punch bowls, two coffee pots, six cans, a sugar dish, a sugar basket, two sauce boats, eight salt cellars and spoons, two sets of castors, a cruet, a large waiter, two middle sized waiters, four small castors, a cream boat, four chaffing dishes, a tea kettle, a 'reine' two pudding dishes, a fish slice, a sucking bottle, a large sauce-pan, four ragout spoons, two large sauce spoons, three marrow spoons, seven dozen knives and six dozen and eleven forks, eleven old-fashioned table spoons, two dozen dessert spoons, three pair of tea tongs, two tea strainers, one mustard spoon, one dozen new teaspoons, eleven second-best teaspoons, seven old teaspoons, five children's spoons, a large camp spoon, two small camp spoons, a camp cup, a broad candlestick."

One can well visualize the splendor of "Westover" on occasions of "great dinners" and visits from notables. Small wonder that the Marquis de Chastellux, when he was a guest at "Westover" in 1782, should thus describe it in his *Travels:* "There are magnificent houses at every view, for the banks of the James River form the garden of Virginia. That of Mrs. Byrd surpasses them all in the magnificence of the buildings, the beauty of its situation, and the pleasures of society..."

The frequently mentioned porringer was a small

dish having straight sides and sometimes ears. Bigelow states that it is more than likely that by the beginning of the eighteenth century porringers were used in
the Colonies as sugar bowls, as were small bowls and
caudle cups in England, before the covered sugar bowl
came into vogue. Perhaps the Virginian liked his
porridge all the same. Perhaps too, he used his porringer for heating brandy and other liquors, as some
writers have suggested.

Canisters were metal boxes for holding tea, coffee,
or spices. Bigelow quotes Mr. Charles K. Jackson,
author of *History of English Plate,* for his definition
of the frequently mentioned quaint tea caddy of our
ancestors. Says Mr. Jackson: "Caddy (a corruption
of catty from *kati,* the Malay word for a pound) the
term applied to the small box, containing about one and
one-third pounds, in which tea was originally imported
from England, is the name in general use for the box
or can in which tea is kept for use." Not until early
in the eighteenth century were silver caddies in general use, and among the first Virginians to own one was
that lavish host and spender, Alexander Spotswood.

Salvers, which William Fitzhugh referred to as
"salvators" were trays, usually heavy, and of considerable capacity; beakers were large wide-mouthed cups
or goblets; and chafing dishes, or braziers, such as
William Byrd owned, usually consisted of a shallow
bowl with pierced and removable bottom plate, and a
shallow compartment beneath, which had pierced
sides. The brazier was supported by three small feet,
and a corresponding number of scroll brackets above
its rim served to hold the plate hot.

In her valuable book, *Early American Silver,* C.
Louise Avery states that in medieval times the standing

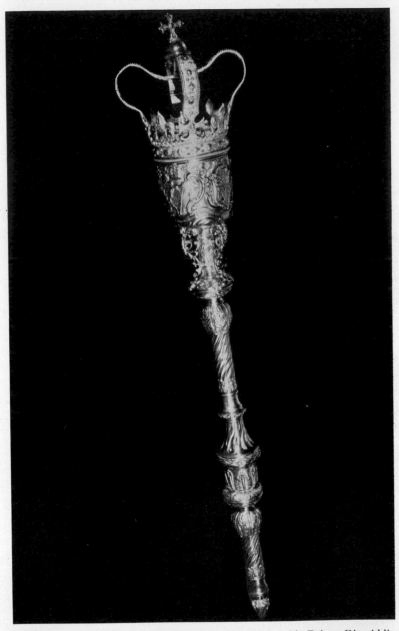

Historic Silver Mace of Norfolk, Gift of the Honorable Robert Dinwiddie, Lieutenant Governor of Virginia, to the Borough of Norfolk, 1753. Courtesy of the Norfolk Advertising Board.

salt, frequently referred to as the "great salt," occupied
a position of first importance at the banquet table, and
was placed next to the host and his honored guest. In
the course of time it lost much of its prestige, and at
the close of the seventeenth century passed out of use
altogether, being replaced by the trencher salt.
Trencher salts were used at the individual's place at
the table, and became increasingly popular during the
eighteenth century. Many English salt cellars in Virginia today are "tripods"—having a circular bowl with
a rounded bottom resting on three feet. The rim of
these is usually gadrooned. Gadrooning was one of the
most characteristic features of silver decoration from
the latter half of the fifteenth century until late in the
sixteenth, and was symbolic of hospitality.

Reposing in a great vault of a time-honored bank in
Norfolk, is the most historic piece of silver in Virginia
today—a Silver Mace, presented to the ancient
Borough of Norfolk in 1753 by the Honorable Robert
Dinwiddie, representative of the Crown, and Com-
mander-in-chief of the Dominion from 1751 to 1758.
With the exception of the Mace of the State of South
Carolina, Norfolk's is the only mace in America in-
herited from Colonial times.

How this historic mace, magnificently wrought from
pure silver, escaped the ravages of wars and the dese-
cration of subsequent raids; lay buried in a humble
garden in a neighboring town during the Revolution;
its whereabouts unknown up to the beginning of the
War Between the States—to be found years later
amongst a heap of rubbish in a state of sad neglect and
disrepair—is a story of sheer adventure.

But first, what did the mace symbolize, and for what
purpose was it intended? In medieval times, the mace

was used as a war-club, and was fashioned with a spiked metal head capable of crushing through the heaviest coat of armor. Thus, prior to the fifteenth or sixteenth centuries, maces were classed distinctly as weapons of war. Later they were used largely by military leaders, and in time came to be regarded solely as a symbol of authority.

The earliest ceremonial maces were intended to protect the person of the King, and were carried by sergeants-at-arms, a royal bodyguard established by Philip II of France. Eventually, the ceremonial use of maces became more popular, and as a consequence, the tendency to make of them elaborate accoutrements of office. Thus began the complete evolution of the mace. Warlike blades, knobs and spikes gradually disappeared, giving way to peaceful ornamentation. The enrichment process continued for years, precious metals and stones often being used in the creation of maces, and later engravings, heraldic devices, and other elaborate embellishments. By this time the mace had become a work of art rather than an instrument of cruelty and offense, but never lost its supremacy as a symbol of authority.

During the Restoration in England, many famous maces were designed for use, notably those of the Houses of Commons and Lords, and of the City of London, all of which are in use today. In the Jewel House of the Tower of London there are eight maces, once used by British Kings and Queens. Eighteenth century maces followed closely the lines of these maces. Norfolk's magnificent mace, attributed to Fuller White, famous jeweler and silversmith of London, bears the date 1753, and is said to be similar in form and detail-work to the mace used in the British House of Commons, which was the symbol of authority of the speaker, and was made in 1649.

Lieutenant-Governor Dinwiddie, with his wife and two daughters, arrived in Virginia on November 20, 1751. He remained for seven years, before being relieved of his post at his own request. His correspondence reveals a deep interest in the colonists, and a great degree of distress at their sufferings at the hands of the French and Indians. Certain it is that the Minutes of the Common Council of the Borough of Norfolk clearly indicate that those who composed it regarded Governor Dinwiddie's gift of the Mace as a token of peace and good-will, and an evidence of the affectionate esteem in which he held the Borough of Norfolk.

The Mace of Norfolk is made of pure silver—an exquisite and truly resplendant ornament of office. The actual figures and details of the Mace were described in a pamphlet published in Norfolk several years ago, and are as follows:

"The Mace weighs approximately one hundred and four ounces (six and one half pounds avoirdupois). There are nine sections which are screwed together to form the complete mace, which is forty-one inches long. The head is in three sections, and the staff is in six, bearing the letters 'F. W.' (initials of the maker); also the prescribed hallmark, a lion rampant, proof of the standard fitness of the silver.

"The staff is twenty-eight inches long, of irregular sizes, and averages two and one half inches in diameter. It is elaborately ornamented with leaves and scrolls. The bowl or head of the Mace is cylindrical, seven inches in length and five and a quarter inches in diameter. The top is slightly rounded, and on it, under the open work of the crown, are the Royal Arms of Great Britain in the reign of George II, the letters G and R, the usual mottoes, being between the lion and the unicorn.

"Around the largest part of the bowl are the emblems of England and Scotland, France and Ireland, each of these being in a separate panel, while in the fourth are the combined quarterings of Great Britain. Ornamentations consist of the Rose of England and the Thistle of Scotland growing on the same stem, and the Fleurs-de-lis of France and the Harp of Ireland. There is also a crown in each compartment over the emblems.

"The bowl is surmounted by an open crown, eight inches across, which is formed by four bands united at the top to support a globe, which in turn supports a standing cross. In a gracefully curving line around the base of the cylinder is the inscription in Roman letters: 'The Gift of the Honourable Robert Dinwiddie, Esquire, Lieutenant Governor of Virginia, to the Corporation of Norfolk, 1753'."

While the feeling of the colonists regarding all royal insignia naturally ran high at the time of the Revolution, the Mace was still venerated. Thus when Norfolk was burned by Lord Dunmore in 1776, the Mace and some public documents were among the few valuables to escape the conflagration, having been sent to Kempe's Landing (the present Kempville) where, according to tradition, the Mace lay buried in an obscure garden, even as Lord Stirling and his Royal Highland Regiment raided the town.

Truly it may be said of this venerable silver symbol of authority, that it has heard "the tumult and the shouting die"—has seen "the captains and the kings depart"—and withal, has witnessed the transition of Norfolk from a mere trading village to a port of world-wide commerce, and like the ancient borough itself, has passed through the baptism of fire, battle, and plunder.

At "Wilton," which has been restored by the Colonial Dames in Virginia, and is used as the Society's headquarters, one may see the exquisite silver tea caddy which belonged to Governor Alexander Spotswood, and is over two hundred years old. This lovely

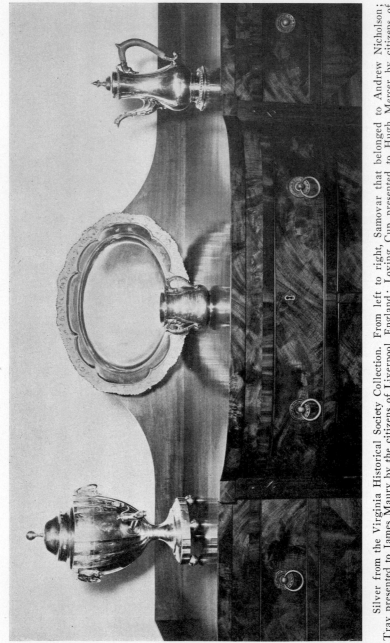

Silver from the Virginia Historical Society Collection. From left to right, Samovar that belonged to Andrew Nicholson; Tray presented to James Maury by the citizens of Liverpool, England; Loving Cup presented to Hugh Mercer by citizens of Princeton, N. J. and Coffee Pot, engraved with the Byrd crest, a falcon, and bearing the English hallmark and date-letter 1765, from "Westover." Courtesy of The Virginia Historical Society.

old piece is elaborately carved, and is engraved with the Spotswood arms and crest.

Several notable pieces of early Virginia silver are in the Virginia Historical Society, the most interesting being a silver coffee pot which belonged to the Byrds of "Westover." This beautiful old piece bears the English hallmark and date-letter of 1765, and is engraved with the Byrd crest, a falcon. The handle is of wood, and circling the top and the base is a beautifully executed gadroon border. Another handsome piece is a large silver samovar which belonged to Andrew Nicholson of Virginia, who married Judith Wormeley.

There are several later pieces of great beauty and interest. One of these is a handsome silver tray with a *repoussé* border, which belonged to James Maury, a kinsman of Virginia's illustrious son Matthew Fontaine Maury, "Pathfinder of the Seas." The tray was a gift from the citizens of Liverpool, England, in 1829, and is inscribed as follows:

"Presented by the Merchants and other Inhabitants of Liverpool, to James Maury, Esquire, late Consul of the United States of America in that town, as a mark of general respect on his removal from an office which he had honorably held for forty years."

One of the loveliest pieces of silver in the Society's collection is a loving cup presented to the great-grandson of General Hugh Mercer, beloved citizen of Fredericksburg and friend of Washington's, who served with distinction in the Continental Army, and fell mortally wounded at the Battle of Princeton fighting for the cause of liberty in the country of his adoption.

Hugh Mercer was the son of a Scottish clergyman of Aberdeenshire. After his graduation in medicine, he served as a surgeon in the army of the Pretender, Prince Charles Edward, but fled Scotland after the Battle of Culloden, and settled in Pennsylvania. Here he met George Washington during Braddock's expedition, and they became such staunch friends, that on Washington's suggestion and invitation, he moved to Fredericksburg.

In this old Virginia town, Mercer met and married the fair Isabella Gordon, and moved to her home "The Sentry Box." He had opened, and continued to operate an Apothecary Shop in Fredericksburg, which has been restored and is one of several monuments to his memory in the old town. Washington kept a desk in the back of Hugh Mercer's Apothecary Shop, where he worked whenever he came to Fredericksburg, and Mercer's old books carry many quaint notations of purchases made by Washington's mother, such as a "dose of bark" etc. When, in September 1775, four nearby counties organized for defense, Hugh Mercer was chosen Colonel of the "Minute Men." In the Revolution he was commissioned Colonel of the Third Virginia Regiment, and at the time of his tragic fall at the Battle of Princeton, had risen to the rank of a General.

The loving cup presented to his great-grandson is of generous size, lined with gold, and has three handles. The inscription reads:

"Presented January 3, 1897 by Mercer Engine Company, Number Three, Princeton, New Jersey, organized 1847, To Hugh Mercer, born August 4, 1893 at Richmond, Virginia, Great-grandson of General Hugh Mercer, the honored martyr of American Independence, who fell mortally wounded at the Battle of Princeton, January 3, 1777."

The Southern Colonies were not so opposed to

"worldly things" as their New England neighbors, and as is evidenced by the costly household furnishings, silver plate, and wearing apparel which wealthy Virginians ordered from London, shared none of the Puritanical sentiments such as John Adams expressed in a letter to his wife, when he wrote: "If I had power I would forever banish from America all gold, silver, silk, velvet, and lace."

Yet, strangely enough, it was New England that gave to this country her earliest silversmiths, and superb craftsmen they turned out to be. Not least among them was a young man whose daring ride in the cause of American freedom has been immortalized in the thrilling lines of Longfellow's *Midnight Ride of Paul Revere*.

Countless Museums throughout the country, as well as private collectors, own valuable examples of Paul Revere's beautiful work. His teapots, especially, are considered silver classics, and have been imitated by later silversmiths in many parts of the country. In the Museum of Fine Arts, Boston, there is a most beautiful silver tea service which was made by Paul Revere (1735-1818) and presented to Edmund Hartt of Boston, along with a silver tankard and jeweled watch.

Edmund Hartt was that sterling New England figure who built the frigate *Boston* and the still more famous *Constitution*. He was an original trustee of the Mechanic Charitable Association, and lived on quaint Ship Street in Boston, opposite his shipyard, which today is known as "Constitution Wharf."

The tea service, which consists of an oval pot and tray, a cream pitcher on a square plinth base, and an urn-shaped sugar bowl with top, is inscribed:

"To Edmund Hartt Constructor of the Frigate Boston. Presented by a number of his fellow citizens as a Memorial of their sense of his Ability Zeal and Fidelity in the Completion of that Ornament of the American Navy. 1799."

The identical inscription is engraved on a silver tankard which was presented to Edmund Hartt at the same time as the tea service; a treasured and beautiful old piece now owned by William H. Hartt of Portsmouth, Virginia, a direct descendant of Edmund Hartt. All of the Hartts have been bred in the tradition of the American Navy, and the Paul Revere tankard, now one of many treasured heirlooms in the Hartt home on Court Street, in Portsmouth, has passed from father to son for five generations.

The memory of a delightful afternoon spent in this hospitable and cultured home is still fresh in my mind; a chill February afternoon without, yet warm and bright within from a glowing fire that sent its blue and crimson flames darting up the chimney. Seated close by the cheerful fire, the gracious *chatelaine* of the Hartt household—Mrs. William H. Hartt, told me the history of the Hartt family. Nearby a tempting tea table, resplendant with old silver and exquisite china, and laden with all manner of delicacies, beckoned us.

I was handed the Paul Revere tankard that I might see the famous silversmith's mark, and read the interesting Hartt inscriptions that fill an entire side of this wonderful piece of old silver. Since I was interested in old, historic things, I was also shown a large, round, wax seal bearing Queen Anne's arms, which originally was attached to a land grant issued by the Queen to one of Mrs. Hartt's ancestors in Princess Anne County, Virginia, over two hundred years

Silver Ale Tankard made by the famous patriot and silversmith, Paul Revere. Presented in 1799 to Edmund Hartt, builder of the frigates *Constitution* and *Boston,* by a number of citizens of Boston. This handsome piece of silver has been handed down through five generations of the Hartt family, whose names are engraved on the tankard, and is today owned by William H. Hartt, of Portsmouth, Virginia.

ago; also a letter written by Stephen Decatur to a "Virginia Hartt" when the latter was commander of the Portsmouth Navy Yard. There was much, so much, to remind one of the romantic and historic past, in this gracious and hospitable home.

Not all fine silver that adorns Virginia homes today, came from England, or New England. The South had at least one notable firm whose beautiful creations in silverware have gained for it an international reputation. To Samuel Kirk and Son of Baltimore, belongs the distinction of being the oldest makers of silverware in the United States, according to a little booklet entitled, *The Story of the House of Kirk,* in which the history of this famous firm is given as follows:

"In 1815 Samuel Kirk, of Doylestown, Pennsylvania, a silversmith of Quaker ancestry, came to Baltimore. He opened a small shop on Market Street, afterwards Baltimore Street, on which street, and not far from the original location, the firm continued in business until 1925 when they moved to their present location at Charles and Franklin Streets. The business has descended from father to son for three generations, with the fourth generation as an officer of the present company."

Through both parents Samuel Kirk descended from English silversmiths. His father traced his ancestry to John Kirk, the son (and second of the name) of Godfrey Kirk, of Chesterfield Monthly Meeting, England. Through his mother, Grace (Child) Kirk, Samuel Kirk sprang from a long line of English goldsmiths, who were also bankers, tracing back to Sir Francis Child, Lord Mayor of London in 1669, who was also a practical goldsmith and founder of the Child Banking House.

Samuel Kirk, founder of the House of Kirk in Baltimore, purchased in August, 1815, of F. Lucas, Jr., his neighbor, an account book which had three unruled fly leaves. "At the top of the first page that was ruled for keeping accounts, he made his first entry under the date of August second or fifth (day not clear), 1815." And thus dawned the beginning of one of this country's foremost firms of silversmiths.

In the notable collection of early Kirk silver are several historic and beautiful objects wrought from crude silver by the skilled hands of Kirk craftsmen. Among them are two beautifully fluted goblets, with a delicately carved rim and base, known as the "La-Fayette Goblets." These were ordered by the celebrated Frenchman during his visit to Baltimore in 1824, and were presented by him to David Williamson, a prominent resident of Baltimore, at whose estate "Lexington," LaFayette had been entertained. The goblets are appropriately inscribed.

Another prized trophy made by the House of Kirk is the Silver Spade, made for the City of Baltimore, and used by Ferdinand Foch, Grand Marshal of France and Commander-in-Chief of the Allied Armies during the World War, in breaking ground for the War Memorial Building, during the Marshal's visit to Baltimore on November 22, 1921.

When the citizens of Maryland wished to honor those in command of a great battleship named for their State, they had the House of Kirk make a complete dinner service and plateau, which they presented to the Cruiser *Maryland*. This magnificent silver service is of exceptional beauty and historical interest, for each piece is embellished throughout by scenes depicting the historical places and events of the counties and cities of Maryland, and is entirely hand-carved. The *pièce de résistance* of the complete service is the great center-piece, or plateau which is surmounted by two spread eagles, with the coat-of-arms of the State of Maryland and historical scenes carved in bold relief.

Virginia has ever honored her distinguished sons by presenting them with swords, in recognition of achievements in their chosen field. While in Richmond during the summer of 1930, Rear Admiral Richard Evelyn Byrd was presented with a magnificent silver sword by the citizens of Virginia as a token of their pride in his aerial explorations. On the blade is etched the Admiral's name and a record of his flights to France, to the North Pole, and over the Antarctic Continent. On the silver scabbard his ships are shown pushing through the ice floes, and his plane, the *Floyd Bennett,* is portrayed in flight over the South Pole.

Some day, these magnificent tributes in silver will take their places beside other historical pieces in Museums, and new and brighter links will be added to the already dazzling chain that forms the saga of silver. For like a glistening thread, interwoven in the fabric of human experience, silver has always touched the hand of man.

From a silver chalice and paten, a band of storm-tossed English settlers took their first communion, "beneath an olde saile" that was their first church at Jamestown, on a spring day in 1607. And on a summer day in the year 1776, a band of American patriots, gathered in convention at Philadelphia, dipped their pens in a silver inkstand—still preserved at Independence Hall —and affixed their signatures to a document destined to go down in history as one of the greatest declarations of man—The Declaration of Independence.

Old China

"*There's a joy without canker or cark,*
There's a pleasure eternally new,
'T is to gloat on the glaze and the mark
Of china that's ancient and blue."

—ANDREW LANG.

CHAPTER XII
Old China

HERE are dreams to be dreamed, and fancies to be woven around a piece of old china. And oftimes memories to be evoked! Romance and mystery cling to an old cup, plate, or teapot, whose maker and past owners are veiled in uncertainty; and if the piece be genuine Wedgewood, Lowestoft, Spode, or Bristol, so much the better, for the beautiful tea sets and punch bowls, vases and pitchers, plates and platters, carrying the irrefutable marks of the great potters and factories of almost two centuries ago, have about them a charm and fantasy—beauty and loveliness—that can never be put into words.

The smell of the sea clings to old Lowestoft; green tea and ginger, sandalwood and spices, to old blue Canton and Willow-ware; the pleasant aroma of savory foods to old Spode. About a cracked and faded India china punch bowl is the rich fragrance of brandy and curaçao, cloves and cinnamon, lemon and nutmeg, madeira and malaga, rum and mandarin oranges, and all of the other wines and rich ingredients that went into Colonial punch.

Even a faded, cracked, and unidentified cup and saucer holds a certain fascination for the lover of old china. With the gift of imagination, one can open the door which leads to places and people belonging to our imperishable past, and say with all earnestness, "Perhaps Benjamin Franklin or George Washington sipped tea or coffee from this very cup; perhaps it once belonged to a lovely old set, brought out of England or China; perhaps it was the cherished possession of a beauty-loving woman who helped to carve a nation out of a wilderness; perhaps it once lay buried in some old-fashioned garden, while a battle raged and the enemy was pillaging everything in sight." There are a hundred fancies one can weave around a homely old cup and saucer!

The very name of "Wedgewood" at once suggests a beauty and elegance seldom found in other china. "Lovely as are the porcelains of Chelsea, Derby, Bow, Plymouth, and Worcester," writes N. Hudson Moore in *The Collector's Manual,* "as mere artistic productions, they yield the palm to the work of one man. None of these porcelains mentioned were the product of a single mind; they were the result of experiments by many.

"On the other hand, the great Wedgewood invented most of his own products, formed the first specimens with his own capable hands, and directed and controlled those vast works which were the growth of his own genius. He disputes with Palissy for the position of 'greatest potter.' "

Josiah Wedgewood was born in Burslem, Staffordshire, England, in 1730. Like many another genius, he was the son of poor parents; received little education, and at the age of eleven went to work in his brother's factory. An incurable lameness forced him to give up the potter's wheel, and he removed for a time to Stoke, where he entered into partnership with persons in his own trade. Here his talent for ornamental pottery was first displayed. In 1759 he returned to Burslem and set up a small manufactory of his own. As his business improved, he turned his attention to white stone-ware and to the cream-colored ware for which he became famous.

Wedgewood's earliest wares were the tortoise-shell and highly colored green-glaze. These were followed by the perfected cream-colored "Queen's Ware" which name he gave to this especial kind of pottery in honor of Queen Charlotte, who it is said, visited his factory and admired his works. Wedgewood's blue-and-white jasper wares and balsates, with their exquisite cameo medallions, are among his most beautiful creations.

Alice Morse Earle, in her superb book *China Collecting in America,* says that a few of Wedgewood's cameo medallions found their way to America, and it is interesting to know that the great potter himself, sent as a gift to Thomas Jefferson three of his most exquisite medallions—two oval and one oblong in shape. These were in blue and white jasper, with mythological designs. The largest, says Mrs. Earle, was twelve inches long and six inches wide, and bore the lovely design of Cupid and Psyche with troops of attending loves. Jefferson had them set in the front of the great mantel in the dining room at "Monticello," but an unkind fate awaited them there. One of the medallions is said to have fallen to the floor and shattered to bits, while the other two were dislodged and stolen. Today, three similar Wedgewood medallions are inserted in the mantel in the dinning room at "Monticello," but these were placed there after Jefferson's occupancy.

One of the first things Wedgewood set out to do, after he inherited a fortune of *one hundred dollars* at the age of twenty one, was to make handles for knives and forks in mottled pottery, agate, and tortoise shell ware, which he supplied to the hardware manufacturers of Birmingham and Sheffield. Sets of antique knives and forks with handles by Wedgewood, are as difficult to find today as the proverbial needle in a haystack. They were considered "elegant additions" to one's dining room, where they were displayed in their oftimes handsome wooden cases, and as can be imagined, were costly possessions.

In Portsmouth, Virginia, such a set of knives and forks are among the prized heirlooms belonging to one of the town's most prominent residents. The original set, numbering eighteen knives and forks with beautiful handles of mottled blue and white china, repose today in the tall velvet lined polished wooden box in which they were delivered to their owner. As is frequently the case, not a single mark of identification can be found on any of the pieces, so it is impossible to prove that the handles are the product of the great Wedgewood, but several authorities on ceramics who have examined carefully each of the pieces, attribute them to the master potter.

These priceless antiques originally belonged to John Montgomery, of Londonderry, Ireland, who with his nephew Charles Montgomery, came to America early in the eighteenth century. The elder Montgomery settled in Carlisle, Pennsylvania, where he became a leading citizen and patriot of town and State. His nephew settled in Virginia, and today, many of their descendants bearing the name of Montgomery as well as of Diemer, Morrison, Edmiston, Harris, Davidson, and Somerville, are scattered throughout the United States.

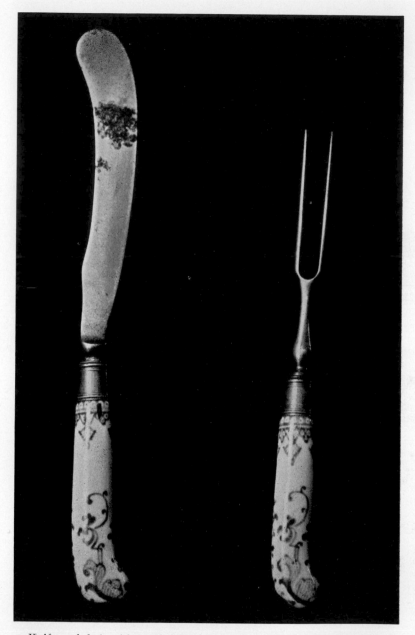

Knife and fork with mottled blue and white china handles attributed to Wedgewood. These rare old pieces belong to a set of eighteen pieces, originally owned by John Montgomery, of Carlisle, Pennsylvania, and now owned by a descendant living in Portsmouth, Virginia.

In a fascinating old journal covering many pages, and written in flowing script three quarters of a century ago by a granddaughter of the *émigré* John Montgomery, one meets the great and near-great of Colonial America. For "Happy Retreat," the Montgomery home in Carlisle, was the rendezvous of many notable men.

Through the pages of this personal, yet historic journal, one has intimate glimpses of Benjamin Franklin, who sipped coffee (when patriotism forbade tea!) with John Montgomery and his wife; of Major André, who, while a prisoner on parole in Carlisle, spent much of his time in this hospitable house; of George Washington, a warm friend of the family and a frequent guest at "Happy Retreat;" of the celebrated Scotch divine, Dr. Charles Nesbit, first president of Dickinson College, who spent his early weeks in Carlisle in the Montgomery home, and of Robert Davidson, D. D. who succeeded Dr. Nesbit; of Colonel James Morrison and Colonel Edmiston of the Continental Army, who married daughters of John Montgomery; of Albert Gallatin, an intimate friend, who while American Minister to France, purchased in Paris the brocaded satin cushions which long adorned the parlor at "Happy Retreat;" of LaFayette who was "an honored guest" in the Montgomery home during his visit to the United States, and who "always remained a fast friend" —and many, many others.

About these old knives and forks rests a nimbus of chronicle and romance. Few treasured possessions in American homes today have known such intimate contact with great men as these priceless old pieces, with their beautiful blue and white china handles, gently curving rounded steel blades, and quaint two prongs.

What of Lowestoft? Surely no one make of fine china was ever so veiled in mystery, or the subject of such prolonged controversy as this delicate and lovely bluish-white pottery, with its exquisite designs of birds and flowers and coats-of-arms. *Oriental* or *English?* This has been the burning question for years. Mrs. Earle quotes numerous authorities on old Lowestoft in her book, *China Collecting in America,* but it was written almost half a century ago. Mrs. Moore, in her *Manual,* which is a later book, has this to say of Lowestoft:

"For over half a century such pitchers" (Helmet Pitchers) "and other china of similar paste and decoration have gone under the name of 'Lowestoft,' and have been the delight and pride of hundreds of collectors. It is only within the last few months that it has been definitely decided that no such ware was either made or decorated in England, but that it is entirely of Oriental manufacture. At the little English town of Lowestoft have been unearthed fragments both of moulds and bits of pottery, which go to prove that the ceramic products of that town were no different from what was made in other English towns at the same period."

"All this pot and potter" I leave to the authorities on ceramics; I am content to love old china for its own sake; for the romance and history and tradition woven around it; for its bold or fragile beauty, and the insight into human nature it affords me.

The pieces of Lowestoft most frequently seen in America are parts of tea services, punch bowls, pitchers, coffee pots, mugs, and occasionally vases. The latter are usually found in two shapes: cylindrical with suddenly flaring top, or a vase with small base that bulges sharply in the center, and as suddenly contracts to a small neck. Often the border is of clear cobalt blue, adorned with gold stars or a "meander" pattern in gold.

"These vases" writes Mrs. Earle, "in sets or garnitures of three or five pieces, graced the mantel of many a 'parlour' a century ago, and were frequetly decorated with initials or coats-of-arms." She uses as one of her illustrations, one of the beautifully shaped and decorated vases with blue, brown, and gold decoration, given by LaFayette to Cadwallader Jones, of Petersburg, Virginia. These vases have the impressed basketwork design encircled in blue and gold, and are almost identical to the three shown in the accompanying illustration, which belong to Miss Eliza Roy of Fredericksburg.

Here are examples of "old Lowestoft" at its loveliest; the famous bluish-white background, decorated with bands of cobalt blue and gold stars, and in the wide blue circle framing delicate baskets of flowers, a trailing design of gold leaves. Each vase has a removable top, and on each top rests a tiny animal—weird looking little creatures, one of which appears to be a ram, another a lizard, and the other a dog.

These old vases have a history all their own. They were brought from China in 1798 by young William Thornton of Fredericksburg, to his mother Mrs. Robert Wellford, the former "Widow Thornton." The proud mother took her newest treasures and placed them on the parlor mantel of her home, and there they have remained for almost a century and a half, with the exception of five years, when they lay buried in the backyard of the Wellford House during the raging battles of the War Between the States. Their present owner, Miss Eliza Roy of Fredericksburg, is the daughter of Mary Catherine Wellford and James H. Roy, and inherited the vases from her mother.

It is a recognized fact that Lowestoft was the most desirable and fashionable china in early Federal times, both in the North and the South. Mrs. Earle reminds us that "Such was the dinner-service of the Carrolls of Carrollton, with bands of rich brown and gold and a pretty letter C. Such was the family china of William Morris; of John Rutledge, with the initials J. R. and the shield and eagle; and the tea-service of John Dickinson, with blue and gold bands and his initials."

That George Washington was a lavish spender has been amply shown by the many orders for costly wearing apparel he sent to England, as well as his heavy purchases of fine furniture at the *vendue* held at "Belvoir." But not until after the close of the Revolutionary War do we find him manifesting an interest in fine china. Attractive advertisements in Maryland and Virginia newspapers doubtless had much to do with this, although as Ada Walker Camehl points out in the *Blue-China Book,* "The years of Washington's life spanned the periods between pewter and porcelain as articles of table use in America, the close of the War of the Revolution rather definitely marking the transition."

It is well known that Washington owned and used pewter, many of his pewter plates and dishes being engraved with his initials or crest. But after peace had been restored to a war-racked country, our first President found leisure to indulge in—shall we say hobbies—and develope new interests, one of which most certainly was "china collecting." Appealing indeed were the newspaper advertisements of Washington's day, announcing the arrival of vessels from the

Orient, and listing their cargoes of china, teas, and rich stuffs, to be sold at "Public Vendue."

Thus do we find Washington writing from "Mount Vernon" on August 17, 1785, with characteristic prudence and emphasis on economy, to Colonel Tench Tilghman, to make certain purchases for him of goods just imported in the ship *Pallas,* "if great bargains are to be had," and specifying certain articles of china he desired, "with the badge of the Society of the Cincinnati if to be had."

The announcement in the *Baltimore Advertiser* of the arrival of the *Pallas,* and the sale of her cargo which was to follow, read thus:

"On Tuesday evening last arrived here, directly from China, the ship *Pallas* commanded by its owner Capt. O'Donnell. She has on board a most valuable Cargo consisting of an extensive Variety of Teas, China, Silks, Satins, Nankeens, &c., &c. We are extremely happy to find the Commercial Reputation of this Town so far increased as to attract the attention of Gentlemen who are engaged in carrying on this distant but beneficial Trade. It is no unpleasing Sight to see the Crew of his Ship, Chinese, Malays, Japanese and Moors with a few Europeans, all habited according to the different Countries to which they belong, and employed together as Brethren; it is thus Commerce binds and unites all the Nations of the Globe with a golden Chain.

"To be sold at Public Vendue at Baltimore on the first of October next (1785) in Lots The Following Goods Just Imported in the Ship *Pallas,* direct from China: Hyson Teas, of the first Quality in Quarter-Chests and Canisters of about 2¼ lb each; Hyson Tea of the second sort in Chests; Singlo, Confee, Hyson-Skin, and Gunpowder Teas of the first Quality in Chests; and a large Quantity of excellent Bohea Tea; Table-Sets of the best Nankin blue and white Stone China; white stone and painted China of the second Quality in Sets; Dishes of blue and white Stone China 5 and 3 in a Set; Stone China flat and Soup Plates; Breakfast Cups and Saucers of the best blue and white Stone China in Sets; Evening blue and white Stone China Cups and Saucers; Ditto painted; *Ditto with the Arms of the Order of Cincinnati;* Bowls—best blue and white Stone China in Sets; blue and white Stone China Pint Sneakers; Mugs—best Stone China in Sets; small Tureens with Covers; Wash-Hand Guglets and Basons.

"Brown Nankeen of the first and second Quality; plain, flowered and spotted Lustrings of all Colours; Satins, the Greatest Part Black; Peelongs of different Colours, in whole and half Pieces; Sarsnet of different Colours; embroidered Waistcoat Pieces of Silks and Satins; Silk Handkerchiefs, very fine, and 20 in a piece; spotted and flowered Velvets; painted Gauzes; Bengal Piece-Goods and Muslins, plain flowered and corded; Silk Unbrellas of all Sizes; elegant Paper-Hangings; japanned Tea-Chests; Ditto Fish and Counter Boxes; Sago; Cinnamon and Cinnamon Fowers; Rhubarb; Opium; Gamboge; Borax; very old Battavia Arrack in Leagures; with Sundry other Articles; the enumeration of which would take up too much Room in a Public Paper."

The invoice of goods to be purchased by Tench Tilghman for General Washington included

"a sett of the best Nankin Table China; Ditto best Evening Cups & Saucers; a sett of *large* blue and white China with the badge of the Society of the Cincinnati if to be had; Dishes, say half a dozen more or less; one Doz. *small* bowls blue & white with the badge of the Society of the Cincinnati if to be had; six Wash hand Guglets & Basons with the badge of the Society of the Cincinnati if to be had; six Large Mugs or three mugs & three jugs; a Quarter Chest best Hyson Tea; a Leagure of Battavia Arrack if a Leagure is not large,"

and several items in silks and nankeens.

By comparing General Washington's order with the goods advertised in the cargo of that treasure-laden ship *Pallas,* it will be seen that Washington obtained many of the items he desired, particularly his set of best Nankin table china, best evening cups and saucers with the badge of the Society of the Cincinnati, mugs, wash-hand guglets and basons, the chest of best Hyson tea, and leagure of Battavia Arrack. The quaint obsolete names of the china articles enumerated in the

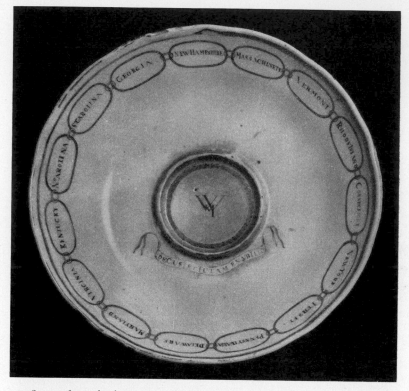

Saucer from the famous set of "States China" given to Martha Washington by "Mr. Van Braam" and so designated in her will. Courtesy of the Virginia Historical Society.

Lowestoft Vases brought from China in 1798 by William Thornton of Fredericksburg, to his mother, Mrs. Robert Wellford (the "Widow Thornton"). Owned by Miss Eliza Roy of Fredericksburg, a descendant.

ship's cargo, and the General's order, excite one's curiosity today. What, for instance, was a "guglet" and a "sneaker"? The former was a little jug, possibly blue or brown or white, and a sneaker ("good old Addisonian English") was originally a small-sized drinking mug or beaker. It will be noted that Washington boldly ordered *mugs* instead.

The personal possessions of famous people have always aroused interest. Mary, the mother of Washington, owned several sets of china which she designated in her will as "my blue and white tea china" and "my red and white tea china." The blue set she bequeathed to her grandson Felding Lewis, and the red set to her granddaughter, Bettie Carter.

Martha Washington possessed a quantity of valuable china, including a handsome set presented to her by Count de Custine in 1792. This set had come from his own factory at Niederweiler, near Pfalzburg, in Lorraine, and was presented by the Count in behalf of himself and ten other officers then stationed at Colchester. It was delivered to "Mount Vernon" the day before the officers were to dine there, and was evidently sent as a token of esteem and appreciation of the hospitality the General and his Lady had so often accorded the officers of the regiment.

An even more interesting set, and one that has long claimed the attention of antiquarians, is known as the Martha Washington "States China" which she refers to in her will as "the set given me by Mr. Van Braam." It is known that one Captain Van Braam, a native of the Netherlands, was a friend of Washington's youth, and taught the future President the art of fencing, so the natural supposition for years has been that he presented the set to Mrs. Washington. Recent disclosures however, point to another Van Braam as the donor—a wealthy merchant and ship owner who had the set made in China, and there adorned with Martha Washington's initials and the names of fifteen American States, and brought by him to America in the hold of his own ship.

Several pieces of this set are in the National Museum in Washington, the Metropolitan Museum, and *one saucer* is in the Virginia Historical Society, but Ada Walker Camehl states "the White House collection is without a specimen."

There are believed to have been between forty and fifty pieces in the original set, which doubtless was for a complete dinner service, for Lossing describes cups and tureens, plates and saucers, on which were "painted in delicate colors a chain of thirteen large and thirteen small elliptical links" with the name of one of the original thirteen States in each large link. The number of links and States he mentions is erroneous; there are *fifteen* long and fifteen short links instead of thirteen, Kentucky and Vermont having at that time (1796) been added to the thirteen original States.

Around the edge of the saucer in the Virginia Historical Society, is a faintly discernible border of blue and gold. Beneath this, encircling the upper part of the saucer is the chain of fifteen long and fifteen short links painted in delicate colors. Within each of the large links is the name of one of the following states: New York, New Jersey, Pennsylvania, Delaware, Maryland, Virginia, North Carolina, South Carolina, Georgia, Kentucky, New Hampshire, Vermont, Connecticut, Massachusetts, and Rhode Island. In the exact center of the saucer is the interlaced monogram of Martha Washington—M. W. painted in dark blue against a background of jade green encircled with gold. Beneath this, on a delicately painted ribbon scroll, is inscribed in small letters the motto—*"Decus et tutam ab illo."*

Despite the divergent opinions so often expressed regarding the origin of this celebrated set, and its donor, (LaFayette has even been credited with having presented it to Mrs. Washington, as well as a group of French officers, and the card accompanying the saucer in the Virginia Historical Society reads, "From the set of porcelain presented to Mrs. Washington by the Society of the Cincinnati") no china in American collections is more highly prized than the surviving pieces of this famous set. Proud indeed should Virginians be that at least one undamaged piece is preserved in their Historical Society.

The most favored of all china in the eyes of the early Virginia or Massachusetts housewife, was the "old blue Canton ware," and many a treasured set filled Fredericksburg and Salem cupboards. Mary Washington's blue and white china was of this make, and there were others in Virginia, like Zaccheus Collins, who in 1750 imported from China a beautiful fifty-piece set of "Blue Canton" for his daughter Elizabeth, wife of Richard Bland Lee, who bought heavily of this lovely old ware.

In the Virginia Historical Society, one may see the bold blue pieces belonging to this almost two centuries old set that Zaccheus Collins ordered from Canton for his daughter. Time has not dimmed their lustre or faded their colorful blue designs. Here are shining piles of plates in three sizes, soup bowls and saucers, great platters as broad as they are long, covered vegetable dishes and gravy boats, large round bowls of un-

usual depth, covered cookie and ginger jars, and long
deep tureens whose covers have pineapple knobs. To
look at this fascinating old set, is to appreciate to the
full the words of Mrs. Earle: "You can buy blue
Canton today, but it is not old blue Canton."

The set has passed through many hands in this dis-
tinguished family; hands we may be sure that handled
each piece with pride and affection. From Elizabeth
Collins Lee the set passed to Ann Matilda Lee, wife
of Dr. Bailey Washington, then to their daughter,
Elizabeth Lee Washington. It next passed to a niece,
Ann Washington Ready; to her sister, Alice Matilda
Ready, and lastly to their cousins, Elizabeth Collins
Lee and J. Collins Lee, who in turn presented it to the
Virginia Historical Society in memory of Richard
Bland Lee and Elizabeth Collins Lee.

In Virginia, china tea sets were much more in evidence than silver ones, and since the earliest tea pots
used in England were of Oriental porcelain and
pottery, the same may be said of those used in Virginia. When William Byrd visited the Spotswoods
at their Germanna "palace" it will be remembered
that a brace of tame deer caused quite a stir of excite-
ment in that poised household, when one, spying his
own figure in the pier glass, sprang over the tea table
that stood under it, making "a terrible fracas among
the china," as Colonel Byrd describes it.

When tea was no longer a popular beverage in the
colonies, and the Virginia patriots drank coffee instead,
doubtless many an old teapot was replaced by one intended to hold the richer drink. Fithian entered in
his diary from "Nomini Hall" the following amusing incident, which speaks eloquently for the staunch
patriotism of "Councilor" Carter:

"Something very merry happened in our palace this Evening. Mrs. Carter made a dish of Tea! At Coffee she sent me a dish—and I and the Colonel both ignorant. He smelt, sipt, look'd! At last with great gravity he asks, 'What's this?'. 'Do you ask Sir?'. 'Poh!' and out he throws it, splash, a sacrifice to Vulcan."

John Harrower, the tutor of Colonel Daingerfield's children at "Belvedere" on the Rappahannock, though not so learned as his contemporary at "Nomini Hall," also kept a sprightly diary of "the doings" of the Daingerfields, and the happenings at "Belvedere."

Of his bountiful board, he writes:

"Our victualls are all dressed in the English taste. We have for breakfast either coffee or Jaculate and warm Loafe bread of the best floar. We have also at table warm loaf bread of Indian corn, which is extremely good, but we use the floar bread always at breakfast. For Dinner smoack'd bacon, or what we call pork ham, is a standing dish either warm or cold. When warm we have greens with it, and when cold we have sparrow grass. We have also either warm roast pig, lamb, Ducks or chickens, green peas or anything else they fancy. As for Tea, it is not drunk by any in this Government since July 1, nor will they buy two shillings worth of any kind of East India goods, which is owing to the differences at present betwixt the Parliament of Great Britain and the North Americans about laying a tax on tea."

An interesting and naive recital of pre-Revolutionary life and sentiment in Virginia.

The sturdy settlers in the Valley had little or no china. Wooden trenchers served them long and well, and when delft first made its appearance, they looked askance at this glazed blue earthenware that brightened their dull looking tables. Kercheval, in his *History of the Valley of Virginia,* says:

"In our whole display of furniture, the delf, china, and silver were unknown. It did not then, as now, require contributions from the four corners of the globe to furnish the breakfast table . . ."

When pieces of blue delft found their way into the

homes of these staunch settlers, their reaction was one
of disdain, if we may accept Kercheval's statement.
He writes:

"The introduction of delf ware was considered by many of the
backwoods people as a culpable innovation. It was too easily broken,
and the plates of that ware dulled their scalping knives . . . tea ware
was too small for men, but might do for women and children."

Without realizing the fact, these pioneers were shar-
ing the feeling of Addison, who in 1713 wrote, "China
vessels are playthings for women of all ages."

Among the interesting pieces of china in the Valentine Museum collection are a small cup and saucer
that once belonged to John Wickham of Richmond.
According to tradition, these two dainty pieces are part
of a set that was purchased for the entertainment of
Thomas Moore, the young Irish poet, when he visited
Virginia in 1804. If this be true, the set was indeed
of a most unusual design, for the cup and saucer, which
are of white porcelain, are dotted with what seem to
be hundreds of tiny gold stars.

Toom Moore must have found his host and hostess
charming people. John Wickham was a brilliant
lawyer and a gentleman of exquisite manners, and was
afterwards described by his young Irish friend as "fit
to adorn any court." Mrs. Wickham was conspicuous
in Richmond society for her beauty and personal accomplishments, and her cameoesque features and delicate coloring are said to have been unsurpassed by any
woman of her day in Virginia.

If the tiny gold stars on the fragile cup and saucer
could but speak, what a fascinating recital they would
give of the talk that passed between John Wickham—
famous for his sarcasm and wit—and his talented young
Irish guest!

Fifty-piece Dessert Service made by the Brothers Honoré, of Paris, for Andrew Stevenson of Richmond, Minister to England. Each of the pieces is painted individually. The large urns were referred to in the Stevenson inventory as "ice pails with cones to match." This set was purchased by Mann S. Valentine. Courtesy of the Valentine Museum.

The most impressive and unusual china in the Valentine Museum collection is the beautiful fifty piece dessert service made to order for Andrew Stevenson of Richmond, who was Minister to England from 1829 to 1831. The manufacturers were the Brothers Honoré of Paris, and the decoration of each piece is individual. The service is of hard paste porcelain, each piece having a deep maroon border with a narrow gilt edge, while in the center is an individual hand-painted design, either of fruits or flowers. There are three dozen plates, six compotes, two cake stands, two sauce boats, two fruit baskets, and two very unusual large urns, described in the Stevenson inventory as "Ice pails with cones to match." Among the fruits painted separately on the different pieces are pomegranates, pears, grapes, cherries, peaches and plums, while the flowers include roses, lilies, dahlias, violets, chrysanthemums, sweet peas, asters, lilacs, cowslips, apple blossoms, geraniums, pansies, primroses, and hydrangeas. This beautiful set was purchased in 1848 by Mann S. Valentine, and deservedly belongs in a Museum.

When one thinks of "Scenic Plates" one instinctively thinks of old blue or pink *Staffordshire*. For by far the greatest number of American scenes delineated on plates and platters, bowls and pitchers, went to "The Potteries" in the English County of Staffordshire—Burslem, Cobridge, Stoke-upon-Trent, Hanley, and Tunstall, while the names one most frequently finds on the back of old Staffordshire wares are those of Adams, Jackson, Clews, Ridgeway, Wood, Stevenson, Tams, Mayer, and Green. Frequently interesting old specimens are unmarked, but this fact in no wise lessens their appeal in the eyes of those who love old, quaint things.

From Niagara Falls to Natural Bridge, from the Erie Canal to Harper's Ferry, American scenes were indelibly stamped on Staffordshire plates and other pieces, while dozens of prominent American buildings —State Capitols, Churches, Theatres, Custom Houses, Hotels, Banks, Court Houses, as well as Monuments, Scenes of Great Battles, University Sites, Famous Homes, even Railroads, were equally popular subjects.

Virginia proved a happy hunting ground for many well known draftsmen and artists, whose finished designs were promptly transferred to plates and platters by the various Staffordshire potters. Among them was one William Goodacre, a contemporary of Charles W. Burton, both of whom Julia D. S. Snow describes in a valuable article entitled "Delineators of the Adams-Jackson American Views," appearing in a recent issue of the magazine *Antiques,* as having "long been the exasperation and even despair of students of early American art . . ."

Both Burton and Goodacre seem to have been foot-loose and fancy-free (an artist's prerogative, then as now) for they were never long in any one place. During the years 1828-1832 Burton was listed in the New York City Directory as a "draftsman," and after that, completely disappeared from the metropolitan area. The fame of Virginia's Shenandoah region had spread far . . . Whether Burton simply heeded the call of the *Wanderlust,* was lured by the therapeutic virtues of its famous springs, or the beauty and grandeur of its mountain scenery, we shall never know, but we do know that he made a design of its scenic wonders, which both Adams and Jackson used on eight and nine-inch pink plates, captioned *Shannondale Springs, U. S.* and *Shannondale Springs, Virginia.*

Goodacre likewise was listed in the New York City Directory from 1829 to 1835, as a "teacher of drawing," after which he seems to have completely disappeared. But numerous Staffordshire plates bearing his designs vouch for his extensive travels through the East and South, for Goodacre produced a plate for every pilgrimage. His output from Virginia was far more prolific than Burton's. Here he found inspiration for his work in the geologic wonders of Natural Bridge, the beauties of the Potomac from Harper's Ferry, the State Capitol, the University buildings at Charlottesville, and Monumental Church, which he captioned *The Episcopal Church at Richmond.*

Goodacre's delineation of Monumental Church, which is celebrating its one hundred and twenty-fifth anniversary this year, is highly amusing, in that no such edifice as it portrays ever existed. As a consequence collectors and readers have an altogether erroneous impression of Richmond's memorial church, built from public subscription, and dedicated to those who lost their lives in the fire that destroyed the Richmond Theatre on the night of December 26, 1811.

Old Monumental Church is so rich in historic associations that it claims our interest and attention, especially during the celebration of its present anniversary. Built on the site of the Richmond Theatre, it was erected by order of the Common Council as a memorial to the seventy-three persons who perished in the conflagration on the fateful night of December 26, 1811.

Mrs. Vivian Minor Fleming of Fredericksburg, recalls a story often told by her husband's father, Dr. George Fleming of Hanover County, Virginia, concerning his grandfather, George Frederick Augustine

Fleming of "Healing Springs" in Louisa County, and
his visit to Governor George W. Smith of Virginia,
during the Christmas holidays in 1811. Mr· Fleming
was widowed, and his children were with their grand-
parents at "Rocky Mills," so he had accepted the invitation of Governor Smith, and gone to Richmond
for several days. On the night of the twenty-sixth, the
Governor tried to induce Mr. Fleming to accompany
him to the theatre, but he had refused, saying, "No,
Governor, you have here a box of books just come from
England, and I greatly prefer to stay at home and look
them over." So Governor Smith left his friend, and
light of heart, went to his doom.

There is also the story of the beautiful Mary
Homersel of France, whose life was saved by Dr.
Philip Thornton of Virginia, whom she later married.
Judge William Meade Fletcher of "Thornton Hill"
is said to have once read the memoirs—now lost or
destroyed—of this beautiful and unhappy woman, in
which she told of having gone to the Richmond Theatre
on the night of the fateful fire, and of Dr. Thornton
saving her life by lowering her to the ground by her
hair. She is said to have confessed that she married
the doctor out of gratitude, and that her life was very
lonely and unhappy.

After the burning of the theatre, John Marshall was
appointed chairman of the committee to receive sub-
scriptions toward the erection of a suitable memorial,
which was to be a church built on the site of the burned
theatre. Five thousand dollars was subscribed by the
City of Richmond and paid from the city treasury,
while John Marshall entered his name at the top of
the list as follows: "J. Marshall, $200. provided there
be twenty-five as high."

We may safely assume that there were, for soon thereafter a prize of five hundred dollars was offered to competing architects for the most appropriate and acceptable design for a monumental edifice to the lamented victims of the Richmond fire. The winning contestant was Robert Mills of Philadelphia, a young architect and *protégé* of Thomas Jefferson, former pupil of James Hoban who designed the White House, and one-time draftsman for Benjamin Latrobe.

Mills submitted several successive designs, the first of which—though never produced in structural form is the church that appears in Goodacre's drawing on Jackson's plates. The first thing that catches one's eye is a monument-like tower rising like a column of smoke to the left of the familiar dome, with a spire piercing the sky. Obviously, Goodacre did not take the time or the trouble to see the church for himself. The logical assumption is that he either had access to Mills' various designs, or saw pictures of them, and chose at random the one he liked best, or thought correct. Jackson is believed to be the only potter who used this delineation of *The Episcopal Church at Richmond,* which makes the little seven-inch plate doubly interesting and valuable.

Isaac Sturdevant of Boston was the master builder of Monumental Church, and the Reverend Richard Channing Moore, later Bishop of Virginia, its first Rector. Among the first pew-holders was Chief Justice John Marshall, who also served as a vestryman. To-day, visitors to the church have pointed out to them the pew occupied by John Marshall and his family, and listen with mingled amusement and delight to the story of this great and simple soul, unlatching the door of his pew during prayers in order to stretch his long legs! Young Edgar Allan Poe, with his foster-parents the John Allans occupied pew number eighty-three, from which vantage point the wistful-eyed boy used to spell aloud the golden letters above the chancel. LaFayette, too, worshipped here on his visit to Richmond in 1824. Truly the feet of great men have trod the aisles of this old church.

Some recently discovered papers and church records give intimate glimpses of old Monumental's early history, and of Richmond in the "eighteen-twenties." The Sunday School, which opened in October 1817, was the first in the city. Originally the membership was composed exclusively of the city's poor. These young unfortunates were not only taught religion and morals, but the "three R's" as well. According to the original constitution, "the pupils must appear with clean face and hands, their hair combed and as decently dressed as their circumstances will permit."

The old church records which antedate street numbers in Richmond, record addresses in this quaint manner—"next door to the poor house" or "across the street from Mr. Brown's pharmacy." As to the Sunday School progress, there are occasional entries such as "Attendance poor today. Streets very muddy." Yet from this church and its school came four Bishops of the Episcopal Church, a score of missionaries, and many who have taken on the mantle of leadership in religious and civic affairs; and from it two churches have been formed: historic St. Paul's and All Saints.

What memories are aroused by a piece of old china! That lovable American, Banjamin Franklin, whose famous maxims and sound logic are as immortal as the man himself, shared George Washington's fondness for blue china, and while he was in London sent quantities of it home to his wife. On one of these occasions he wrote her that letter containing the oft-quoted lines:

"I also forgot to mention among the china a large fine jug for beer to stand in the cooler. I fell in love with it at first sight; for I thought it looked like a fat jolly dame, clean and tidy, with a neat blue and white calico gown on, good-natured and lovely, and put me in mind of—somebody."

It was said of that prince of collectors—Horace Walpole,

"China's the passion of his soul,
A cup, a plate, a dish, a bowl
Can kindle wishes in his breast,
Inflame with joy or break his rest."

Charles Lamb, too, found time in his busy and brilliant career, to know and love all kinds of china, confessing as much in the *Essays of Elia,* when he wrote:

"I have an almost feminine partiality for old china. When I go to see any great house, I inquire first for the china-closet, and next for the picture-gallery. . ."

When we learn to "fall in love" with a homely jug, like the lovable Franklin; think enough of a set of china to record in our wills the source from whence it came, as did Martha Washington; give to a pair of treasured old vases a place of permanence and honor in our homes; and strive, with Oscar Wilde, to "live up to our best blue and white plates"—then perhaps we shall recapture some of the lost romance and adventure, beauty and loveliness, our ancestors found in their old pieces of Canton and Lowestoft, Staffordshire and Spode.

A Pair of Old Dueling Pistols

"Cowards die many times before their deaths;
The valiant never taste of death but once."

—SHAKESPEARE.

CHAPTER XIII

A Pair of Old Dueling Pistols

THE day of the duel dawned centuries ago, probably when the German tribes invaded Europe and men were compelled "to fight out their differences with one another." Buckle, in his *History of Civilization in England,* attributes the practice to chivalry, with France as the *locale* in which it reached its "polite perfection" and the peak of its popularity.

Early in the fifteenth century dueling was general throughout France, and in the sixteenth so spirited that seconds fought each other on the side. During the reign of Henry of Navarre (1553-1610) it is estimated that in eighteen years time between four and six thousand persons were killed in this fantastic practice. Some French kings are credited with having opposed ducling, while others promoted it, believing that it tended to maintain an *esprit militaire* among the people.

In England, Buckle found no evidence of any single duel being fought earlier than the sixteenth century, and even then very few until the last half of Queen Elizabeth's reign. The "hot Scots" who followed King James to Westminster were, it seems, a peculiarly sensitive lot, and arrived in England well equipped with "short Spanish swords, dirks, and pistols." Finally, James I had to "warn them by proclamation."

Under James' son Charles I, dueling flourished and

grew in frequency after the Restoration. Oliver Crom-
well—grim man that he was—refused to permit such
foolishness, but that "Merrie Monarch" Charles II,
patron of sports, did, as well as his successors. Queen
Anne's reign witnessed much fighting. "My Lord
Mohun" of Thackeray's *Henry Esmond,* who beyond
the pages of fiction was the very real Charles Mohun—
peer of Devonshire, had a crimson record. Early
on a foggy morning in November 1712, he fought the
Duke of Hamilton in Hyde Park, both of them losing
their lives in the futile fight.

The open field of honor was not always the scene of
combat. Writes Don C. Seitz in *Famous American
Duels*: "Duels were fought in strange and desperate
ways—across tables, in locked rooms, and in the dark,"
and adds that many had as their *raison d'être* silly
causes. "Lieutenant Sterne, father of the Reverend
Laurence Sterne of *Tristram Shandy* fame, was run
through by Captain Philips, of Handyside's Regiment,
in a row that began over a goose. Lord Byron's father
killed Mr. Chaworth, at the Star and the Garter, when
they disagreed over the extent of their respective land
holdings."

The great lexicographer, Dr. Samuel Johnson, de-
plored the decadence of prize-fighting, and unwisely
endorsed dueling. All too soon he had good reason to
regret his sanction of this evil practice, for ironically
enough, Sir Alexander Boswell, son of his friend and
biographer, met his death in a duel. Thus the duel
continued to take its toll, *ad infinitum.*

The early colonists brought many English customs
and fashions with them to Virginia, but happily dueling was not among them. Though duels were frequent
after the Revolution, they were practically unknown

in the colony up to this time; so much so that only two are known to have been actually fought. The first of these was between a sea captain named Edward Stallinge and Captain William Eppes, in the year 1619, and took place in Charles City County at a spot known as "Dancing Point." Stallinge was the victim—Eppes the victor. The second duel took place five years later, in 1624, when George Harrison died from a wound between the knee and garter from the sword of Captain Richard Stephens.

There were other challenges and casualties in the colony, perhaps the most notable pre-Revolutionary duel being that fought by Colonel John Chiswell of Hanover County, and Robert Routledge, a Scotchman, in the old Tavern at Hanover Courthouse in 1766.

Colonel John Chiswell belonged to a prominent Virginia family, his father, John Chiswell, having been Clerk of the General Court, and a resident of Hanover County, where he died in 1737. The younger Chiswell had married Elizabeth Randolph, daughter of William Randolph of Turkey Island, and had thus allied himself with one of the most notable families in Virginia.

From 1745 to 1755 Colonel John Chiswell represented Hanover County in the House of Burgesses. In 1757 he discovered the New River lead mines in what is now Wythe County, where he opened mining operations. It has been claimed that this was the first lead mined on the continent; certainly, during the Revolution, these mines supplied lead for the patriots. A few miles from the mine a fort was built for protection against the Indians and was named Fort Chiswell, in honor of Colonel Chiswell.

Robert Routledge was a Scotch gentleman—probably a refugee and supporter of the Pretender, for Chiswell is said to have called him a "rebel Presbyterian." He was not well known in Virginia, whereas Chiswell was, to say nothing of being wealthy and belonging to the aristocracy. The bar-room at old Hanover Tavern was the scene of the fracas, and according to an old account, after Chiswell slew Routledge, "he wiped his bloody sword on a cloth, and sat down and drank a bowl of bumbo." Bumbo was a punch made of many strong ingredients, and said to be a very potent drink.

There was considerable "class feeling" throughout Virginia over this brutal killing, and fuel was but added to the smouldering fires of resentment, when Chiswell, after having been refused bail by the county court, was bailed *en route* to jail by three members of the General Court—John Blair, Presley Thornton, and William Byrd. All three are said to have been relatives of Chiswell, and were bitterly attacked for their interference.

In the end, his prosecutor was chosen in the prevailing custom by lot, and fell to John Blair, Jr., an intimate friend, to conduct the case. But a kindly fate intervened for both, for Chiswell, brooding over the tragedy, took his own life, and thereby wrote "finis" to the case.

Another duel to claim widespread attention in Virginia, particularly throughout Tidewater, was that which was fought by young William Thornton and Francis Fitzhugh Conway, late in December of 1803 at "Alum Spring Rock," two miles from the Court House in Fredericksburg.

William Thornton was the young son of John Thornton of "The Falls," near Fredericksburg, and his wife Catherine Yates. As the "Widow Thornton" she had married Dr. Robert Wellford, retired surgeon in the English Army, who had come to America during the Revolution, and at the close of the war settled in Fredericksburg.

Young Conway's parents lived at "Mount Zion" in Caroline County, and were among the most prominent residents in the community. Both young men were favorites in society, and highly esteemed by all who knew them. As frequently happened of old, the tastes of each led them to seek in marriage the same lady. She was none other than the charming Nellie Madison, a niece of President James Madison, who afterwards married a Mr. Willis of Gloucester County.

Nellie Madison was a frequent visitor at "Chatham," the hospitable seat of the Fitzhugh family across the river from Fredericksburg, and here the young rivals —Thornton and Conway—frequently paid court to her, their visits often falling on the same evening. According to descendants of the Thornton-Wellford family now living in Fredericksburg, it was while calling at the home of Mr. Byrd Willis in Fredericksburg that some unpleasantness arose between young Thornton and Conway, which led to the challenge that resulted in the fatal duel.

The mortal field was once again the favorite rendezvous of other combatants of the day—"that even pathway at the foot of Alum Spring Rock." John Spotswood Wellford acted as second for his half-brother William Thornton. At the word "fire" two shots sounded almost simultaneously. Both men were mortally wounded, but young Thornton was able to ride back to Fredericksburg, where he died in one of the upper bed-chambers of his step-father's home on Caroline Street. The old Wellford house is still standing, and I have had pointed out to me the tragic death-chamber by the present owner, Miss Eliza Roy of Fredericksburg, whose mother, Mary Catherine Wellford married James H. Roy.

I am indebted to Miss Elsie W. Lewis, also of Fredericksburg, for the privilege of being allowed to see and copy a torn and yellowed clipping from the *Virginia Express* of Fredericksburg, dated December 29, 1803, which reads as follows:

> "Swift as occasion, I myself will fly, and
> Earlier than the dawn, wake thee to freedom."

"With infinite regret, we communicate to the public, an event, the most distressing in its nature, and fatal in its consequences of any within the compass of our recollection.

"On Monday last Mr. William Thornton and Mr. Francis Conway met, in consequence of a previous misunderstanding, in the neighborhood of this town, and sorry are we to announce that the event proved fatal to both parties. In the fatal bout they both departed this life.

"By their untimely fate two weeping Mothers are left to deplore the loss of two dutiful sons, their children two affectionate brothers, and society two most promising citizens. The surviving relations are in a situation easier to be imagined than described.

"We sincerely regret the frequency of a custom so prevalent in our country, and hope the melancholy catastrophe, here related, will prevent others from endangering their own lives, or embittering the days of their surviving relatives."

Two traditional beliefs have followed this tragic duel for more than a century. One is that there was found on the person of William Thornton at the time of his death, a miniature of Nellie Madison. The other relates to a dream which the mother of young Conway had, the night before the dawn that witnessed the fatal duel.

Neither of Francis Conway's parents had any knowl-

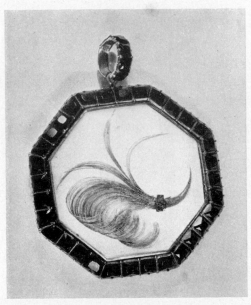

Gold locket, with jet border and opal face, made to commemorate a fatal duel. This locket belonged to Mary Thornton of Fredericksburg, whose brother William Thornton was killed in a duel with Francis Conway, who also sustained fatal injuries. The locket is inscribed—"William Thornton, born 24 Sept. 1772, died 27 Dec. 1803. You that have lost a Brother pity me." Against the opal facing of the locket is a titian lock of hair, presumably that of the beloved brother. Owned by Mrs. M. R. Turnbull of Richmond, a descendant of John Spotswood Wellford of Fredericksburg, half-brother of William Thornton.

edge of the impending conflict, but on the morning of the fatal day, Mrs. Conway is said to have appeared very agitated as she took her place at the breakfast table. When asked by her husband why she seemed so distressed, she told him of a dream she had during the night, in which a man on a white horse had hastened to the house, bringing a message that their son had been killed. Mr. Conway refused to share his wife's feeling of alarm, and did all in his power to calm her. A short while later, as she stood by one of the front windows, she fell to the floor in a faint. Rushing to her side, her husband lifted her in his arms, and as he turned to walk away, looked out of the window. There, riding at full speed was a man on a white horse, bringing the death-message foretold in the dream.

In the possession of Mrs. M. R. Turnbull, of Richmond, there is an exquisite gold octagonal locket, originally belonging to a sister of young William Thornton, whose inscription commemorates this fateful duel and the tragic death of a beloved brother. There are two interesting sides to this unusual and beautiful old locket; the one on which is inscribed the sister's lamentation, and the other, which reveals beneath a small oval of glass, a lock of William Thornton's hair—a beautiful titian-gold lock. This old locket was inherited by Mrs. Turnbull (the former Mary Spotswood Carmichael of Fredericksburg) from her parents, Lucy Dickinson Ashby and Charles Carter Carmichael. The latter was the son of George French Carmichael and his wife, Mary Wellford, whose father was John Spotswood Wellford, son of Dr. Robert Wellford and his wife, the "Widow Thornton," and a half-brother of William Thornton.

The duel between Aaron Burr and Alexander

Hamilton, in which the latter lost his life, is generally considered the most famous duel in American history. But a later conflict—a *duellum* in the strictest sense of the word—was to fire the imagination of the American public, and cause more genuine grief than any duel which had ever taken place on American soil, or has since taken place.

This was the ill-fated duel between James Barron and Stephen Decatur in 1820, which resulted in the death of the gallant young Decatur, whose brilliant naval career had made him a hero in the eyes of the American people. Few duels, either at home or abroad, aroused Virginians as did this one, for Barron was born in Hampton and therefore a native son, while Decatur had married a Norfolk girl, and by ties of marriage and long residence, was considered a son by adoption.

The early career of James Barron paled into insignificance beside that of Stephen Decatur, whose daring exploits at sea had sky-rocketed him to fame at the age of twenty-five. In addition, he had charm and *savoir-faire,* and an ease and grace of manner which but served to increase his popularity.

When the impudent and imprudent Bey of Tripoli declared war on the United States, U. S. Commander Richard Dale of Portsmouth was ordered to the Mediterranean with four ships—one of which, the U. S. S. *Essex,* under Captain Bainbridge, had Stephen Decatur on deck as first lieutenant. The fearless feat of young Decatur in recapturing and burning the U. S. S. *Philadelphia,* February 16, 1804—"under the very nose of the Bey of Tripoli," and without the loss of a single man, although one hundred and forty one cannon were turned upon them, was declared by Admiral Nelson to be "the most daring act of the age." Stephen Decatur was but twenty-five years old at the time.

Less than two years later, the world still ringing with his praise, Stephen Decatur, in command of the U. S. S. *Congress,* dropped anchor at Old Point Comfort, with its old-fashioned square yard-arms and spotless decks. Decatur reported to President Thomas Jefferson, his arrival, and that he had brought with him from across the Atlantic, the Ambassador of the Bey of Algiers, and awaited orders.

In the interim, Luke Wheeler, Mayor of Norfolk, and one of the city's wealthiest merchants, with a party of distinguished citizens crossed Hampton Roads to officially welcome Decatur and his party, and personally extend to him an invitation to visit Norfolk. The invitation was accepted, and the very next day Stephen Decatur and other members of his party were sumptuously entertained at the Wheeler home.

If, before meeting him, Susan Wheeler had already fallen in love with the hero of the hour, certain it is that on this brilliant occasion, when her eyes rested on him in the flesh—attired in all of the splendor of his full-dress naval uniform—gold lace, gold braid, and a shining sword adding splendor to the already spendid figure that Decatur naturally was—she realized, as all about her must have realized, that in fact and not fancy, she had lost her heart to the young officer. A grand ball followed the Mayor's dinner, and when the visitors returned to their ship, Stephen Decatur knew too, that he had lost his heart that evening.

On March 8, 1806—six months and three days after Stephen Decatur had first dropped anchor at Old Point Comfort, Susan Wheeler became his wife, the ceremony being performed by the Reverend Benjamin

Porter Grigsby, pastor of the Bell Presbyterian Church in Norfolk. Happy and triumphant years followed, with Norfolk considered by both Decatur and his wife as "home."

On January 1, 1819, Stephen and Susan Decatur bade a permanent farewell to Norfolk as a place of residence, moving to Washington where he had built an imposing house facing LaFayette Square on H Street, one block from the White House and two blocks from the house of Mrs. James Madison. Little did either of them dream at the time that Stephen Decatur would have but one year to live in his new home.

Susan Decatur, as the wife of an internationally famous and tremendously popular man, entered at once into the gay and strenuous life which those in the inner circles of Washington society invariably lead, and soon was recognized as one of the most charming and captivating young hostesses in the cosmopolitan capital.

But these gay days were short-lived, and it seems tragic indeed, that on the very eve of Stephen Decatur's lamented death as the result of his duel with James Barron, his young wife should have gone through all of the graces of a brilliant hostess, and entertained at a notable reception, totally unaware that her husband was pledged to fight a duel at sunrise. And doubly tragic, that the debonnair Decatur should do the honors of the perfect host, with never a suggestion of his gruesome sunrise date.

James Barron was the son of Commodore James Barron of the Virginia Navy during the Revolutionary War, and was born in Hampton, Virginia, in 1768.

The series of heated letters which passed between Barron and Decatur and were the direct cause of the fatal duel, were but the aftermath of Captain Barron's suspension from the American Navy. As Naval Commissioner, Stephen Decatur had vigorously opposed Barron's efforts to secure re-instatement on the ground that Barron had not made proper efforts to re-enter the sevice in 1812. The heated correspondence that followed, in which Decatur was correct, though not conciliatory, led to Barron's challenge.

Never forgetting the true meaning of *noblesse oblige,* Decatur, in deference to his opponent's faulty eyesight, is said to have selected the shortest distance—eight paces—and stated privately that he would aim low to avoid mortal injury. At the first exchange of shots, both men fell, Barron wounded in the thigh, and Decatur through the abdomen.

When they had first met on the "field of honor" at Bladensburg, Maryland, just outside of Washington, Barron had said to Decatur, "I hope we will be better friends in the next world than we have been in this." To which Decatur replied, "I have never been your enemy, sir."

Now, with the fatal shots having been fired, Decatur, struggling to stand erect while his hand went to his right side, finally crumbled to the ground, uttering next to his last words—"I am mortally wounded, at least I believe so. I wish I had fallen in the defense of my country."

Nearby, Barron was also lying in a pool of blood. As Bainbridge and the attending physicians lifted Decatur, and carried him passed Barron, Decatur spoke for the last time—"I hope you will forgive me." To which Barron replied, "With all my heart."

Rushed to his home in Washington, Stephen Decatur's suffering increased, and in the arms of his grief-stricken young wife he died at ten-thirty o'clock— March 22, 1820—at which hour, the evening before, he had done the honors of a princely host.

So intense was the feeling of the general public at the time of Decatur's death, that it found expression in the words of the *National Intelligencer* of Washington: "Mourn Columbia, for one of thy brightest stars has set—a son without fear and without reproach."

A Pair of Old Dueling Pistols—gruesome and sinister; pistols that played a ruthless rôle in a duel that caused the death of one of America's most gallant and distinguished sons—Stephen Decatur. Is it not incredibly strange that with Museums clamoring for such historic weapons, the very pistols used in this famous duel should today be in Virginia, in the city of Norfolk that knew and loved Stephen Decatur so well?

For several years these old pistols were exhibited in the Myers House in Norfolk, but at the present time are in the possession of their owner, Mrs. Barton Myers.

The pistols repose in their original case—a long narrow wooden box, lined with felt and equipped with various small compartments. Two interesting old labels still cling to the inside of the case, conspicuously placed at the top so that all who behold the gruesome weapons therein, will know something of their manufacturer.

The largest and oldest label bears the name, address, and patent of the London manufacturer, while the

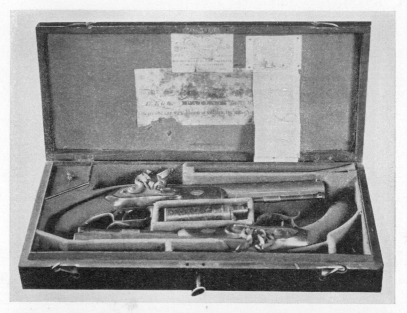

These are the pistols Barron and Decatur used in their famous duel; one of them, in the hands of Barron, killed Decatur. Owned by Mrs. Barton Myers of Virginia Beach. Norfolk Advertising Board photograph.

whole is offset by the royal insignia of Great Britain.
It reads:

No. 132 Strand.   London.

D. Egg   Patent   Gun Maker

To His Majesty, Prince of Wales, Duke of York.

The smaller and later label reads:

Joseph Spratley

Gun   Maker

Has on hand

Guns, Pistols, Locks and Mounting

of every description.

Norfolk, Virginia.

Six years after the Barron-Decatur duel, John Randolph of "Roanoke" and Henry Clay met on Virginia soil at a spot above the Little Falls bridge in Fairfax County, and faced each other in a duel which well enough might be called "A Comedy of Errors," for happily it lacked all of the bitterness and bloodshed of the Barron-Decatur feud.

While a member of the United States Senate, Randolph had characterized the coalition between Henry Clay and John Adams as a union of "the blackleg and the Puritan." This invidious use of two of the chief characters in Fielding's *Tom Jones* brought about a decided uproar in political circles. There was no mistaking their identities: Adams was the "Puritan" and Clay the "blackleg."

Of the incident, H. A. Garland, Randolph's biographer wrote: "Mr. Clay was not a man of such forbearance and Christian virtue as to permit a gross imputation on his motives to pass unnoticed. He was

compelled to act. Randolph . . . had been the evil
genius that from the beginning stood in the way of his
aspirations." The result was that the Secretary of State
challenged his vindictive foe to mortal combat, selecting General Thomas S. Jesup to bear his message.

Seconds were chosen and proceeded to arrange the
details of the duel. The place, and the date—Satur-
day afternoon, April 8, 1826, were decided upon.
Virginia had a law prohibiting dueling, a fact pointed
out to Randolph by Thomas H. Benton, a mutual
friend of his and Clay's, who was to be one of the
party. Randolph is said to have replied that as Clay
would be the only one to shoot, the statute could in no
wise affect him (Randolph).

As the day of the duel approached, Randolph showed
a surprising calm, and on repeated occasions when
visited by friends, was found reading Milton's *Paradise Lost*. On one of these occasions, Colonel James
Hamilton of North Carolina was the visitor, and Randolph is quoted as having said to him:

"Hamilton, I have determined to receive without returning Clay's
fire; nothing shall induce me to harm a hair of his head. I will not
make his wife a widow or his children orphans. Their tears will be
shed over his grave; but when the sod of Virginia rests on my bosom,
there is not in this wide world one individual to pay this tribute
upon mine."

The hour set for the rendezvous was half-past four.
Randolph lived in Georgetown, not far from the
chosen scene of conflict. A final visit from Benton,
who was *en route* to the "field of honor" found Randolph making elaborate preparations for the worst.
He had sent to the local branch of the United States
bank for some gold coins and a check covering his
balance. Benton was given a sealed envelope—to be

opened in the event of Randolph's death—otherwise to be returned; also a note to be read before reaching the field. This last contained Randolph's request that nine gold coins be taken from his pocket, three of which were to go to Blanton, three to Tatnall, and three to Colonel Hamilton.

Thus, with matters settled, and his destiny hanging in the balance, Randolph and his second proceeded to Virginia in a carriage, Benton following on horseback. "The sun was just setting behind the hills of Randolph's own Virginia," wrote Colonel Hamilton. "Here were two of the most extraordinary men our country in its prodigality had produced, about to meet in mortal combat."

The chosen spot was a small depression of open ground, screened from view by a thicket of trees. Clay saluted Randolph courteously, the latter returning the gesture graciously. General Jesup was repeating instructions, when Randolph, adjusting the butt of his pistol to his hand, fired accidently. The muzzle was pointing downward—almost to the ground. Clay promptly remarked, generously and truthfully, that the shot was clearly an accident, "and it was so unanimously declared."

"Another pistol was immediately furnished; and an exchange of shots took place, and, happily, without effect upon the persons. Mr. Randolph's bullet struck the stump behind Mr. Clay, and Mr. Clay's knocked up the earth and gravel behind Mr. Randolph, and in a line with the level of his hips, both bullets having gone so true and close that it was a marvel how they missed."

From the sidelines, Benton and the others had been watching tensely. Surely now, whatever honor had been involved in the affray was satisfied. But Clay would have no intervention; what had transpired was "child's play" and he demanded another fire.

"When the word was given" writes Don C. Seitz in *Famous American Duels,* "Clay fired, his ball lodging in the gravel, as before, but perforating the skirt of Randolph's coat *en route.* Randolph fired in the air and called out: 'I do not fire at you, Mr. Clay!' At this he stepped forward and offered his hand. They met halfway and shook hands, Randolph remarking jocosely, as Benton relates it, 'You owe me a coat, Mr. Clay.' 'I am glad the debt is no greater,' was the hearty response." Colonel Hamilton's version follows:

"The moment Mr. Clay saw that Randolph had thrown away his fire, with a gush of sensibility, he instantly approached Mr. Randolph, and said with an emotion I can never forget: 'I trust in God, my dear Sir, you are untouched; after what has occurred, I would not have harmed you for a thousand worlds'."

Randolph had narrowly escaped a serious wound, the ball cutting close to his thigh. In the Virginia Historical Society, preserved with countless other historical treasures, is the white flannel coat (now yellowed with age) which John Randolph of "Roanoke" wore in this duel. The discerning visitor soon discovers the tear on one side of the coat, caused by the bullet from Henry Clay's pistol, and if he fails to notice it, the spot is called to his attention.

At the conclusion of the deeply touching reconciliation between Clay and Randolph, the latter asked Benton for the sealed envelope he had given him as they left Georgetown. Opened, it was found to contain Randolph's check for a thousand dollars which was to have been used, had Randolph been killed, to bury him in Virginia, "Under his patrimonial oaks."

In his written instructions, Randolph had specifically forbidden his interment in Washington, and had he met his death on the so-called "field of honor" his eccentricities would have followed him to the grave, for he had requested that one hundred hacks should follow the funeral procession. The gold pieces he intended should be turned into seals for his three friends, and he afterwards facetiously remarked to them, "Gentlemen, Clay's bad shooting shan't rob you of your seals. I am going to London and will have them made for you." And he kept his promise.

A duel which stirred post-war Richmond to the very foundations, and is talked about to this day in the older circles of Richmond society, was the fatal combat between Page McCarty, "a dashing journalist of those days," and the gallant young Confederate soldier, John B. Mordecai.

On a fair spring day in 1873, there appeared in the Richmond *Enquirer* the following poetic lines:

"When Mary's queenly form I press, in Strauss' latest waltz,
I would as well her lips caress, although those lips were false;
For still with fire love tips his darts, and kindles up anew
The flame that once consumed my heart, when those dear lips were true.
Of form so fair, of faith so faint, if truth were only in her,
Though she would be the sweetest saint, I'd still feel like a sinner."

This amorous bit of verse was attributed to Page McCarty, and was supposed to refer to a renowned belle and beauty of Richmond, the fair Mary Triplett, to whom McCarty was known to have long paid court. Young Mordecai knew and admired her as well, and as would be expected of a knight errant of old Virginia, deeply resented what he considered no less than a public insult to this muchly admired young woman.

Mordecai at once challenged McCarty to a duel, but friends intervened and the matter was momentarily dropped. However the fates decreed differently, for shortly thereafter, the two men met in the Richmond Club, at the corner of Third and Franklin Streets. As a result of this *contretemps,* Mordecai again challenged McCarty, the challenge being accepted. Dr. H. J. Eckenrode, writing in the Bicentennial issue of the Richmond *News Leader* on "Richmond in the Reconstruction," gives the following version of the fatal conflict:

"The two men met on May ninth, appropriately enough behind Oakwood Cemetery. Mordecai's seconds, 'Buck' Royall and W. R. Trigg were long prominent in Richmond; his surgeon was the famed Hunter McGuire. The weapons were navy revolvers, and the distance ten paces. They fired, without effect. They fired again, and Mordecai fell mortally wounded and McCarty badly hurt.

"Nothing had been done about duels before; the 'code of honor' prevailed. This time it was different. The seconds were taken to jail, charged with murder, and were finally admitted to bail. McCarty was tried, convicted of manslaughter, and sentenced to a fine and imprisonment. Because of his wound, which still troubled him, the Governor pardoned him of the prison sentence. However he was a ruined man; he had to leave Richmond."

The dawn of a new era was at hand in Virginia. The day of the duel belonged to the irrevocable past.

The Ancestry of the Doll

"Frontenac tells me that you desire patterns of our fashions in dress. I send you therefore some model dolls."
—HENRY IV OF FRANCE TO MARIE DE MEDICI. 1600.

"Yet for old sake's she is still, dears,
The prettiest doll in the world."
—CHARLES KINGSLEY.

CHAPTER XIV

The Ancestry of the Doll

IN Virginia, where one's ancestry is an *all-important matter,* the doll should feel perfectly "at home," for she boasts an ancient lineage that goes back to the Pharaohs. Proof of the doll's antiquity is attested by Egyptian, Greek, and Roman remains, among which small figures and objects of wood, clay, ivory, and bone, have been found in children's graves and identified as dolls.

In the British Museum there is a notable collection of these same dolls, estimated to be four thousand years old, and therefore conceded to be the oldest known dolls in existence. Discovered by archaeologists in the tombs of Egyptian children, the accompanying legend is that they were placed in the arms of the dead child at burial, so that it might be amused and entertained when it reached the spirit world.

The doll is the oldest toy known to mankind, and is to be found among all nationalities and tribes, even of the most remote antiquity. Among the American Indians a child's doll appears as an image of deity—fashioned of wood, held as sacred, and intrusted to a child only during the time of religious instruction. Similar dolls, carved to represent the masked dancers who impersonate the gods, are used throughout the Pueblo area of the United States, in Arizona and New

Mexico, and in a derivative form among the Pomo in California.

So great is the respect with which dolls are treated among the Pueblos, that their sale is forbidden. The Navajo, who occupy the adjacent territory, look with fear and superstition upon the Pueblo doll, and use a wooden effigy representing a Hopi doll to work evil upon the enemy.

The Eskimo and Northern Indians make dolls for their children from ivory, bone, and mammoth teeth, dressing them in fur and hide, while the beaded buckskin dolls of the Plains and other Indians are believed to have been inspired by white influence. In ancient Peruvian graves, small clay dolls have been found, perfectly clothed.

In Japan, a primitive type of child's doll consists of a shaved willow stick with shavings or string for hair, and paper clothes, an obvious adaptation of the shaved willow sticks formerly set up on the banks of streams as scape-goats, at the annual purification ceremony. An actual scape-goat doll which was fed and dressed and treated as though alive, was given to mothers in Old Japan to ward off evil from their children.

Apart from these "magical" dolls, little Japanese girls have common-place dolls as well as ceremonial ones. The latter are never played with, but kept for formal exhibition at the Girls' Festival which is held in May of every year. These dolls are symbolic of the Imperial Court, and are magnificently dressed.

In Korea, little girls never know what it is to receive a manufactured doll, but make their own by cutting a bamboo pipe stem five inches in length, in the top of which they put long grass, salted and made fine like hair. These dolls are never given a face, but sometimes a little white powder is pasted in its place. They are dressed in clothes like those worn by a woman, and sometimes a pin made by the children themselves, is placed in the hair. In Korea, the Children's Festival takes place every year in April, celebrated in Japan as the birthday of Buddha.

In India, where infant marriage prevails among the Hindus and Mohammedans, elaborately dressed dolls are paramount among the presents given a child-bride at marriage. Throughout the Mohammedan East the use of dolls is general, despite the law of Islam which forbids the representation of the human figure. It is told that when the nine year old wife of Mohammed Aisha, entered his harem, she brought her dolls with her, and, according to legend, the Prophet himself played with them!

Dolls are never given to children as toys in Bagdad, Mohammedan mothers seeing in every doll the spirit of evil, and therefore fearful lest they should bring misfortune upon their children.

In China, dolls are made to represent mandarins, war-lords, soldiers, peasants, women, children—even actors! In Persia, little girls make their dolls out of pieces of folded cotton which they clothe and mark with features.

In darkest Africa, the doll is a familiar object, even common-place, certain forms being peculiar to certain regions, although their use by children is somewhat complicated by magical observances.

Among the Fingo of the Orange Free State, a girl is given a doll when she becomes of age which she keeps until she has a child. Following this, her mother gives her another doll, which she also keeps until she has a second child. These dolls are naturally looked upon as sacred and are never played with.

Today in France, Italy, and other Catholic countries in Europe, Toy Fairs are held in the streets, and purely secular dolls are sold side by side with toy images representing the Virgin Mary, Joseph, the Holy Infant, and other saints associated with the season of the Nativity.

For many years the Netherlands and the Tyrol were among the leading centers of the doll industry in Europe, the importation of dolls into England at one time being almost exclusively from the Netherlands. Thus not an unusual name for a doll was a "Flanders Baby." These old Flemish or Dutch dolls were made of wood with neatly formed faces and somewhat garish dresses, the less expensive ones having wooden legs.

One of the quaintest dolls known to collectors is the fascinating "Peddler Doll" which originated in England in 1780, and continued to be produced until well into the 1800's. These intriguing dolls were possibly inspired by prints such as Wheatley's *Cries of London* series. In any event, an authentic picture of the early nineteenth century English peddler has been preserved for posterity through the medium of these amazingly equipaged dolls, several notable examples of which are now in privately owned American collections.

A notable example of the late eighteenth century Peddler Doll is in the celebrated collection of Mrs. DeWitt Clinton Cohen of New York City. This doll, elaborately attired in bonnet, shawl, and flaring bombazine skirt, carries a tray overflowing with miniature gadgets of every conceivable kind. Here one beholds a veritable salmagundi of wares: pierced paper patterns for cross-stitch mottoes, a rolling pin, string

A trio of famous dolls in the "Virginia Room" of the Confederate Museum. From left to right, "Aunt Phyllis" whose head is made from a hickory nut; wooden doll named "Hercelia", dressed in 1845 and owned by Mary Susan Wright, of Essex County, Virginia; and "Ann Blaws", the childhood treasure of Mary Braxton Cocke, of "Bremo" on the James. Courtesy of the Confederate Museum.

of pearls, hoods and scarves, a diminutive mortar and pestle, crocheted knitting bags, pewter ware, and whatnot.

That Peddler Dolls are today considered rare and expensive oddities may be gleaned from the following advertisement which appeared several years ago in the magazine *Antiques:*

"An extremely rare Pair of shell peddler dolls, the bodies of which are wood and the faces wax, in perfect original condition excepting that a few tiny shells are missing from the man's arms. Price delivered, one hundred and twenty-five dollars."

The majority of dolls made about 1860 were the long slender type, with kid or cloth bodies and heads of china or *papier-mâché*. Later came the beautiful wax dolls with curly hair, eyes that opened and closed, and the magical inside apparatus which enabled them to say "Mama" and "Papa."

Still later came the wooden-bodied jointed dolls invented by a Frenchman named Jumeau, and at first manufactured exclusively in France. Soon Germany appeared on the business horizon as a serious competitor for this type of doll, making similar ones in all details though less costly.

Prior to 1914, most of the German dolls sold in the American market were made in the village of Sonneberg, in the Thuringian forest. Here the industry can be traced back to the seventeenth century. In making the dolls the work is divided among members of a household, the father molding the different parts of the doll, the mother painting them and making the wigs, while the children put the parts together. After completion, the dolls are taken to a general collecting house.

The typical German doll, true to the ideal of the

Ewig-Weibliche, has the bulging pink cheeks, light blue eyes, flaxen curls, and symmetrical pearly smile that were the standard of beauty in the pre-flapper period.

As to the exotic doll, it is Italy, and not France, who has contributed this long-lashed, slightly sophisticated beauty to the markets of the world. She is known and sold the world over as the "Lenci Doll"—made of felt and dressed as an enticing mantilla-draped coquette, or, quite the opposite—as a wee little miss ready for a walk with her nurse in Kensington Gardens or the Bois. An expression of haunting allure is ever on the face of this bewitching beauty, the utter antithesis of the fixed stare and prosaic expression of its German cousin.

Scandinavian dolls are quite apt to be on sleds or skis, or else riding in the kayaks of the North, dressed in fur-trimmed peasant costumes or else snugly wrapped in furs.

Russia's contribution to the Doll Kingdom, as seen at the great fairs and in the cities, is both modern and old-fashioned. The former are jointed dolls, gorgeously dressed in the various brilliant colors that blend themselves into fanciful peasant costumes, while the latter, known as the "Matrioska Doll," is made of wood and typifies the comfortable peasant woman, wearing her bright kerchief and apron, looking much the same as her great-grandmother did before her, with her waistline uninhibited by present-day fashions.

During the last fifteen years there has been an ever-increasing vogue for making and manufacturing dolls in the likeness of famous persons. The doll presented to Princess Astrid, late Queen of the Belgians, on her arrival in Brussels as the bride of King Leopold III, is described as having been a perfect likeness of this beautiful princess, whose tragic death soon thereafter, brought to a sudden close one of the few real romances of European royalty.

A later doll of more international popularity, which attracted wide attention, was the Parisian miniature model of Colonel Charles A. Lindbergh. According to the correspondent of the *New York Times,* writing from Paris June 19, 1927,

"The first Sunday of the fortnight preceding the *Grand Prix* was an occasion for an outburst of charitable functions in Paris. Among the drawing cards at these functions, Colonel Charles A. Lindbergh's prestige continued in the front rank. Lindbergh dolls, which were an excellent likeness of his blond head and even produced his winning smile, went like hot cakes for five hundred francs each, and many more could have been disposed of had they been offered."

One of these original dolls was sent to Colonel Lindbergh's mother, Mrs. Evangeline Lindbergh, and she in turn presented it to the Jefferson Memorial in St. Louis, Missouri, where the thousands of Lindbergh trophies are housed. So great were the number of dolls sent to Colonel Lindbergh from different countries, it has been necessary to display them in one large group.

There are forty-five dolls in the entire collection, of which twenty-one are German, nine Japanese, six French, and nine American. The German dolls are made of wood, very small in size, and classified as follows: "Six little dolls with long skirts, to be used as egg-warmers; four little dolls on corks; four ballerinas, and seven sets of boys and girls to be used as ornaments."

The Japanese group include two "Asakusa Dolls," exquisitely made, representing the Japanese in various ceremonial gowns and postures; two warrior dolls in full military regalia; one bisque warrior doll, and two girl dolls dressed in brilliant red satin kimonas. Practically all of the Japanese dolls sent to Colonel Lindbergh by his Nipponese admirers came in satinwood boxes, with sliding glass panels—typical examples of Oriental artistry.

The French dolls in the Lindbergh collection present a variety of type. The most interesting of them all, is, of course, the aviator doll fashioned in his own image. Made entirely of felt, this doll and others like it, were auctioned in Paris at a benefit for the French War Blind, each bringing as large a sum as five hundred francs.

Not to be outdone by other nations, American admirers added nine interesting dolls to Colonel Lindbergh's collection, most of them dressed to represent the Colonel and his Lady, in their now-familiar flying togs.

Probably the oldest and most famous doll in America today is "Letitia Penn II," who lives in Montgomery County, Maryland. This enchanting doll dates back to 1699, the year in which William Penn sailed from England for America on the *Canterbury,* bringing with him the doll chosen by his daughter Letitia, for a little friend in Philadelphia.

Despite her age, "Letitia Penn II" seems to have successfully defied the ravages of time, and whenever she appears in public is invariably the cynosure of all eyes. She measures twenty inches in height, is slim waisted and generally slender, while her coiffure features a full high brow with the hair drawn back from the face. Letitia wears a court dress of the late seventeenth century made of softly tinted striped brocade and velvet, the full skirt flaring by means of a tremendous hoop, and all in all, she is a very elegant lady!

The oldest known doll in Virginia, and one of the

oldest and quaintest in this country, is owned by Mrs. William W. Richardson of "Little Berkeley," Hampton, Virginia. This little seven-inch doll has a composition head, kid body, bisque hands and feet, and an elaborate coiffure painted black. She wears her original dress and pantalets, the delicate gauze-like material now threadbare and yellowed with age, yet seen beneath glass in an ornate gold frame, she looks very much the part of the real Colonial Dame.

This unusual doll was brought from England to America around two hundred years ago by Mrs. Richardson's great-great-grandmother Maria Hardyman, who married Robert Harrison of Prince George County, Virginia, and during her long span of years has become quite a celebrity in the doll world.

Not only has her picture appeared in the *New York Times* and *D. A. R. Magazine,* but it was also used as one of the illustrations in Mary Newton Stanard's book, *Colonial Virginia, Its People and Customs.* Several years ago, this diminutive doll was exhibited with other notable American dolls at the Pratt Institute in New York, and during the entire time of her absence from Virginia, was insured for the sum of fifteen hundred dollars.

Other celebrated dolls in American collections include one known as "Mehibitable Hodges," which was brought from France to Salem, Massachusetts, in 1724 by Captain Gamaliel Hodges for his little daughter; also the delightful "Alcott dolls" which belonged to the author of *Little Women.* The hair on each of these dolls' heads is said to have been the actual hair of Jo, Meg, Beth, and Amy, whose life's story went into Miss Alcott's beloved book.

In the Confederate Museum in Richmond, there is a

small but fascinating group of dolls, all of which are redolent of *ante-bellum* days in Virginia and the South. The most celebrated doll in the entire collection carries the number "310" and is a titian-haired enchantress named "Nina." Without doubt she is the proudest possession of the Florida Room, and is considered the most historic doll in the entire Southland.

Nina is an unusually large doll, measuring a full yard in length. Her beautiful well rounded head, neck, and broad shoulders are of a plaster composition, while her hair, eyebrows, and lashes are painted a rich copperish-red. Her eyes too, are painted a brilliant blue, and her cheeks and lips are the color of coral. Whoever made Nina intended her for a vixen, and one does not marvel that her beauty so bewitched sentries and officers alike, that she successfully served her purpose as a carrier of quinine and morphine to sick soldiers "behind the lines," during the harrowing years of the War Between the States.

It is as a gay deceiver rather than a bewitching beauty that Nina rests her claim to fame. Carried in the arms of General Patton Anderson's small niece during the war, both the doll and her young owner passed many a sentry's vigilent guard, looking so utterly innocent and beguiling, that never once in their entire career were they suspected of carrying contraband goods.

Nina's body is as soft as a rag doll's, and presumably is stuffed with cotton. Her large beautiful head is held securely on with tape, yet can be removed from her body in a few minutes time. It was by this means that Nina was able to successfully conceal quantities of quinine and morphine, which were stuffed in the hollow of her head.

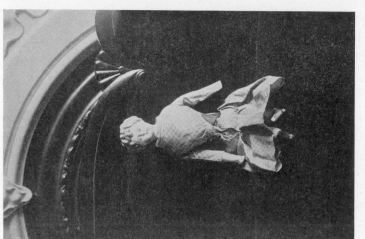

Winnie Davis Doll. Owned and dressed by the daughter of the President of the Confederacy. Courtesy of the Confederate Museum.

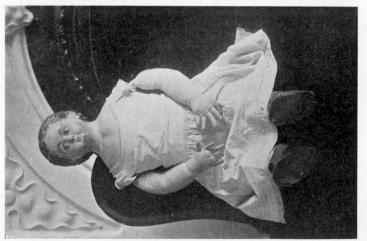

"Nina" in whose head quinine and morphine were secreted, and carried to sick Confederate soldiers "behind the lines", during the War Between the States. Courtesy of the Confederate Museum.

After the collapse of the Confederacy, this famous doll became a much loved member of General Anderson's household, passing from his niece to his little daughter. Sixteen years ago Nina was presented to the Confederate Museum by General Anderson's two children, James Patton Anderson, Jr. and Margaret Bybee Anderson of Palatka, Florida, and today, smiles contentedly from a large glass-enclosed cabinet in one of the upstairs rooms of the former White House of the Confederacy.

Other interesting dolls in the collection include a small indestructible wax doll which was dressed during the War Between the States by the wife of General A. P. Hill, and presented to her cousin, little Lizzie Lightfoot of Virginia; a slender wooden doll made in England, and named "Hercelia," which was dressed in 1845 in a typically Southern dress and bonnet—which she still wears—and given to Mary Susan Wright, the young daughter of James Wright of Essex County, Virginia; and an unusually beautiful doll with bisque head which was dressed by Winnie Davis and treasured by her throughout her life. Naturally this doll is given precedence over the others in the Museum collection, and carries the number "1." Does not a great Southern organization owe its very name to her? For remember, it was in Atlanta, Georgia, on that memorable first day of May, 1886, that Jefferson Davis, ex-President of the Confederacy, addressed a wildly enthusiastic audience, introducing his daughter Winnie as the "Daughter of the Confederacy."

There are so many historic, interesting, and quaintly dressed dolls in the Confederate Museum collection, one scarcely knows when to end in describing them.

The oldest and one of the largest dolls in the Virginia

Room is known as "Mary Scotia," who is said to have been ninety years old when she was given to the Museum in 1916. This quaint doll originally belonged to Miss Mary Sperry of Winchester, Virginia, and is credited with having had many thrilling adventures during the years 1861-65. Mary Scotia looks to be a yard tall, her face is of a plaster composition with painted black hair and eyes, and her arms and legs are of kid. She wears an old-fashioned dotted Swiss dress, elaborate slippers, and lacks nothing in the way of accessories, which include a silk hand-bag, an ivory fan, and a necklace of coral beads.

Another large doll which has a Staffordshire glazed china head, glossy black hair and rosy cheeks, is named "Ann Blaws." She was the childhood treasure of little Mary Braxton Cocke of historic "Bremo" on the James, which was patented by Richard Cocke in 1639.

The most recent acquisition to the Museum's collection is a lovely large doll in a remarkable state of preservation, whose name is "Grace Darling." She is handsomely gowned, and has the familiar glazed china head, jet-black painted hair and rosy complexion, which seem to have been the standard of doll beauty prior to and during the War Between the States.

This interesting doll was named for Grace Darling, the daughter of an English lighthouse keeper, who by her daring in helping her father to rescue from a raging sea, the crew of nine men on the wrecked steamer *Forforshire* in 1838, became quite a celebrity on both sides of the Atlantic. For her act of bravery, Grace Darling was presented with a purse of three thousand five hundred dollars, publicly subscribed; and long years after her death her name must have stirred the imagination of many a child, for one little girl in

Virginia, Sophia Strauss, named her loveliest doll for the English heroine.

It was in Culpeper, Virginia, in the year 1862, that a Confederate soldier who had been wounded in battle, was taken to the home of Mr. and Mrs. Strauss and nursed back to health. As a token of gratitude for all that this kind family had done for him, he presented the doll who later became Grace Darling to their little daughter, who has treasured and kept her in perfect condition for seventy-seven long years. A few months ago, Mrs. L. Z. Morris of Richmond (she who was Sophia Strauss), gave Grace Darling to the Confederate Museum, that she might take her rightful place in the ranks of other famous dolls belonging to the era of the Southern Confederacy.

The dress Grace Darling wears is made from the material of a dress worn by Mrs. Morris' mother while living in Culpeper in 1856, and is in a remarkable state of preservation. It is of a handsome quality of black bengaline with broad satin stripes, and rose-point lace is used effectively around the neck and sleeves. So clean and shiny is Grace Darling's pretty face and head, one finds it very very difficult thinking of her as belonging to that vanished day of Joseph Hergesheimer's *Swords and Roses*.

In 1932, the year of the George Washington Bi-Centennial, one of the largest American doll manufacturers brought out a George Washington doll, and not to overlook the General's Lady, a Martha Washington doll also. Both dolls are identical as to expression, size, and workmanship. The General measures nine inches in height; is made of a non-breakable substance now generally used by all American doll manufacturers, and has the perfectly coiffured white wig, so indispensable to the members of Colonial society in America.

"George Washington" is as fastidiously attired as was the great American whose likeness he bears. His costume consists of a tri-cornered hat; a meticulously fashioned Colonial suit including coat, fancy vest, lace ruff, knee breeches; white hose and black slippers with silver buckles. One feels that the General, who was a firm believer that dress was an important badge of rank, would give a nod of approval to this authentically groomed doll which commemorates the two hundredth anniversary of his birth.

Few, if any American made dolls have attained the widespread popularity that "Shirley Temple" dolls have so long enjoyed. Aside from their tremendous sale in this country, these dolls are manufactured by sub-licensees of the original company in half a dozen foreign countries including Australia, Canada, England, France, Poland, and Holland, while South Americans—particularly the Argentines, have bought them on par with Americans.

Other dolls fashioned in the likeness of famous young people include the "Dionne Quintuplets," which have grown up just as fast as the little sisters in Callander, Ontario; also the "Princess Elizabeth" dolls which are dressed in the proper English fashion, with a miniature golden coronet crowning their blond heads. Nor have doll manufacturers overlooked the field of fiction, for among the most recent new-comers to the realm of dolls are "Scarlett O'Hara" dolls, as bewitchingly beautiful and exquisitely gowned as was the incredible heroine of *Gone With the Wind*.

Aside from numerous well known American doll manufacturers whose products have been largely responsible for popularizing and expanding the sales of American made dolls, there are several individuals whose unusual doll creations have not only brought them personal recognition, but have contributed in no small measure to the ever increasing charm, individuality, and value of American dolls.

One such artist is Miss DeWees Cochran of New York City, whose "Portrait Dolls of Real Little People" represent one of the most valuable and distinctive contributions yet made to American doll history and manufacture. Miss Cochran describes these as "real American physiognomies worked out from a great number of pictures and models, with body proportions of normal children—something original to American made dolls."

These dolls are first modelled in plasticine, then a plaster cast is made in which the composition is moulded by hand and finished with a tedious process of sand papering and fillers. The doll is completely handmade, modelled to resemble any child, with any expression desired. The head is of very durable light weight composition practically unbreakable; body of silk jersey, and the wig of real hair, woven in a ventilated manner exactly like a child's. The hair may be combed and brushed if desired, and the doll's clothes are exact replicas of the child whose image has thus been fashioned into a doll. These dolls sell from fifty to sixty-five dollars each, and as can be imagined, will be priceless heirlooms in generations to come.

Another widely known maker of dolls is Miss Helen Siebold Walter, of Staunton, Virginia, familiarly known as "The Doll Lady." Perhaps this interesting appellation was given Miss Walter because she not only creates unusual dolls, but collects old and historic dolls as well. She is best known for her ingenious "Mayflower Pilgrim Dolls" which she originated for the Mayflower Hotel in Washington, D. C. For this especial group Miss Walter has worked out eight characters: John Alden, Priscilla Mullins, Captain Myles Standish, Elder Brewster, Governor Bradford, Madam Alice Southworth (his second wife), John Winslow and Mary Chilton.

Equally as popular as the Mayflower dolls, are the Southern Darky Dolls—"Just Folks"—a special group of slave dolls which Miss Walter originated for the Williamsburg Restoration. These quaint dolls were inspired by the will of Lieutenant Governor Francis Fauquier of Virginia, which was discovered among some old Williamsburg papers. The part relating to Governor Fauquier's slaves and their disposal, Miss Walter had copied in the old *Caslon* type, and each box that contains a Williamsburg slave darky doll also contains one of these excerpts. The dolls are named after the beloved slaves of Governor Fauquier: Aunt Sukey, Uncle Tidus and Piccaninny Sall make up a black family, while a brown family includes Mam' Mary, Uncle Lancaster and Child Jemima.

The "Just Folks" Darkey dolls are made in both black and brown sateen. They have a variety of typical faces and are colorfully costumed. Even the kinks of the piccaninnies are hand-wrapped with cord, in exactly the manner that colored mammies wrapped the hair of their little ones in *ante-bellum* times.

Mrs. T. L. Yarrington of Brook Hill, Virginia, is another talented person who has shown great versatility in creating the most unusual dolls from the humble corn shuck. The finishing touch to these delightful dolls is a coat of lacquer, or several coats, depending on the number of colors desired, and the doll's identity and costume. What is now a serious profession with Mrs. Yarrington, began as a mere pastime, and to date she has made hundreds of these dolls, representing Pamunkey Indians, a Darky Cotton Picking Group, and innumerable characters from story-book land, including Tom Sawyer and Huckleberry Finn, Snow White and the Seven Dwarfs, Raggedy Anne, Red Riding Hood, and ever so many others.

Doll collecting has long been a hobby among royalty. Queen Victoria is said to have been extremely fond of dolls, so much so that she began collecting them from all parts of Europe. Today, her remarkable collection, numbering almost a hundred, is housed in the Victoria and Albert Museum in London. Recently a well known London firm advertised for sale "a charming pair of dolls, made in 1840 to represent Queen Victoria and the Prince Consort in their wedding robes, priced fifty dollars the pair."

Another royal doll collector was the late Dowager Queen Marie of Roumania. Her celebrated collection is estimated to far surpass that of Queen Victoria's, containing over one thousand dolls dressed in national and historic costumes, many of which emphasize the costumes of the Roumanian peasant, while others illustrate the method of Roumanian manufacture.

Most of the royal personages of Europe contributed to this collection, making it one of the most valuable in the entire world. Practically every country is represented, some of the dolls dating back to the fifteenth century, with exact reproductions of the fashions of that period, while others represent their donors in early life.

Numerous are the materials which have gone into the

making and manufacturing of dolls since their earliest inception: wood, clay, ivory, bone, mammoth teeth, sticks, stone, shells, beads, wax, cloth, cotton, silk, shavings, saw-dust, china, plaster, wish-bones, felt, kid, bisque, procelain, *papier-mâché,* cornshucks — even nuts!

And numerous too, are the likenesses in which they have been fashioned, the purposes which they have served. In the home they are not only playthings, but door-stops, telephone screens, pin cushions, tea cozies, egg-warmers; in times of war disguises for concealing secret messages and dope, and in the world at large, ministers plenipotentiary from the courts of fashion!

At the beginning of the eighteenth century, fashionable mantua-makers received their ideas of the changes of fashion from Paris by means of dolls, which were dressed in the height of style and sent to New York on the fast sailing packets. In *The Social History of Flatbush,* Gertrude Vanderbilt gives a charming pen-picture of this custom. She writes:

"As early as 1712, these dolls, dressed in the fashion of the day, were sent from Paris to London. We have a vivid remembrance of the old age of one of these fashion-plate dolls which had been sent from Paris to a fashionable mantua-maker in New York. When the dress had changed as to style, the dress-maker sold the doll to one of her customers, and Miss Nancy Dawson passed into the obscurity of humble dollies who had never been sent as ministers plenipotentiary from the courts of fashion."

In the Valentine Museum in Richmond there is an enchanting doll known as "Miss Lena" which was brought from Paris to Virginia by little Miss Lena Dandridge, sometime between 1866 and 1870. One suspects that this elaborately accoutred doll was intended to play a similar rôle to that of Miss Nancy

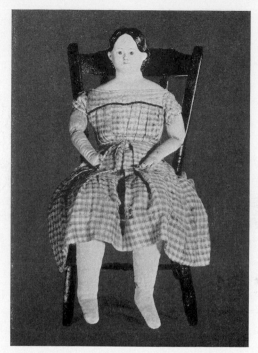

"Ninny" who knew a happy and "sheltered life" for three-quarters of a century, in an old home on Church Hill in Richmond, where she was played with by several generations of Richmond children. For many years she was owned by Miss Carolina H. Ellett, and was presented to the Valentine Museum by Miss Elizabeth Wright Weddell of Richmond, a later owner.

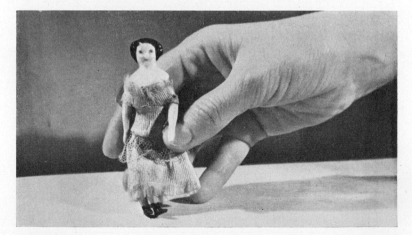

Three-inch glazed china doll dressed by Mrs. Robert E. Lee for a Confederate Bazaar in Lexington, from material of a silk bonnet belonging to Martha Washington. Courtesy of the Valentine Museum.

Dawson, for Miss Lena boasts such an amazing wardrobe it is difficult to think of her as ever having been destined solely for the nursery.

Included in her original wardrobe, the following articles remain intact, and a very inseparable part of Miss Lena's past they are. One parasol with ivory handle; one red leather chatelaine containing scissors, thimble, pin-cushion; several lace-edged linen handkerchiefs; one pair of eye-glasses; lorgnettes; one red leather pocketbook; one silk fan with ivory sticks and handle; one hooded cape; one paisley shawl; three hats; one pair of tan leather laced shoes; one pair of London gaiters; underclothes, including pantalets and petticoats; several pairs of cotton stockings; two pairs of kid gloves, white and tan; dresses galore, the loveliest of which is a ball dress of rose colored taffeta over a foundation of white net and lace; and various impedimenta including an ivory bird cage, a set of ivory dominoes, *et cetera.*

From little Miss Dandridge, "Miss Lena" passed to Miss Mary Gibson, who later presented her to the Museum. The doll belongs to the period of the eighteen-sixties, and is of French make; her body is of kid with jointed legs, and her head is of bisque. She is slender and graceful, with blue eyes and taffy-colored hair, and measures seventeen inches in height.

There are other interesting dolls in the Valentine Museum whose costume, history, age, or quaintness, at once arouse the visitor's interest. Mrs. Margaret Dashiell has contributed a group of "Period Dolls" beautifully gowned. Among them is one named "Madame Paradise" after that eccentric lady of old Williamsburg, who had such a *penchant* for hats she is credited with having bought or borrowed every new hat that arrived in the old capital, yet, paradoxical as it may seem, refused to wear them because they disarranged her hair. One of the most amusing anecdotes that the visitor to old Bruton Parish Church hears, is that of Madame Paradise, who was wont to walk down the aisle of the church to her pew with a small African attendant following at her heels, carrying her newest hat on a velvet cushion, that the parishioners might behold her latest triumph in millinery.

Also there is the little doll with wooden head and arms, elaborately dressed in red brocaded silk trimmed with green fringe, which was played with almost a hundred years ago (1847-1850) by little Martha Turpin of Richmond. In another room sits "Miss Dolly Madison," one of the largest dolls in the entire Museum group. This old doll was purchased shortly after the War Between the States in Petersburg, Virginia, for little Ann Henry Reed, and cost the astonishing sum of one hundred and fifty dollars in Confederate money. Because of Dolly Madison's great weight and height, her small owner dragged her around by the feet, tearing beyond repair her original dress, and wearing off the paint on the back of her head.

And last but not least, there is "Ninny." She too, is an *ante-bellum* doll, and almost, if not as large as Dolly Madison. So far as I know, Ninny is the only doll in Virginia whose head, features, and broad shoulders bear all of the earmarks of being a *Greiner Patent Head*.

According to existing records of the United States Patent Office, the first doll patent was issued on March 30, 1858, to Ludwig Greiner, of Philadelphia. Greiner was a German toy manufacturer and claimed that his heads were "so substantial they will not break by falling." In a recent issue of the magazine *Antiques* there is a detailed article dealing with Greiner's patent, and profusely illustrated with Greiner doll heads. To look at any one of these is to behold Ninny's perfect twin, and what is infinitely more important, at the base of Ninny's neck there is an oblong square impression, identical with the oblong label used on all Greiner heads.

None of Greiner's heads boasted of beauty. As Eleanor Hudson points out, "Their foreheads were invariably high, their noses small, their mouths—perhaps in deference to the rosebud simile—preternaturally small and suggestive of selfishness. Cheeks and jowls and double chins were excessively fat. If the coiffures were not mere painted simulations (which Ninny's is) one might arrange them to cover the invariably unsightly and boblike ears. The eyes were wide open in a fixed stare. Parhaps in early youth the complexions of these damsels were a redeeming pink and white," but she continues "they were not immune against the discoloration of time." Ninny is proof of this statement, for her pristine freshness vanished long ago, and the glow of youth and innocence has "yielded to the sallow hue of age and hard experience," as Miss Hudson expresses it.

But withal, Ninny is a very arresting figure, seated in a child's rocker in one of the upper rooms of the Museum. About her are several other dolls, but it is somehow Ninny who catches your eye, and holds it. Her head and broad shoulders are of *papier-mâché* reinforced with fabric (here the wise Greiner struck a happy combination that saved many a dropped dolly from a fractured cranium), while her body is of cloth stitched at the joints.

Ninny wears a quaint grey homespun dress, and her expression is one of calm complacency. Perhaps there is a good reason for this (Greiner notwithstanding), for Ninny knew a happy and "sheltered life" for three quarters of a century, in an old home on Church Hill in Richmond, where she was played with by several generations of Richmond children. Her devoted owner for many years was Miss Carolina H. Ellett, and she was presented to the Museum by Miss Elizabeth Wright Weddell of Richmond, a later owner.

Quite the loveliest doll of my acquaintance is one named Adrienne Beaumont. She is the symbol of beauty and romance, and unlike most of her Virginia contemporaries, boasts no historical associations. One glance at her court dress of cream-colored *mousseline de soie* and rose taffeta, the glittering brilliants that hang from tiny holes pierced in her ears, her elaborate coiffure, and features as clear-cut as a cameo, and you realize that here indeed is "a Lady of Quality."

Who is she you ask, and where does she live? The latter is easily answered, for Adrienne Beaumont is spending the twilight of her days in Virginia, in a large white-columned home on a shaded avenue in Richmond, with her beloved companion and owner, Mrs. Margaret Dashiell.

Like many another celebrated beauty, Adrienne Beaumont has a past—a past that is veiled in mystery. Several years ago Mrs. Dashiell bought her from a friend who owns an antique shop. Then, as now, the doll was wearing her court dress and glittering earrings, but had nothing else to commend her, for such requisites as pedigree, past history, age, and worst of all—a name—were lacking.

What matter? The doll belonged to the *noblesse—*

"Adrienne Beaumont." Owned by Mrs. Margaret Dashiell of Richmond.

of this fact there has never been any doubt, so without deliberation or delay she was given the name of Adrienne Beaumont, a name which long years ago belonged to a beautiful girl in New Orleans who was a dear friend of Mrs. Dashiell's mother.

When you enter a room graced by this beautiful doll's presence, you at once forget that she is inanimate; suddenly she becomes alive, and you begin to feel the subtle charm and necromancy which Adrienne Beaumont weaves about all those who come near her.

"What an exquisite creature she is!" you exclaim. "Why she is the Marquise de Pompadour and Comtesse DuBarry in miniature!" And so she is. Her head, broad shoulders, arms, hands, and tiny feet are of bisque; her lovely almond-shaped eyes are as blue as *lapis-lazuli;* her hair is painted a soft gold, and altogether she is the personification of beauty, grace, and poise. In length she measures fifteen inches, her body is of kid, and her tiny feet are snugly fitted into high heel slippers. To behold her for only a few seconds is to be guilty of breaking the Tenth Commandment.

There is a legend which is destined to follow Adrienne Beaumont wherever she goes; a very lovely legend I think. Many years ago, in one of the large capitals of Europe, there lived a beautiful woman whose name was known to high and low alike. One day, as she was being driven through the streets of Paris in an open carriage, she was seen at close range by a doll-maker's apprentice.

So dazzled was the young man by the woman's beauty, that he rushed to his employer's shop, and while the vision of loveliness was still fresh in his mind, set to work to model a doll in her image. Throughout the long hours of the night and well into the next day, the young apprentice worked unceasingly on his model. When at last his task was finished he could scarcely believe his eyes, for there before him was a doll bearing such a striking likeness to the beautiful lady of his dreams, that it might easily have been her own image, reflected in a diminutive mirror.

Fame came to the apprentice overnight, and soon he was master of a shop of his own. Always he kept his beautiful doll on display in his shop window, and steadfastly refused to part with her, though many tempting offers were made him if he would but agree to sell.

On a cold winter's evening, long years after the doll-maker had first started in business for himself, he sat in his shop resting after a hard day's work. Outside the landscape was a miracle of white, and so heavily was his front window curtained with snow, the old man could scarcely see the familiar glow of the corner street-light opposite his shop. Weary from his labors, and lost in reverie, the doll-maker soon fell asleep.

Suddenly, he was aroused from his slumbers by a knock at his door. Who could be wanting to buy a doll at this hour of the night? Well, he would see. Slowly making his way to the door, the old man finally opened it. "Good evening, Monsieur," said a soft and lovely voice. "Good evening, Madame," replied the old man, looking somewhat astonished into the face of an old, but still beautiful woman.

"You will pardon me, Monsieur, for troubling you at this hour of the night, but the doll in your window— I wondered if I might look at her closely. Always during the day people are standing in front of your window gazing at her. I too, have been guilty of that very act, but somehow, I cannot quite explain it—what

I have seen has never quite satisfied my curiosity. Now that the street is deserted, I thought perhaps I might look at her from your shop window, but the snow has covered the glass, and I cannot see her clearly. Would you mind if I stepped inside, just for a few minutes?"

"Not at all, Madame," replied the doll-maker. "Please do, for it is very cold." And so, with no further ceremony, the old man closed the door behind his visitor, and going to his front window, removed the doll from its accustomed place, and handed it to her. Neither of them spoke for several minutes, while the woman looked long and lovingly at the doll, whose cameo-like face was as fresh and as beautiful as the day the young apprentice had made her.

"Yes," she murmured, as if talking to herself, "I was right. The soft golden hair, the eyes, the mouth, they are the same. Ah! even the diamond drops that fell from your dainty ears. How well do I remember them. And the dress, it too is the same, the very same that you wore your last evening at the Tuileries. Can it really be that I see you as you were then, Mignon Daubigny?"

The old man stood a few paces away, speechless and amazed. Had he dreamed this scene, or was it real? He must make sure. "Madame," said the doll-maker, looking searchingly into her eyes, "the doll—she resembles someone you knew long ago?"

"Yes, Monsieur, she does. A very striking likeness." And rising to go, she added, "And now, thank you, and goodnight."

"Pardon, Madame," said the old man, faltering for words to restrain her from going. "I am soon to close my shop and retire into the country. The doll has long since served her purpose. Would you not honor me by accepting her as a gift?"

"But Monsieur,"—

Walking up to the old woman, the doll-maker handed her the doll which she had only a few minutes before held in her hands.

"She is yours, Madame Daubigny. She has always belonged to you."

"But Monsieur, you *knew?*" she murmured, almost in a whisper.

"Yes, Madame. I knew from the first." And walking to the door and opening it, he added, "And now, goodnight."

Without a word she turned from him, and pressing the doll close to her heart, walked out into the night from which she had come.

INDEX

INDEX

Kingsley, Charles, 290.
Kirk, Godfrey, 239.
Kirk, Grace, 239.
Kirk, John, 239.
Kirk, Samuel, 239.
Kneller, Sir Godfrey, 80, 82, 83.

L

La Fayette, General, 12, 24, 26, 29, 45, 64, 134, 151, 240, 249, 251, 257, 266.
Lamb, Charles, 266.
Lancret, 84.
"Laneville," 87, 161.
Lang, Andrew, 244.
La Prade, Mrs. W. W., 81.
Latrobe, Benjamin, 265.
Laurens, Lieutenant Colonel, 154.
Laydon, John, 168.
Lear, Colonel, 132.
Lebrun, 84.
Lee, Ann Matilda, 258.
Lee, Elizabeth Collins, 258.
Lee, General George Washington Custis, 132.
Lee, Henry, 188.
Lee, J. Collins, 258.
Lee, Mary Custis, 132.
Lee, Mildred, 94.
Lee, Colonel Richard, 186, 223.
Lee, Richard Bland, 257.
Lee, General Robert E., 2, 3, 94, 133.
Lee, Mrs. Robert E., 132.
Leedstown, 128.
Leigh, Watkins, 116.
Le Mayeur, Dr. John Peter, 118.
Leopold, 298.
Lexington, Mass., 109.
Lewis, Ann, 137.
Lewis, Attaway, 137.
Lewis, Daingerfield, 137.
Lewis, Elsie W., 276.
Lewis, Colonel Fielding, 12, 103, 136, 137.
Lewis, Fielding, 255.
Lewis, Fielding III, 137.
Lewis, Major George Washington, 136, 137.
Lewis, Colonel John, 102, 103, 104.
Lewis, Lucy, 137.
Lewis, Warner, 225.
Lewis, Zola, 137.
"Lexington," 240.
Library of Congress, 17.
Lightfoot, Lizzie, 301.
Lincoln, President, 89, 90.
Lindbergh, Charles A., Colonel, 297, 298.
Lindbergh, Mrs. Evangeline, 297.

Lisbon, 210, 212.
"Little Berkeley," 48, 299.
Liverpool, England, 235.
Lockwood, Joshua, 188.
London, 79, 80, 107, 111, 127, 146, 157, 158, 159, 182, 183, 223, 237, 239, 287, 309, 310.
Long, Dr. Crawford Williamson, 29.
Longfellow, Henry Wadsworth, 21.
Lossing, 256.
Louis XIII, 84.
Louis XIV, 84.
Louis XV, 70.
Louis XVI, 204.
Louvre, The, 85, 88.
Lowestoft, 250, 252.
Lowestoft, England, 250.
Lowther, Margaret, 44, 45.
Lowther, William, 44.
Lukis, Fredericka, 24.
Lydgate, John, 38.
Lynchburg, Virginia, 26, 194, 196.
Lyttleton, Lord, 207.

M

Macauley, Lord, 185.
Mackenzie, George Norbury, 168.
Macky, Robert, 173.
Madison, Dolly, 19.
Madison, James, 116, 275.
Madison, Mrs. James, 280.
Madison, Nellie, 275, 276.
Malone, Mildred, 8.
Maozane, Kumagai, 71.
Marat (Citizen), 89.
Marie Antoinette, 70, 88, 204.
Marlborough, Duke of, 79.
"Marmion," 136, 137.
Marshall, John, 5, 6, 15, 25, 116, 137, 264, 265.
Marshall, Thomas, 6.
Martin, Colonel Thomas Bryan, 173, 174.
Mary, Queen of Scots, 55, 69.
Mary Washington Cottage, 161.
Mason, Mrs. Ann, 188.
Mason, George, 154, 156.
Mason, George (Great Grandson), 156.
Mathews, Captain Francis, 187.
Maury, James, 235.
Maury, Matthew Fontaine, 235.
Maximilian, Emperor of Mexico, 73.
Maxwell, James, 60.
Mayflower, The, 110, 167.
Mayo Memorial Church House, 25.
Mayo, Mrs. Stephen Decatur, 81, 82.
McCarty, Arthur Peyton, 87.
McCarty, Mrs. Arthur Peyton, 86, 87.

McCarty, Page, 287, 288.
McClellan, General, 90.
McCormack, Helen G., 27, 28.
McGuire, Dr. Hunter, 288.
McKim, Ruby Short, 58, 59.
McLeod, Mary, 207.
Mercer, General Hugh, 235, 236.
Merrimac and *Monitor,* The, 89, 90.
Metropolitan Museum, 85, 137, 256.
Mettauer, Dr. Francois Joseph, 29.
Mettauer, John Peter, 29, 30, 31.
Michaux, Judith, 121.
Mignards, 84.
Miller, Dr. Joseph, 19.
Mills. Robert, 265.
Mohun, Charles, Lord, 272.
Monroe, James, 116.
Montgomery, Charles, 248.
Montgomery, John, 248, 249.
Montezuma, 218.
"Monticello," 151, 247.
Monumental Church, Richmond, 119,
    263, 266.
"Moons Mount," 87.
Moore, Bishop Richard Channing,
    frontispiece, 15, 25, 265.
Moore House, 154.
Moore, N. Hudson, 128, 130, 141, 182,
    189, 246, 250.
Moore, Thomas, 260.
Mordaunt, Charles, 83.
Mordecai, John B., 287, 288.
Morris, Mrs. L. Z., 303.
Morris, William, 252.
Morrison, Colonel James, 249.
Moseley, Colonel, 107.
"Moss Neck," 87, 161.
"Mount Airey," 159.
"Mount Vernon," 18, 28, 113, 114,
    131, 132, 145, 149, 151, 160, 175,
    252, 255.
"Mount Zion," 275.
Murray, John (Earl of Dunmore),
    194, 195, 196.
Murray, Margaret Ann, 36.
Museum of Cairo, 54.
Museum of Fine Arts (Boston), 237.
Mussolini, 220.
Myers, Mrs. Barton, 282.
Myers House, 282.

N

Napoleon, 203, 204, 206, 208, 210, 211,
    212, 213.
Napoleon III, 118.
National Museum, 173, 256.
Natural Bridge, Va., 263.
Nelson, Admiral. 278.
Nelson, Fannie Page, 87.

Nelson, Sallie, 44.
Nesbit, Dr. Charles, 247.
New Amsterdam, 171.
"New Market," 153, 158.
Newmarket, England, 116.
New Orleans, La., 85, 86, 313.
Newport, Captain Christopher, 168.
New Town, 107.
New York, 24, 26, 44, 45, 85, 87, 137,
    152, 188, 299, 305, 308.
Nicholas, Harrison Trent, 194, 196,
    198, 199, 200.
Nicholas, John Scott, 198.
Nicholson, Andrew, 235.
Niederweiler, 255.
"Nomini Hall," 102, 103, 108, 159,
    258, 259.
Norfolk, Va., 36, 107, 117, 128, 231,
    232, 233, 234, 278, 279, 280, 282.
Norton, "Widow," 196.

O

Ogle, Cuthbert, 158.
Oldfield, Mrs., 83.
Old Point Comfort, 279.
Old Sweet Springs, 209.
Oneida (ship), 23.
Osgood (ship), 105.
Oxford, Lord, 83.
Oxford, England, 21.
Oxford University, 167.

P

Page, Gabriella, 94.
Page, John, 6, 44, 45.
Palatka, Florida, 301.
Palissy, 244.
Pallas (ship), 253.
Paradise, Madame, 309, 310.
Paris, 84, 204, 210, 212, 249, 261, 308.
Parke, Colonel Daniel, 79.
Parke, Lucy, 80.
Patterson, Elizabeth, 203, 205, 206,
    207, 208, 209, 210, 211, 212.
Patterson, Mrs. William, 203, 208, 209.
Patterson, William, 203, 206, 208, 209,
    210.
Peachy House, 133.
Peale, Charles Wilson, 15, 16, 18, 19,
    20.
Peale's Museum, 19, 20.
Penn, Letitia, 298.
Penn, William, 146, 298.
Pennsylvania, University of, 30.
Pepys, Samuel, 39, 56.
Pepys, Mrs. Samuel, 38, 39, 56.
Peterborough, Lord, 83.
Petersburg, Virginia, 251, 310.